Sociology of Religion

MW00824554

The first sociology of religion textbook to begin the task of diversifying and decolonizing the study of religion, *Sociology of Religion* develops a sociological frame that draws together the personal, political and public, showing how religion – its origins, development and changes – is understood as a social institution, influenced by and influencing wider social structures.

Organized along sociological structures and themes, the book works with examples from a variety of religious traditions and regions rather than focusing in depth on a selection, and foregrounds cultural practice-based understandings of religion. It is therefore a book about 'religion', not 'religions', that explores the relationship of religion with gender and sexuality, crime and violence, generations, politics and media, 'race', ethnicity and social class, disease and disability – highlighting the position of religion in social justice and equality.

Each chapter of this book is framed around concrete case studies from a variety of Western and non-Western religious traditions. Students will benefit from thinking about the discipline across a range of geographical and religious contexts. The book includes features designed to engage and inspire students:

- Up-to-date and comprehensive analysis of engaging and accessible material
- 'Case Examples': short summaries of empirical examples relating to the chapter themes
- Visually distinct boxes with bullet points, key words and phrases focusing on the context
- Questions suitable for private or seminar study
- Suggested class exercises for instructors to use
- Suggested readings and further readings/online resources at the end of each chapter

Following a review and critique of early sociology of religion, the book engages with more contemporary issues, such as dissolving the secular/sacred binary and paying close attention to issues of epistemology, negotiations, marginalities, feminisms, identities, power, nuances, globalization, (post) (multiple) modernity (ies), emotion, structuration, reflexivity, intersectionality and urbanization. This book is essential reading for undergraduate and postgraduate students exploring the sociology of religion, religion and society, religious studies, theology, globalization and human geography.

Abby Day is a Professor of Race, Faith and Culture in the Department of Sociology at Goldsmiths, University of London. She is also an international expert in the social scientific study of contemporary religion with particular interests in gender, generations, ethnicity and in decolonizing knowledge. She is a trustee of the *Sociological Review*, an editorial board member of *Religion*, peer reviewer for several journals and funding agencies, and past Chair of the British Sociological Association's religion section.

Sociology of Religion

Overview and Analysis of Contemporary Religion

Abby Day

Routledge
Taylor & Francis Group

LONDON AND NEW YORK

First published 2020
by Routledge
2 Park Square, Milton Park, Abingdon, Oxon OX14 4RN

and by Routledge
52 Vanderbilt Avenue, New York, NY 10017

Routledge is an imprint of the Taylor & Francis Group, an informa business

© 2020 Abby Day

British Library Cataloguing-in-Publication Data
A catalogue record for this book is available from the British Library

Library of Congress Cataloging-in-Publication Data
Names: Day, Abby, 1956– author.
Title: Sociology of religion: overview and analysis of contemporary religion / Abby Day.
Description: Abingdon, Oxon; New York: Routledge, 2021. |
Includes bibliographical references and index.
Identifiers: LCCN 2020039470 (print) | LCCN 2020039471 (ebook) |
ISBN 9780367151874 (hardback) | ISBN 9780367151911 (paperback) |
ISBN 9780429055591 (ebook)
Subjects: LCSH: Religion and sociology–Textbooks.
Classification: LCC BL60.D37 2021 (print) | LCC BL60 (ebook) |
DDC 306.6–dc23
LC record available at https://lccn.loc.gov/2020039470
LC ebook record available at https://lccn.loc.gov/2020039471

ISBN: 978-0-367-15187-4 (hbk)
ISBN: 978-0-367-15191-1 (pbk)
ISBN: 978-0-429-05559-1 (ebk)

Typeset in Times New Roman
by Newgen Publishing UK

Contents

Preface

As one of the most important social forces in any society, religion is both visible and invisible, accepted and rejected, feared and desired. Its ideas, beliefs, values and practices inspire people to perform great, and often terrible, acts. Armies are mobilized and stood down, money spent and withdrawn, treasures amassed and stolen, human rights awarded and transgressed, citizens empowered and subjugated, governments elected and overthrown, health and sickness addressed and ignored, natural environments protected and destroyed, all in the name of religion.

As this book went to press, the world was shuddering with the horrific impact of a pandemic. Lives, livelihoods, faiths and certainties were shattered. Some religious leaders sought to help and calm people; others stoked divisions and encouraged false cures. And yet, not enough people understand how to interpret religion's public or even political role or how to work within a complex socio-religious, multi-faith, multi-identity world. Who, then, will help repair the damage religions often create, or work with them to help resolve wider societal problems? Perhaps you will.

Readers of this book are interested in religion's relationship with such issues as social justice, politics, human rights, economies, public goods and media. This book is designed to help students, often new to the subject of religion and sociology more widely, to use a sociological imagination to understand religion's social influence and role. The chapters are designed to identify practical examples and use contemporary theories to help understand them.

The text's sociological frame draws together the personal, political and public, showing how religion – its origins, development and changes – is understood as a social institution, influenced by and influencing wider social structures. Organized by sociological structures and themes, the book works with examples from a variety of religious traditions rather than focusing in depth on a selection, and foregrounds cultural practice-based understandings of religion. It is therefore a textbook about 'religion', not 'religions'.

The book develops argument and evidence to provide necessary description to enliven ideas, offer in-depth knowledge from numerous sources, create a comparative, problematising schema and suggest several ways forward. Attention to agency and structure, legitimations, history, reproductions, power and economy are important components of a 'sociological imagination'. Readers will engage with contemporary issues, such as dissolving the secular/sacred binary and paying close attention to issues of epistemology, negotiations, 'race', feminisms, identities, sexualities, power, nuances, globalisation, (post) (multiple) modernity (ies), emotion, structuration, reflexivity, intersectionality and urbanization.

Further, in response to widespread and increasing critiques, many universities now conduct detailed course reviews to ensure curricula, approaches, styles, readings and theories reflect diverse populations. A new criterion that is gaining attention is what is sometimes known as liberating, or decolonializing, the curriculum. That means including authors who have been historically muted: women, people of colour, scholars from emerging economies. As a white, middle-class *cis* woman I speak from an unfair, privileged position, and I try to address that. I hope that process is reflected in the textbook as I have worked hard to review all themes to extend the usual bibliographic sources and case studies. All first names are included in the bibliography to make more apparent the author's assigned or acquired gender. The reason for this is both practical and ethical: knowledge is enriched through widening the scope and I recognize that the dominance of white men within the discipline, and higher education more widely, reflects gender and racial inequality more generally. This causes structural problems and micro-aggressions for students and staff from other backgrounds and impoverishes the knowledge we create.[1]

Chapter themes, style and content are derived from my own national and international lectures and publications on religion (sociological and anthropological) during the last 20 years, a comprehensive analysis of sociology of religion programmes at universities worldwide, a recent review of texts used for teaching the sociology of religion and detailed, constructive feedback from anonymous peer reviewers.

The theories included here, like any theory, are open to revision. A critical reading of theory, and any evidence that underpins it, is necessary and forms an important part of academic work. Criticality is a task and skill expected of scholars and students in any field. Right now, that is more important than ever. But how do you do it? Most students new to the field may be perplexed by their lecturers' demands to be critical, and so I have written this book with that in mind throughout, always asking questions, pointing to potential flaws, suggesting the reader thinks more.

The theory that is presented to university students on courses will be in lecture, book and journal paper form. Most new students will have never seen a 'journal paper'. That is because academic publishing is a niche operation for academics who want to get their ideas and research read by other academics. The journal articles are long, upwards of 7,000 words, written in formal prose and in a language familiar to other academics, but not to new students. The chapters here work with material from both books and journals and the extended bibliography points readers to the source. If students decide to follow the suggestions and read from the bibliography, my advice is to try not to panic. The first time you read one of these academic journal papers it will be unfamiliar and may be confusing, but in time you will become accustomed to it. Start slowly, check new terms and ask yourself throughout: what is this paper about? What are the key points? Where is the evidence? Why does it matter?

Chapters in this book relate to each other, and readers will often see cross-references. Some teachers may present an individual chapter to be read in isolation, and the book has been written to allow that to happen fairly seamlessly.

My potential list of people to acknowledge became so lengthy and unwieldy that I no longer knew where to start or end. Perhaps that is the greatest feeling of thanks – I'm so lucky to have had so many research participants, students, colleagues, co-authors/editors, book contributors, friends, publishers, reviewers and other professional associates who have all been so generous and so interesting, wise and often funny over the years.

Word length would never permit me to list them all, and then I would await with dread the realization that I had left someone off the list. Cowardly, perhaps, but I will restrict these published thanks to those specific individuals at institutions I joined as my career developed from student to author, researcher and teacher, first at Lancaster University, then Birkbeck, University of London, University of Sussex, University of Kent and Goldsmiths, University of London. For consistent and outstanding intellectual and emotional support my thanks to Linda Woodhead, Hiroko Kawanami, Simon Coleman, Gordon Lynch, Jeremy Carrette, Adam Dinham, Bev Skeggs, David Oswell, Vikki Bell and Dan Nyland.

Finally, this book would never have been written had Routledge Commissioning Editor Emily Briggs not approached me initially and then supported my conviction that it should be transparently assertive with a widening, de-colonizing agenda. Undoubtedly, there is more work to be done and I look forward to readers' critiques and suggestions. I am grateful to her, Lakshita Joshi, Jane Robson, and all colleagues at Routledge for their professional expertise. I am also grateful to Alex Peters-Day for detailed editorial assistance and advice, and to Dr Kim Harding and Dr Danny Zschomler for providing additional literature reviews and analysis on topics of politics, disability and secular supernatural. Any errors or omissions that remain are wholly my responsibility.

Abby Day
Goldsmiths, University of London
August 2020

Note

1   For a review of practical steps being taken in universities, see Abby Day, Lois Lee, David Thomas and James Spickard (eds), *Doing Diversity in Academia: Practices and Pitfalls*. Bristol: Bristol University Press.

Part I

Mapping the field

Chapter 1

What is a sociology of religion?

Religion is an institution created by people; sociologists are interested in how and why humans create and practise it. This book has been written for university students who are studying religion from a social scientific perspective, many for the first time. It is not an apparently neutral, fact-laden textbook, but my overview and critical analysis of important themes dominating the field of study, and an exposure of some that have been ignored or silenced.

The ideas and analysis have arisen from my own teaching and research, a review of sociology of religion syllabuses worldwide, detailed review of my proposed chapters by peer reviewers (for whose feedback and recommendations I am most grateful), involvement in the field's main international academic organizations (mainly the Sociology of Religion study group in the British Sociological Association and the Association for the Sociology of Religion) where many of these ideas, particularly concerning a critical feminist turn, and decolonizing and liberating the curriculum, have been discussed.

The decolonizing agenda, taking 'colonization' as both material and epistemic means to suppress and reinforce 'otherness' (Said 1978) has rightly been gaining pace and its influence will be seen throughout this book. The institutions of the Global North and West remain dominated by a small elite, with a much narrower set of perspectives and interests than are found in diverse populations. People from a small set of identity-categories – crudely equated to 'white men of the Global North' – still dominate the production and dissemination of academic knowledge in teaching, writing and research. This distorts the knowledge that universities produce, ill-serves students from non-dominant groups and threatens the humanistic values on which the modern university is founded (see e.g. Day et al. 2021; Bhambra et al. 2018; Connell 2018; Mbembe, 2016; Santos 2014; Mignolo 2011; Encarnacion et al. 2010).

Ideas that have become 'taken for granted' in the sociology of religion need critical exploration, even – or especially – when presented by one of the 'masters': the subordination of human agency to structure; the apparently universal search for meaning; a turn to individualization; the universality and timelessness of religion, women being more religious than men, religion's disappearance or loss of significance; an apparent decline in morality being linked to decline of religion; and so on. Those are often untested, and frequently lazy, tired concepts that need to be subjected to review and analysis.

In this chapter, we will consider three main questions. What constitutes a discipline of 'sociology'? What is 'religion'? Why is there such a strong relationship between the two?

Inventing sociology

There is a phrase in the Christian Bible that in the beginning there was the 'Word', and the 'Word' was made flesh. Sociologists think the opposite: in the beginning (were such a thing as a 'beginning' even imaginable), there was flesh and flesh made words. Humans created language and with language came categories that are seemingly so real that they are taken for granted, such as gender, or race, or religion. Sociologists did not invent categories. Centuries before the word 'sociology' was spoken, the Greek philosopher Aristotle (Durkheim and Mauss 1963) argued that categories are human constructions which not only classify phenomena, but structure our thinking about them.

The anthropologist Rodney Needham, (1972, vii–xlviii) in his introduction to Durkheim and Mauss's essay, criticizes the authors for not developing or providing more evidence for that idea, but welcomes it (Needham 1972, xxxiv) nevertheless for drawing attention 'for the first time in sociological enquiry, to a topic of fundamental importance in understanding human thought and social life' and, in his words, providing a theoretical contribution that 'has been to isolate classification as an aspect of culture to which sociological enquiry should be directed' (Needham 1972, xi)

Durkheim and Mauss's argument was significant to those in circles beyond the social scientific. It expressly countered claims by the influential philosopher Immanuel Kant, who argued that human beings uniquely possessed a mental structure that existed *a priori* (Kant 1881). Durkheim and Mauss took the opposite position and went one step further. Not only did they say that all categories are social and not the product of any one individual, but that the first stage in such social classification would be a religious one as people attempted to explain their worlds, probably by marking a difference between people and something thought to be beyond people.

Thinking with words

Students of the sociology of religion may find it helpful to keep the term *a priori* in mind when reading books about religion as it identifies a particular, and important, line of argument. The Latin term means 'from the earlier', and is used in philosophy to denote something that is inherent, existing before being acquired by the senses. Its opposite, a sense-derived experience, is often called *a posterior,* a Latin term meaning 'from the later'. Sociologists generally assume that knowledge is formed from experience, and does not exist pre-socially. When sociologists of religion describe something – an idea, a need, an emotion – as *a priori* or inherent, they are usually drawing on their theological background rather than a sociological training.

Durkheim and Mauss also opposed James Frazer (1890), arguing that he thought people were divided into clans by something pre-existing. Durkheim and Mauss said that people classify things because they are divided by clans. These distinctions are important because exploring how social worlds are created is one of the principal aims of sociology. Sociologists work to make the familiar unfamiliar, exposing social constructions of what may be otherwise taken-for-granted, appearing 'natural' or 'common sense'. 'Common sense' and 'nature' are often terms for received, socially constructed and hegemonic 'wisdom'. Deconstructing those ideas and exposing their background agendas have been the defining marks of feminist analysis, beginning in the 19th century. Suffragette, novelist and sociologist Charlotte Perkins Gilman (1899) made an observation that was rare at the time: such taken-for-granted assumptions about nature are gendered, with an apparently natural social order depending largely on the unpaid labour of women as care-provider and nurturer. Insufficient numbers of social scientists then or now have retained that focus, and the apparent distinction between private and public spheres, and reproduction/production are essentialized concepts that have, as will be discussed throughout this book, important ramifications for religion.

Gilman was writing in a period of rapid social change, when the consequences of empire and the industrial revolution, for example, were having significant global impact. She and many other female and non-white sociologists have generally been ignored in what has become the sociological 'canon', or accepted 'foundational' or, in a gendered manner of speaking, 'seminal' works.[1]

Thinking with words

Essentialize is a critical term for sociologists. Think first of the noun 'essential', meaning that which defines the set of which it is part. Water is an essential resource for human survival. When the word is turned into a verb and used critically, 'essentialize' means to convey that something is an essential part of something else, when it is not. People may reduce women's role as care-givers to something apparently natural by essentializing gendered care. A statement like 'caring women create strong societies' makes the notion of care essential to the female condition. Your teachers and examiners will notice if you essentialize during your writing and guide you to think more critically.

Sociology is thus concerned not only with what may be explained about society, but with the methods of explaining that, both theoretically and empirically. What is explained, how, and by whom? Who decides on how knowledge is created? As sociologist Michael Mann put it, it is dangerous to make assumptions about what is a 'fact':

> Analysis cannot merely reflect the 'facts'; our perception of the facts is ordered by mental concepts and theories. The average empirical historical study contains many implicit assumptions about human nature and society, and commonsense concepts derived from our own social experience – such as 'the nation,' 'social class,' 'status,' 'political power,' 'the economy.'
>
> (Mann 1986, 3–4)

Mann was interested in how societies operate through the manifestation and distribution of power. He noted that religion traditionally had more power than states or armies because it gave people in a large geographical area a sense of collective identity, producing 'a particular way of organizing social relations' (Mann 1986, 21).

While it is therefore striking, it should perhaps not be surprising that many early socio-logical thinkers chose to investigate religion. Several of those figures were instrumental in what has been regarded as the beginning of social thought, with the French social theorists Auguste Comte and Émile Durkheim deliberately rejecting speculative phil-osophy as a legitimate means of understanding human life, instead turning to science and society, identifying what Durkheim called 'social facts'.

The turn to describing ideas and behaviours through society has many roots, but a prime one often appearing in contemporary sociology and the sociology of religion is the era of the Enlightenment. This 18th-century, western European period, also known as the Age of Reason, will be familiar to most readers and I therefore will not provide a detailed history lesson. The reason for raising it here, however, is to prepare the sociolo-gist of religion for some of the most heated debates, and often quietly held assumptions, in the field. Put crudely, the Enlightenment is regarded with respect by those who favour its valorization of reason and prominence of the secular over religious, and criticized strongly by those who see it as the beginning of a harsh period of industrialization, cap-italism, positivism, and loss of enchantment, even innocence. An accusation of 'enlight-enment thinking' is not to be taken as a compliment.

Randall Collins (1994, 16–17) describes this period as the point where social scientific thinking began, housed both in universities and the comfortable salons of the wealthy:

> It was the first time that thinkers tried to provide *general explanations* of the social world. They were able to detach themselves, at least in principle, from expounding some existing ideology and to attempt to lay down general principles that explained social life.

The continued rise of universities gave the opportunity for ideas relating to history, economy and the social sciences to develop as their own spheres of research and writing, known as 'disciplines'. In the following sections, I discuss several themes arising from those new disciplines that have significantly influenced sociology and the sociology of religion.

Materialism and the social

One of the most astute observers of societies, and a master storyteller, was Karl Marx. Understanding basic concepts of Marxist theory is important for a sociologist of reli-gion for several reasons. One is the impact he and his collaborator (and financial backer) Friedrich Engels had on scholars and lay people alike: *The Communist Manifesto* (Marx and Engels 1848) is only outsold by the Bible. Another reason is how Marxism inspired some of the most significant social changes in the 20th century: widespread revolutions across the world included Russia 1917, China in 1925 and 1949, and the Cuban Revolution of 1959, as well as underpinning mixed economies of the 20th cen-tury. Sociologists and other scholars have criticized Marx on many grounds, not least of these being a recognition that he universalized his theory from a European perspec-tive. Gurminder Bhambra (2007) criticized Marx for describing 'capital' in Euro-centric terms, placing non-European societies as 'other' and failing to analyse economic and non-economic processes of exchange between European and non-European societies.

Marx also failed to consider under his banner of 'exploitation' the role of non-waged slave labour, as authors such as Stephanie Smallwood (2008) discuss.

Other scholars reject Marxist views that ignore the role women play in capitalist economies through their unpaid labour, providing free domestic service to the male worker and raising children to be contributors to the capitalist economy (see e.g. Barrett 1980).

Thinking with words

Materialism has a specific meaning in the context of social theory and philosophy, and should not be confused with a more everyday, normative current term of 'materialistic', or a sociology of religion turn to the 'material'. Materialism is the opposite of 'idealism'; it is a view that all 'facts' and all human history are caused by physical processes. Marx used his idea of 'historical materialism' to argue that all societies and their institutions, including religion, systems of morality, the family and law, are products of economic activity.

Sociologists may then explore why communist societies largely banished religion, and what have been the dynamics of its apparent resurgence and retreat in huge swathes of the globe. There is also the usefulness in some research projects of engaging with ideas of 'the material', for providing insights into interpretations of social class and, more recently, into a trend towards 'spirituality in the workplace' (we'll learn more about that in future chapters). Finally, some people, such as Stuart Jeffries (2012), are observing a return to Marxist thought and principles, particularly in younger generations who believe that capitalism has developed in ways that produce financial disasters.

While usually associated with his development of theories about 'capital', Marx's doctoral thesis was a complex exploration of Greek philosophy, written in 1841 and later published (1901). It is an exposition of how Marx was grappling with the qualities of two schools of Greek thought epitomized by Democritus and Epicurus. As few readers of this text, or its writer, are experts in the dense language and style of 19th-century German philosophy, the detail of his argument will not detain us here: Marx's further work, such as *Das Kapital, 1844 Paris Manuscripts*, and *The Communist Manifesto* are all clearly written and accessible to the average reader. What is remarkable about his doctoral thesis was how it described the problem Marx, and future social scientists, would battle with for decades if not centuries: what is the relationship between human endeavour and wider social influences – between, as sociologists might say today, agency and structure? A religious person might, as Democritus did, divide the world into human or divine impact, while a non-religious person, such as Epicurus, would claim that all is determined by humans both today and, importantly for Marx's thinking, throughout history.

The insight of history's effect was discussed by Marx as 'historical materialism', and this has important resonance for sociologists in general, and sociologists of religion in particular. The question is simple but staggering in its consequence: how do we explain social change? Through the actions, ideas and initiations of a few dynamic people, such as Buddha or the Beatles? Or, as Marx argued, through the way people interact with their material environment? Marx and Engels transplanted ideas from the privileged world of academic philosophers to the here and now, arguing that ideologies were rooted in the material, not only in the minds of people. Any ideas at any one time are to be understood through appreciating the particularities of the social world, and how they are produced by material conditions. Further, they argued, prevailing ideas are related directly to class structure, meaning that dominant ideas in any particular time are the ideas of the ruling class. Such a view would be anathema to future theologians and some sociologists of religion who would argue for *a priori* or pre-social origins of ideas and values, namely that inspired by a divine figure who created people with an inherent sense of morality.

Social scientists usually argue that people's religious preferences are moulded by social structures. For example, some people may lean towards the kind of religion that promises happiness in the hereafter because their lives now are poor and miserable, while others prefer a more esoteric, intellectual religion because they are rich and free from worries about daily survival. While appearing as 'common sense' at first glance, the subtleties and intersectional effects of that argument will be discussed throughout this book, not least because they are implicitly gendered.

Nevertheless, the idea that religion acts to comfort people was precisely its danger, according to Marx, giving rise to his much-quoted phrase that religion was a drug, like opium. Embedded in Marx's choice of words is another glimpse of his philosophy, perhaps used ironically. Opium, at the time of his writing, was a drug used notoriously by the upper classes who discovered it during their imperialistic activities in China and India. It is worth looking at the whole passage, not just the well-known punch line: 'Religion is the sigh of the oppressed creature, the heart of a heartless world, and the soul of soulless conditions' (Marx 1859). At first, this seems quite positive, even complimentary about religion, until he adds: 'It is the opium of the people.' Marxists are usually antagonistic towards religion for that reason, seeing it as a means of drugging people into compliance with the ruling class of property owners. Years later, the sociologist C. Wright Mills summarized this insight as a 'sociological imagination': 'The sociological imagination enables us to grasp history and biography and the relation between the two within society. That is its task and promise' (1959, 6). Mills argued that what people experience in daily life often occurs because of structural changes. He said that such changes increase as our social institutions become more complex, intertwined and encompassing:

> to be aware of the idea of social structure and to use it with sensibility is to be capable of tracing such linkages among a great variety of milieux. To be able to do that is to possess the sociological imagination.

Marx grappled with that association between human lives and wider social structures in his development of his economic, political and sociological ideas, laying down a framework for the transformation of societies through Communism, and also for the study of society through his method.

As will be discussed in more detail in the next chapter, the methods sociologists use are often messy and imprecise, much like the social phenomena we study. When Marx was writing his thesis back in the first half of the 19th century, he was aware of that, but sought to place human experience of the environment at the centre of the intellectual project. First, he argued, humans sense something in their environment; perhaps they feel cold when snow falls. They then try to make an idea of it – snow may make humans cold and therefore influences their lives. This will usually translate into a rule, or belief: snow is dangerous for humans, that is why they build shelters. Taken a step further, the social scientist might decide to conduct research about the types of dwellings in different part of the world based on their climates. This might lead to a theory about the world, such as 'human societies fare better when people can create better shelters', or, perhaps, 'the conditions in which people work depend on the material resources at hand', to 'access to material resources determines human survival and well-being' to 'humans fight over the scarce resources necessary for their survival' to 'a person becomes rich by hoarding resources and controlling those who need them' to 'an effective means of controlling people is through punishment and reward' to 'a belief system that helps people manage control others will give them more permanent power'. Thus, a Marxist sociologist may argue, kings and priests both conflict and conspire to manage the larger masses of people for their own benefit.

The human condition, Marx believed, is formed and framed by work, by *producing*. Marx articulated that idea through proposing a relationship between what people produce and what happens with that production. People should be able to benefit from the results of their labour, as they would, say, from planting crops, harvesting and eating them. But, with the advance of private property ownership, farmers no longer directly benefited from work – the landowner who employed them owned their crops and, as a consequence, their labour. In order to profit from their labour, the landowner – or, capitalist – will pay the workers less than what the goods can be sold for. The difference between what is paid as a wage and what the capitalist can sell the goods for (and accounting for other costs such as building and taxes) is a profit. The profit is generated as what Marx called 'surplus value'.

If Marx had stopped there, he would have gone down in history simply as an economist, but he did not. He took that idea and created wider theories, particularly with Engels, that spoke to politics, sociology, philosophy and religion. His success in making those connections was through his insight that labour and profit are not neutral activities understood through a balance sheet, but lead to human suffering through a process he called 'alienation'. Marx saw the effects of workers being subject to laws of supply and demand just like anything else, leading to them becoming a commodity, just like coal or corn. The consequence of this dehumanization and 'commodification' causes people to be depressed spiritually and physically (Marx 1964). Marx concluded that we are continually influenced by the material world, just as we ourselves are material. Our beliefs, mores, attitudes, consciousness itself, are all products of the material world. Idealists, on the other hand, believe that ideas or beliefs exist independently of the material world and shape human history and material outcomes rather than the other way round. For Marx, there was no God-given or higher self which determines our nature. Marx believed that ceding the power to mediate to this 'fiction' alienates people from their true nature (of being able to self-mediate): 'The more he puts into God, the less he retains in himself' (Marx 1964 109). Marx then asks, to whom does alienated labour belong? The answer is: 'to a man who holds this alien power over the worker' (Marx 1964, 115). Marx believed that capitalists would continue to hold power over the worker and to exploit the worker until the workers themselves forced a change.

The power balance looks, 150 years later, largely tipped in favour of the capitalist in a system usually described as neoliberalism. In Britain and the US there are proportionally more poor people than ever before (Giddens 1998, 270–82). In Britain, traditional industries like coal, steel and shipbuilding declined and for the most part disappeared over the past 30 years, taking thousands of jobs and depressing towns and villages. Members of the working class continue to be sicker and die younger than the more affluent middle class or the moneyed, capitalist class. They die disproportionately of almost everything – heart disease, stroke, suicide, car accidents, work-based accidents, house-fires – in far greater numbers than the others do.

Thinking with words

Capital is a word with several layers of meaning, all linked to ideas of value. Capital is the stuff we have, material or immaterial, that allows us to get what we want. A type of asset, capital may refer to the physical property we own that we can trade on the market – a house, for example, or a factory, but it also refers to the intangible assets we have of education or networks of human people. We may hear people quoting Marx, discussing capital in economic terms, or Bourdieu (1986) who wrote widely about the effects of human capital. What we know and who we know give us the means to advance in society: an education from Eton and a politics degree from Oxford University may give us a certain type of knowledge, but it also signals that we are connected to a powerful institution with powerful people.

Marx's colleague Engels provided more detailed analysis of how the capitalist system affects and is affected by women: see Celia Amorós (1991) for a critical summary.

Shortly before this book was published, data worldwide were showing that people from black and minority ethnic backgrounds have been disproportionately affected by the Covid-19 pandemic. The emerging analysis pointed to socio-economic factors, such as consistent racism, marginalization, crowded living conditions, lower incomes and employment in public-facing occupations.

From material to meaning

It can be helpful here to move from Karl Marx to Max Weber, not because they are diametrically opposed but rather because they focus on two distinct concepts that may be held in juxtaposition, a juxtaposition that has often influenced sociologists of religion and sometimes betrayed a religious bias. What could be more 'religious' than Weber's claim that people are motivated throughout life by a search for meaning?

In reviewing Marx's ideas, the voice of Weber seems to speak in response as Anthony Giddens (1970,1) wrote:

> There are few intellectual relationships in the literature of sociology which present as great an interpretative problem as that posed by the assessment of the connections between the writings of Karl Marx and those of Max Weber. It has been the view of many that Weber's writings – particularly *The Protestant Ethic and the Spirit of*

Capitalism – provide a final 'refutation' of Marx's materialism; others have taken a completely opposite view, considering that much of Weber's sociology fits without difficulty into the Marxian scheme.

Giddens's (1970) analysis of Weber and Marx draws close attention to both Weber's life as an academic theorizing about sociology, but also as a political commentator, writing at a time when Europe was being transformed by political movements which both reflected and opposed Marxist ideas. In Weber's milieu, Marxism was not an abstract theory. Weber analysed capitalism and society in terms of overlapping social spheres, rather than solely the field of economy, and later focused on striving to account for human values, judgement and other 'inner states'.

Weber famously never defined religion, saying it was not appropriate to define such a concept in advance. He did, however, focus on several aspects of society that have had important and lasting effects on the sociology of religion, primarily relating to the place of the individual, meaning, charisma, affinity and disenchantment.

Weber chose to study the role of the individual and religion and how, he argued, it was changing in favour of a more individualized spirituality, a result of increasing rationalization and disenchantment in society as a whole. Although Weber described himself as religiously 'unmusical', he was not implying that he did not understand religion. Weber grew up in a devoutly religious profoundly family. His mother was a Calvinist, which may have influenced his thinking and inclination to write one of his most influential books: *The Protestant Ethic and the Spirit of Capitalism* (1864).

Weber's task in the book was to explore how a Protestant emphasis on self-denial linked to, and perhaps produced, a strong work ethic. He argued that Protestants believed they could not achieve salvation in this world. Salvation, they believed, was only available to the 'elect', and it was impossible to know whether one was elect or not. That led them, Weber reasoned, to perform lives of self-denial and asceticism, where they would lose themselves in hard work, thrift, self-control and rational actions. Often they believed the harder one worked, the more wealth was amassed, which meant that Protestants could recognize a 'godly' person through evidence of their material success. This then related to a sense of 'calling', a certainty that attention to work demonstrated a godly life.

Weber also demonstrated a close affinity to religion through his sole venture into sociological fieldwork – a visit to his family in the United States, members of a strict Christian sect, the Primitive Baptists (Peacock and Tyson 1989). Weber maintained the view, which can be described as *a priori*, that all people share a search for 'meaning'. Religious people, he argued, often face a 'problem of meaning' when bad things happen in a world apparently governed by an omnipotent, omniscient and all-loving god. Often, they seek to resolve the problem of meaning created when their belief in a good god is threatened by bad events. This was described by Talcott Parsons as a core definition of religion where beliefs are 'systems of cognitive orientation relative to problems of meaning' (Parsons 1951, 368).

Weber used the term *verstehen* to describe an understanding of human action, an understanding which could not be derived from using scientific research methods commonly employed in the natural sciences. No study of human action would be complete if the researcher could not grasp, from informants' perspectives, the meaning of their actions. Weber's driving assumption that people are searching for meaning has rarely been problematized. Most scholars in both anthropology and sociology of religion follow implicitly, and sometimes explicitly, a Weberian assumption that all people, always, search for 'meaning' (Weber 1922, 117) (and see Chapter 2 for the implications on method).

Weber's adoption of an individualistic, universalizing search for meaning has strongly shaped the sociology of religion. For example, Weber (1922) proposed that people would feel varying degrees of attraction to, or affinity with, different types of religion, based on a sense of similarities with others.[2] As has been suggested in other work (Day 2005; Woodhead 2001), it is difficult to apply directly to women Weber's theories on why different groups of people are attracted to different kinds of religions as his analysis is based on men's economic conditions and occupations: the warrior, the peasant, the artisan, the missionary, the tent-maker, the prince, the capitalist and so on. Other scholars have pointed to similar issues in trying to reconcile such grand theories with women's experience.

Most theories about religion are largely constructed by men about social contexts dominated by men, where women's voices are subsumed and assumed. When sociology was being formed as a discipline, there were several influential female sociologists who then became muted and hidden. In their book about those significant women, Patricia Lengermann and Jill Niebrugge-Brantley (1998, 1) explain that their book makes three claims:

> that women have always been significantly involved in creating sociology; that women have always made distinctive and important contributions to social theory; and that women's contributions to sociology and social theory have been written out of the record of the discipline's history.

They (Lengermann and Niebrugge-Brantley 1998, 2) point out that any discipline gains an identity through the stories it tells itself about itself. Sociology, they explain, tells its story through the lens of theorists. This, they remind us, is a choice. The story could as easily be told by relating major empirical works or through a discussion of its subdisciplines, but theory lends an important explanatory legitimacy as it directs attention to certain features.

> The history of sociology's theories is conventionally told as a history of white male agency – an account of the theoretical contributions of a 'founding' generation of men [...] This history is presented as an account of the natural way things occurred, a chronicle beyond the powers of human tellers to change.

As such, theories and definitions tend to universalize and marginalize women through ignoring anything specific about their experience and constructs (Bowie 2006). It will also have an effect on the kind of research that is deemed to be acceptable.

While celebrated as a milestone in secularization theory, a glaring weakness in Bryan Wilson's (1966) work, I argue, is its ungendered account, or, more accurately, its neglect of women in society, both scholars and laity: this appears to be a book wholly resting on the performance of men and absence (apart from coded reference) of women. It is striking that at a time of writing in the most significant cultural revolution in living memory, that of the 1960s, women, gender and sexuality were not given a full treatment in the book. Both lay women and women scholars are muted: none appear in Wilson's index, compared to, for example, 31 entries for ecumenicalism, 12 for salvation and 30 for sects. Women scholars are also ignored. Of Wilson's 129 references, only one refers to a woman where he suggests (1966, 75) readers see 'for a popular discussion' Jessica Mitford. Although Wilson discussed the founder of Christian Science, Mary Baker Eddy, he does not cite her own work but folds her into other discussions. When Wilson calls for research on laity, he refers to seminaries or to lay preachers (men) in Anglicanism or Methodism. His coded reference to women is dismissive: problems with laity are because he suggests (Wilson 1966, 130), they 'often persist in commitment for community and family rather than for well-articulated ideological and intellectual reasons'.

Wilson's later work took this coding even further (2001, 44–5) referring to the modern family being 'split apart', with parents insufficiently present to take a role in the moral inculcation of their children. This, he says, is not only because family structures have changed but also because individuals are being encouraged today to 'discover their own identities', to 'be themselves', to 'do their own thing'.

This 'gender-blindness' is a distinctive feature of the sociological study of religion, argued Woodhead (2001, 67–84). She described Weber's idea of the 'iron cage' and Durkheim's concept of 'anomie' as particularly oriented to men because both assume participation in the public, paid-for working realm, a realm from which women have traditionally been excluded. This is an important insight for the future of the church as a social organization, because class and capital not only confer advantage, they also create barriers: 'class concerns boundaries, those distinctions we make between ourselves and others' (McCloud 2007, 2).

Durkheim and the social collective

> The first logical categories were social categories; the first classes of things were classes of men into which these things were integrated.
>
> (Durkheim 1963 [1902], 93)

In his classic study, *Elementary Forms of the Religious Life* (Durkheim 1915) Émile Durkheim proposed that, while the forms of religion may change, becoming more complex over time, religion will always be with us due to its 'ever-present causes' and its continuing function.

Although the *Elementary Forms* was by no means Durkheim's only work on religion – he wrote and lectured about it frequently – it is widely regarded as his 'final word' on the subject and the culmination of all his earlier (and for the most part, consistent) deliberations (Lukes 1973, 482; Pickering 1964, 82–90). It therefore usually serves as the primary source on Durkheim for this work.

Somewhat controversially for theologians, Durkheim rejected the idea that religion derives from a belief in the supernatural or divine beings. Because religion depends on groups of people uniting with shared faith, Durkheim classified magic as not being religion: 'it does not result in binding together those who adhere to it, nor in uniting them into a group leading a common life' (Durkheim 1915, 44). He defines religion as follows:

> A religion is a unified system of beliefs and practices relative to sacred things, that is to say, things set apart and forbidden – beliefs and practice which unite into one single moral community called a Church, all those who adhere to them.
>
> (Durkheim 1915, 47)

Durkheim focuses in *The Elementary Forms* almost exclusively on Australian aboriginal peoples because he believed that, being organized on a clan system, theirs is the simplest form of society, and therefore would have the simplest form of religion (totemism), which is therefore the most 'elementary' religion we can possibly know (Durkheim 1915, 168). Durkheim believed discovering the origins of their beliefs would lead to understanding the causes of religion universally.

Although many have criticized his method (secondary readings of colonial-based reports) and analysis (overly dependent on reductive functionalism, see e.g. Lukes 1973) I intend here to follow closely his line of analysis and conclusions which contributed importantly to both the sociology of religion and the sociology of knowledge, producing a classic 'which continues to afford intellectual excitement and inspiration' (Lukes 1973, 482).

When Durkheim discusses the origin of religion, he tells us clearly he is not discussing 'absolute beginnings' (Durkheim 1915, 8), ultimately a fruitless and unscientific task. Rather, he is concerned with its 'ever-present causes'. Having an 'ever-present cause', however, cannot mean religion was always with us, according to Durkheim's theory. Religion has only been with us for as long as people have gathered in groups, as it arises through the intensity of their group activities. This logic is particularly clear when Durkheim diverts from his analysis of the aboriginal people and briefly describes the French Revolution, caused by the patriotic fever of the collective.

From his premise that religion originates in human gatherings, Durkheim develops his theory of how such events occur and produce religiosity. He examined the gathering of a clan, or sometimes more than one clan within a tribe. A clan is defined as a group of people united under a common totem – an emblem taken after an animal or plant. The clan may be geographically dispersed over a wide area and can gather together for long periods of days or months. The gathering is exuberant, with people feasting, drinking, singing and dancing for hours on end, losing their sense of individual propriety, including their taboos, as participants are swept away by their increasing feelings of intoxication, well-being and interconnectedness.

Eventually, the party ends and the clans disperse. How, wondered Durkheim, can the sense of group identity be maintained? Only by coming together again, says Durkheim, for periodic renewal. But something else has to happen other than just a good feeling to match Durkheim's definition of a religion. What causes the concepts of sacred and profane, the belief system and the 'Church' as a 'moral community'?

In those moments of collective effervescence people feel that they have been transported into a different world. Here, they see the world not as it is in a material sense, but in a symbolic sense. This is, he explains, not simply true with religions: most of the time we imbue ordinary items with sentiments and feelings (Durkheim 1915, 227).

During those moments of collective effervescence, individuals felt a great sense of unity and of something bigger than all of them. But, needing to see what it was, the individuals had to project this 'force' outside of themselves. It could be projected onto anything but in the midst of the excitement it becomes fixed on what people can see all around them – the totem or emblem of the clan (although, Durkheim says, the real force is the clan itself, this is too abstract a reality to conceive 'by such rudimentary intelligences': Durkheim 1915, 220–1). Whatever they project this upon becomes sacred.

Having objectified and sanctified the totem of the clan, certain attitudes and behaviours towards the totem are developed and observed. It also follows that the plants and animals represented by the totem would 'evoke sentiments analogous to those aroused by the emblem itself', as will other things connected with it, including, to some extent, the clan members themselves: 'a sacred character is to a high degree contagious' (Durkheim 1915, 222). From there, Durkheim explains, sub-totems gradually emerge and with the group's cosmological systems (the 'primitive' methods of classification) together form a belief system. The material world thus combines with the moral world and people join together as a moral community, or church.

Durkheim continually reminds us that the system springs from the group, from society: if the totem symbolizes god and society, 'is that not because the god and the society are only one?' (Durkheim 1915, 206).

The function of religion

In this section I will examine the question: what service does religion perform, for whom and for what benefit? There are several functions of religion which can be derived from Durkheim, but here I will focus on social and individual stability. Other main functions can be summarized as 'categories of the understanding' and 'explanations' (Durkheim 1915 9–20, 439–44).

The prime function of religion, according to Durkheim, is social stability. This benefits both society and the individual. Society needs us to participate willingly, which often requires personal sacrifice or contradicts our desires or instincts. If it only gained our compliance through physical means, it could be overthrown through physical means. Rather, it projects its authority or 'moral ascendancy', which in turn commands our respect and obedience. Respect, he argued, is the emotion which we experience when we feel this interior and wholly spiritual pressure (Durkheim 1915, 207). If this pressure is 'spiritual' it must, argues Durkheim, generate the feeling that it comes from a great, external power. It does indeed, he continues, but the power is that of society. The moral authority reflects the morals of society, which are based on socially cohesive ideals.

Religion provides detailed rules and 'interdictions' about how life should and should not be lived. Durkheim prefers the word *interdiction* to taboo, although agrees their sense is the same (Durkheim 1915, 300). He focuses on the negative cult whose interdictions 'are the religious interdictions par excellence' (Durkheim 1915, 302) based on the 'principle that the profane should never touch the sacred' (Durkheim 1915, 302). Although most rules are socially cohesive and cause people to act against their own selfish desires, some interdictions seem to serve no practical purpose. There are practices and rituals which lead at the extreme to asceticism (which serves as a good role model to the rest of society), but at the very least to inconvenience, discomfort, sacrifice and even suffering. That, he argues, is its purpose. The individual must be dominated; 'his' nature must be subdued – not broken, but brought into line with the society. These acts 'strengthen the bonds attaching an individual to the society of which he is a member' (Durkheim 1915, 226): it is the price that individuals pay for the sake of their society (Durkheim 1915, 316).

Something key to Durkheim's thinking, and which has provoked much debate in the sociology of religion, is the sacred-profane duality: the life of society being sacred and the individual life being profane. This is reinforced in religious festivals where ordinary, individual life is suspended in favour of religious activities, thus reinforcing that it is the religious (society/collective) life which is sacred. As it is the society which determines what is sacred, we can look at the society's articulated beliefs – its creeds and other statements which reflect its beliefs. Social stability is therefore maintained through the obedience of society's members. Religious rules and rituals discourage people from acting on their own desires, some of which may be anti-social. People are compliant, not causing the havoc which could lead to the breakdown of order and, ultimately, the society.

A society enjoying the benefit of harmony acts like a well-oiled machine. People act nearly unconsciously or automatically, without having to think through each small daily action, let alone a major moral decision. Many choices are made for them. The rules pervade the minutiae of daily life, reinforcing at nearly every moment the presence of society and thereby integrating the individual within the society. Individuals benefit as well from this stability. Their daily lives can be conducted in a more orderly, predictable fashion.

To depart for a moment from *The Elementary Forms*, the theme of an individual's need to integrate with society was also explored in another of Durkheim's studies, *Suicide*. Here, he proposed three 'social causes' of suicide – egoism, altruism and anomie – which vary according to the degree of integration one feels in society. The most efficacious preventions, he argued, are Catholicism, Judaism and the Anglican Church. The level of detail contained in the rules of these more orthodox religions (as opposed to the more liberal forms of Protestantism) left little room for individual decisions, and integrated the individual better into the religion (Lukes 1973, 208–13).

Every creed begins with the belief in salvation by faith, says Durkheim (1915, 415). Believers feel stronger through an act of communicating with their god, he says, although given that his definition of religion does not depend on the concept of god, we must read here 'society'. But it's not enough to just believe – people need to actively engage with each other in an act of renewal. It is therefore essential for Durkheim that there is a regular gathering. In Western Europe and North America people usually associate this gathering with a church service, but it is not critical to Durkheim's theory that it be a church as we commonly know it. It is just 'necessary that we act, and that we repeat the acts thus necessary every time we feel the need of renewing their effects' (Durkheim 1915, 417).

Implicit here is his idea that individuals will need to 'renew their effects'; that the individual has a need. More than the need for salvation, the need must be a need for the group, otherwise the need could be filled without the group in one-to-one prayer with one's god. In his conclusion, Durkheim says specifically that the religious experience is the experience of society, and that it is society which awakens this sentiment of a refuge, of a shield and of a guardian support which attaches the believer to his cult (Durkheim 1915, 418).

That awakening serves the dual purpose of strengthening the individual by tying him more closely to society through dependency and gratitude. And, with the individual willingly remaining part of society, it satisfies his need for belonging and society's need for stability and cohesion. Durkheim maintained his position that religion should not be defined in reference to a deity.

Sample questions for private study

1 What are weaknesses in Weber's work that fail to explain women's religiosity?
2 Suggest sociological explanations for 'meaning'.

Sample class exercise

Debate the manifestation of 'sacred' in university life.

Notes

1 The way in which men have manipulated knowledge is not simply by ignoring women and citing each other (Ahmed 2012) but through the impact of other 'old boy' alliances. Wilson and Bruce (2016, xi) recounts that David Martin, famous for upsetting secularization theories, wrote (Martin 2013, 141) to the arch secularization theorist Bryan Wilson and agreed to maintain a 'gentleman's agreement'; not to openly criticize each other. How differently might students have viewed the central debates about secularization if these two men had engaged with each other's work in scholarly argumentation?
2 The origin of the term 'elective affinity' was not discussed by Weber but appears, according to several authors (see, e.g. McKinnon 2010) to derive from a novel by Goethe.

Indicative reading

Ahmed, Sara. 2012. *On Being Included: Racism and Diversity in Institutional Life*. Durham, NC: Duke University Press.

Amorós, Celia. 1991. *Origins of the Family, Origins of a Misunderstanding: Toward a Criticism of Patriarchal Reason*. Barcelona: Anthropos.

Bainbridge, William Sims. 1985. 'Utopian Communities: Theoretical Issues.' In *The Sacred in a Secular Age*, edited by Phillip E. Hammond, 21–35. Berkeley-Los Angeles, London: University of California Press.

Barrett, Michèle. 1980. *Women's Oppression Today: Problems in Marxist Feminist Analysis*. London: Verso.

Bhambra, Gurminder. 2007. *Rethinking Modernity: Postcolonialism and the Sociological Imagination*. Basingstoke: Palgrave.

Bhambra, Gurminder K., Dalia Gebrial and Kerem Nişancıoğlu, eds. 2018. *Decolonising the University*. London: Pluto.

Bourdieu, Pierre. 1986. *The Forms of Capital*. Westport, CT: Greenwood.

Bowie, Fiona. 2006. *The Anthropology of Religion: An Introduction*. Malden, MA:, Oxford: Blackwell.

Collins, Randal. 1994. *Four Sociological Traditions*. New York: Oxford University Press.

Connell, Raewyn W. 1997. 'Why is Classical Theory Classical?' *American Journal of Sociology* 102, no. 6 (May): 1511–57. DOI: 10.1086/231125.

Connell, Raewyn. 2007. *Southern Theory: The Global Dynamics of Knowledge in Social Science.* Malden, MA: Polity.

Connell, Raewyn. 2018. 'Decolonizing Sociology.' *Contemporary Sociology* 47, no. 4: 399–407. https://doi.org/10.1177/0094306118779811

Day, Abby. 2005. 'Doing Theodicy: An Empirical Study of a Women's Prayer Group.' *Journal of Contemporary Religion* 20, no. 3: 343–56. https://doi.org/10.1080/13537900500249889

Day, Abby, Lois Lee, David Thomas and James Spickard. Forthcoming 2021. Doing Diversity in Academia: Practices and Pitfalls. Bristol: Bristol University Press.

Durkheim, Émile. 1915. *The Elementary Forms of the Religious Life, a Study in Religious Sociology.* London: G. Allen & Unwin; Macmillan.

Durkheim, Émile. 1993. *Le suicide.* Paris: Presses universitaires de France.

Durkheim, Émile, and Marcel Mauss. 1902 (1963). *Primitive Classification,* translated from the French and edited with an introduction by Rodney Needham. London: Cohen.

Encarnacion, Gutierrez Rodriguez, Manuela Boatca and Sergio Costa, eds. 2010. *Decolonizing European Sociology: Transdisciplinary Approaches.* Burlington, VT: Ashgate.

Frazer, James George. 1890 (1935). *The Golden Bough; a Study in Magic and Religion.* New York: Macmillan.

Giddens, Anthony. 1970. 'Marx, Weber, and the Development of Capitalism.' *Sociology* 4, no. 3: 289–310. 003803857000400301.

Giddens, Anthony. 1998. *The Third Way: The Renewal of Social Democracy.* Cambridge: Polity Press.

Gilman, Charlotte Perkins. 1899. *Women and Economics.* London: Putnam's.

Jeffries, Stuart. 2018. 'The Return of Marxism.' *The Guardian,* 4 July 2012. www.theguardian.com/world/2012/jul/04/the-return-of-marxism, last accessed Aug. 2018.

Kant, Immanuel. 1881. *Critique of Pure Reason.* London: Macmillan.

Lengermann, Patricia M., and Jill Niebrugge-Brantley. 1998. *The Women Founders: Sociology and Social Theory, 1830–1930. A Text/Reader.* Boston, MA: McGraw-Hill.

Lukes, Steven. 1973. *Individualism.* New York: Harper Torchbooks.

Mann, Michael. 1986. *The Sources of Social Power,* vol. 1. Cambridge: Cambridge University Press.

Martin, David. 2013. *The Education of David Martin: The Making of an Unlikely Sociologist.* London SPCK.

Marx, Karl. 1859. A Contribution to the Critique of Political Economy. Moscow: Progress Publishers.

Marx, Karl. 1964. *The Economic and Philosophic Manuscripts of 1844,* edited by Dirk J. Struik. New York: International Publishers.

Marx, Karl, and Fredrik Engels. 1848 *The Communist Manifesto.* London: Pluto Press.

Mbembe, Achille. 2016. 'Decolonizing the University: New Directions.' *Arts and Humanities in Higher Education* 15, no. 1: 29–41.

McCloud, Sean. 2007. *Divine Hierarchies: Class in American Religion and Religious Studies.* Chapel Hill, NC: University of North Carolina Press.

McKinnon, Andrew M. 2010. 'Elective Affinities of the Protestant Ethic: Weber and the Chemistry of Capitalism.' *Sociological Theory* 28, no. 1: 108–26.

Mignolo, Walter D. 2011. *The Darker Side of Western Modernity: Global Futures, Decolonial Options.* Durham, NC: Duke University Press.

Mills, C. Wright. 1959. *The Sociological Imagination.* New York: Oxford University Press.

Needham, Rodney. 1972. *Belief, Language and Experience.* Chicago, IL: Chicago University Press.

Parsons, Talcott. 1951. *The Social System.* New York: Free Press.

Peacock, James L., and Ruel W. Tyson. 1989. *Pilgrims of Paradox: Calvinism and Experience among the Primitive Baptists of the Blue Ridge.* Washington, DC: Smithsonian Series in Ethnographic Inquiry.

Pickering, William S. F. 1964. *Durkheim's Sociology of Religion. Themes and Theories.* Boston, MA: Routledge & Kegan Paul.

Said, Edward. 1978. *Orientalism.* New York: Vintage Books.

Santos, Boaventura de Sousa. 2014. *Epistemologies of the South: Justice Against Epistemicide.* New York: Routledge.

Shilling, Chris, and Phillip Mellor. 2011. 'Retheorising Emile Durkheim on Society and Religion: Embodiment, Intoxication and Collective Life.' *The Sociological Review* 59, no. 1: 17–41. https://doi.org/10.1111/j.1467-954X.2010.01990.x.

Smallwood, Stephanie. 2008. *Saltwater Slavery.* Cambridge, MA: Harvard University Press.

Weber, Max. 1922. *The Sociology of Religion.* Boston, MA: Beacon Press.

Weber, Max. 1958. *The Protestant Ethic and the Spirit of Capitalism.* New York: Scribner.

Weber, Max. 1968. *Economy and Society: An Outline of Interpretive Sociology.* New York: Bedminster Press.

Wilson, Bryan. 1966. *Religion in Secular Society.* London: C. A. Watts & Co. Ltd.

Wilson, Bryan. 2001. 'Salvation, Secularization, and De-moralization.' In *The Blackwell Companion to Sociology of Religion,* edited by Richard K. Fenn, 39–51. Oxford: Blackwell.

Wilson, Bryan R., and Steve Bruce. 2016. *Religion in Secular Society: Fifty Years On.* Oxford: Oxford University Press.

Woodhead, Linda. 2001. 'Feminism and the Sociology of Religion: From Gender-Blindness to Gendered Difference.' In *The Blackwell Companion to Sociology of Religion,* edited by Richard K. Fenn, 67–84. Oxford: Blackwell.

Chapter 2

How do we know what we know?

Introduction

In this chapter the particular problems, debates and patterns that are characteristic of the sociology of religion are discussed, with an emphasis on contemporary epistemological and ethical issues. It is not designed as a primer in research techniques, but as a way to understand the kinds of questions and dilemmas facing scholars in sociology of religion today when confronting arguably the most important question in their research and teaching: how do we know what we know? How are we studying, analysing and creating knowledge for current and future generations?

One of the most common questions, and problems, facing sociologists of religion is: how do we know what religion is and who is religious? We often think of religion as consisting of three Bs – belief, belonging and behaviour – but those do not apply with equal salience and meaning across all religions and societies. Nor does the distinction between 'functional' (what religion does) and 'substantive' (what religion essentially is) definitions of religion. The 'functional' view of religion describes what religion does for wider society and will likely include researching its mechanisms and effects. Theorists discussed in the previous chapter wrote about how religion operated in society, drawing people together as a cooperative group, as Durkheim argued, or masking the pains of capitalism and therefore enabling it to continue in society, as Marx wrote. While sociologists typically research religion in terms of its function, they also accept that it is too easy to simply reduce religion to effect and therefore not show how those effects can be produced by other means. The classic trap is the 'football-is-religion' argument where it can be clearly shown that a group meets frequently and ecstatically to support and praise its object of worship (the football team). Is that sufficient to warrant defining football as religion? Someone holding a 'substantive' view of religion will likely question whether the object of worship has supernatural powers and whether the fans hold beliefs and morals that pre-exist and transcend the experience of the football match. In practice, and analytically, those two categories frequently overlap.

As discussed in the previous chapters, sociologists assume that categories are socially constructed and do not precede society. They create, Peter Berger and Thomas Luckmann argued (1966), socially constructed knowledge through interpreting actions, creating meaningful concepts about those actions, adopting roles as a result and institutionalizing them. James Beckford (2003, 16–19) wrote that many scholars appear to study religion as if it were 'a single, invariant object', whereas he recommends (Beckford 2003, 20) that the best way to discuss religion is not to define 'it', but to consider the 'varieties of meaning attributed to religion in social settings, to discern the relative frequency of the prevailing meanings and to monitor changes over time'.

As with social science in general, academics may use a variety of techniques in studying their social worlds: surveys, questionnaires, interviews, non-participant and participant observation, lived ethnography, multi-sited ethnography, discourse analysis and photo elicitation. The choice of methods is relative to the academic disciplines and orientations of the scholar, the most significant of which may be described as differences between what James Spickard describes as 'generalizers', interested in 'how' large patterns and underlying laws exist, and the 'particularizers', interested in 'what' specific groups of people do and think. While the latter type of scholar may discern a pattern and make connections to other groups or larger theories, their aim is not to uncover or prove laws or 'truths'. Spickard describes a distinction between sociology and anthropology in partly those terms, although there has been considerable shift in the last century. Nevertheless, anthropology's focus of study tends to be on specific groups and their physical, linguistic, cultural and historical characteristics. Sociologists, Spickard adds (Spickard et al. 2002, 145), 'usually follow Durkheim in ruling biology out of court. A *sui generis* social reality resists biological or psychological explanation.' Where anthropology has been traditionally focused on 'culture', sociology has been concerned with 'institutions'; anthropology studied people 'over there' and sociologists studied people 'here'. Those divisions have become increasingly blurred, particularly due to anthropology's reflections on its colonial history, and Spickard reminds us that, while studying people close to home, sociologists are just as easily as anthropologists constructing an 'other', often with the underlying assumption that they are not, but perhaps should be, like 'us'. The contemporary sociologist strives to work without resorting to fixed laws and truths (Spickard 2002, 152):

> Rather than presenting 'the facts', the new ethnography speaks of 'texts', 'discourses', and 'narratives'. Rather than taking the role of omniscient narrator, it touts 'reflexivity', 'pluralism', 'dialogue'. It broods over the impossibility of its knowledge and the inadequacy of its key ideas.

Nevertheless, Spickard (2002, 163–4) concludes, anthropologists have gone further than sociologists to undo the harm of their colonial past and create, through earnest engagements in dialogue, more collaborative, ethical works:

> Post-colonial particularizing anthropology has embraced equality, while much particularizing sociology has not. Anthropological ethnographers once wrote as if they served the Empire, but many do so no longer. Sociological ethnographers, for the most part, still participate in a discourse that honors the middle class.

He warns that a generalizing social science 'produces a clash of worldviews that implicitly belittles religious understandings. And because it does not recognize these understandings' epistemological equality, it furthers the colonial project.'

Religion is 'man' made

One of the first realizations that confronts a sociologist of religion scholar or student is the androcentric nature of the sub-field. Although she is more anthropologist than sociologist, I usually start my classes on this subject by referring to the work of Fiona Bowie (2006). Hers was one of the first texts I read about anthropology of religion, and her forceful exposé of the way the discipline was constructed from a male viewpoint made a strong impression. She pointed out that the pioneers in the field were, literally, pioneers in fields: mostly men, and mostly white men working for northern European governments or private companies. Their goal was to learn about the indigenous peoples in far-flung points of the empire, not to satisfy intellectual curiosity, but to gauge whether they were friendly, had weapons, created goods for trade and, in sum, were likely to be a profitable resource for the wealthier countries of Europe.

The implications of that setting are ethical and epistemological. If a white foreign man from, say, England, were to approach people in a community in, say, Sudan, they were likely to have been greeted by men. If they were allowed to stay in the region and continue their investigations, it was likely they would continue to be in the presence of men, with access to women, children and vulnerable members of the community closely guarded. Following that logic, it becomes inescapable that what the male interloper explored and learned about life in the soon-to-be colonies was not neutrally and unequivocally about 'life' or 'religion', but about visible male life and male religion, tinged with an agenda to consider the usefulness of that knowledge to whatever cause had financed their trip, whether religious, political or commercial.

The 19th-century excursions of men to foreign lands may explain why scholars studying religion spend a disproportionate amount of time on 'ritual' and 'meaning', sharing a 'predominant view of religion as meaning and ritual' (Bender et al. 2013, 10–11), neglecting less visible and, perhaps, equally or more important aspects such as activities not conventionally regarded as religion. I argue that the reason 'ritual' forms so much a part of the study of religion is because it is easy to observe, being mainly a public performance. Those performances may have been interpreted by the early explorers as 'religion' and, if that was the main activity of intense, choreographed community life they saw, it would therefore be their easy conclusion that ritual forms the heart of religion. If, alternatively, they had been able to visit and talk with women, they may have discovered other, significant practices, such as cleaning, food preparation, care for the sick and dying, childbirth, foraging, water collection and other such 'women's work' that formed a major part of a different, but arguably also religious, experience. As Catherine Bell reflected, what is defined as a ritual is often in the eye of the beholder, representing a particular way of looking at world. The associated monolithic terminology and essentialist views of ritual impose 'a powerful set of assumptions about objectivity, religion and other societies' (Bell 2000, 377).

For example, in an ethnographic research project (Day 2017), I was able to visit and work with laywomen in churches, who showed me many aspects of their labours that, for them, were deeply religious. Sharing tea and biscuits with a homeless person, for example, was how, they explained, they performed part of what they understood Jesus to have desired. Cleaning a church in silence was, for many of them, a time of private meditation and prayer where, one woman told me, she had the rare opportunity in her otherwise busy week to be quiet and could listen to her Lord. William Barylo's

(2017) study of young Muslims volunteering in charities showed that their conception of their religion moved well beyond practising ritual to engaging with more diverse and dispersed social fields.

Another preoccupation in the study of religion is the apparent search for 'meaning'. Weber's work has strongly influenced many generations of scholars, not least because he emphasized an apparently universal (and rarely critiqued) search for meaning whereby he discussed:

> the metaphysical needs of the human mind as it is driven to reflect on ethical and religious questions, driven not by material need but by an inner compulsion to understand the world as a meaningful cosmos and to take up a position toward it.
>
> (Weber 1922, 117)

Are we sure about that? Certainly, generations of scholars from Weber through Clifford Geertz (1973, 1966) and Peter Berger (1967) take it as a given and rarely question it, although Weber (1922, 124) sowed some seeds for future dissent by attributing the search for meaning to an intellectual, elite cadre:

> The salvation sought by the intellectual is always based on inner need, and hence it is at once more remote from life, more theoretical and more systematic than salvation from external distress, the quest for which is characteristic of nonprivileged classes . . . it is the intellectual who transforms the concept of the world into the problem of meaning.

Or, as Joel Robbins warns (2006, 218), there is amongst scholars often a need to impute or discern 'meaning' when it is perhaps the scholar, not the research participant, who is seeking it: 'meaninglessness is always something untoward, lobbed in unexpectedly'.

I suggest that such a preoccupation is, again, gendered. Male scholars seem to privilege the contemplation of 'meaning', often at the heart of male-dominated disciplines such as theology, religious studies and philosophy,[1] and incorporate that assumption into their writing, research and teaching. In the next chapter, I will revisit that problem and show how it is beginning to lose its protected space in the field as the study shifts but, for now, it is important to note that issues of ritual and meaning infuse research agendas and the methods that follow.

This is a good example of how a feminist epistemology calls attention to how knowledge is produced, not 'found' as if it is already complete, waiting to be discovered (see e.g. Ackerley and True 2010). Another aspect of a feminist epistemological approach is its embrace of normativity. Rather than continue a (some might say, fictional) goal towards 'objectivity', a normative stance acknowledges the intertwined, subjective nature of research and will take up a position: some kinds of research methods may be simply wrong.

Questioning the questioner

Sociologists sometimes use large-scale methods, such as national surveys, and small-scale methods, such as ethnography. Like any standard methods textbook will teach, the choice of method should be driven by the research question. None is intrinsically better or worse than another, but all have strengths and weaknesses that will become obvious as research continues. For the study of religion, some scholars claim that a completely new stance is required since, the argument goes, the experience of knowing God is like none other and cannot be reduced to a mere questionnaire.

A common phrase that arises in such debates is 'insider/outsider' (see Knott 2010 for a discussion about issues in religious studies). The anthropological insider-outsider distinction (see Lewis, 1973 for an early, and excellent, summary) has been criticized for casting the 'insider' as an exotic 'other' being observed by an apparently objective 'outsider'. Those advocating such a distinction argue only someone with first-hand experience of, say, the presence of a god, would know what that is like to know a god and be religious, and therefore someone who has not had that experience is not qualified to discuss it. That dichotomy has acted in many cases as an effective shield, fending off researchers who wanted to explain religion more in terms of wider social structures. But is it a legitimate claim? It could be argued that there is never a clear insider/outsider distinction in any research project. Let us say, for example, that a woman who self-identifies as an atheist is researching female members of a new religious movement. While she may not have ever experienced the exact type of emotion associated with group worship, she has experienced life as a woman. Is she, therefore, inside or outside that binary? One way researchers address the issue is to be aware of and reflexively address their own positionality (Ackerley and True 2010), taking an intersectional approach to locate the way knowledge is historically and socially located (see Collins 1998, Ryan 2015, 2011) and questioning what, I suggest, may be an obsession with and fetishization of 'objectivity'. Sandra Harding (1991) argues that point and shows how such naturalized claims function to mask exclusions and inequalities. A specific outcome of concerns about position and power is feminist standpoint theory, which goes beyond simply recognizing one's position to actively incorporating it in the research process, recognizing that all stages of the traditional approach, such as the scientific method, are theory-laden, with theory itself being a subjective creation. Importantly, feminists argue that research should begin with and be driven by the lived experience of those being researched: as Harding (1991, 56) said: 'Starting off research from women's lives will generate less partial and distorted accounts not only of women's lives but also of men's lives and of the whole social order.'

A compromise some researchers reach is known as 'phenomenology', whereby the researcher claims to put aside, or 'bracket out' questions such as the veracity or falsehood of a research participant's own religious experience, and concentrate instead on what may be understood as issues outside that individual experience. Sociologists grapple uneasily with such a position, asking how the individual experience can be isolated. Why would it be methodologically any different, they may ask, to study a monk or a murderer? Both are shaped by their social environment. The monk may hear voices and call them words of God and accept them as a revelation: a serial murder may also claim to hear voices and call them the words of a master and accept them as instructions. Why would a researcher 'bracket out' any of that phenomenon on the grounds that they, as researchers, do not hear voices? Critical criminology has become more accepted as an approach than more traditional psychological or forensic approaches to studying crime, mainly through claiming that criminals are not created by physiology or individual psychology, but mostly by the environment within which they live. They therefore look to wider influences, such as economy or cultural artefacts: it is not possible, they would suggest, to isolate an individual as an apparently single, 'criminal mind'.

As Russell McCutcheon somewhat wryly observed (2003, 338) no one would expect to see books are articles with titles such as 'The Insider/Outsider Problem and the Study of Athens' or 'The Insider/Outsider Problem and the Study of Nazism' because, in the first case, there are no living ancient Athenians to study, and in the second case, no scholar is likely to try to create an empathetic relationship with Nazis in order to sympathize with and thereby to some extent legitimize their position.

It is also important to see that some of the most significant, enduring works in sociology of religion, and sociology more generally, have been written by people who were at the outset, or during the course of their research became, partial 'insiders'. Anthropologist E. E. Evans Pritchard (1937), writing in the early part of the 20th century, concluded in his research that a belief in a spirit world, such as witches, was not irrational but acted as a mechanism to create and maintain social cohesion. He famously upset his standing as an 'outsider' with an account of seeing what he described as the light of a witch. Jeanne Favret-Saada (1980), a late 20th-century anthropologist, reported that she felt she had been possessed by a witch spirit in the region of France where she was studying such phenomena.

The highly regarded *Street Corner Society* by William Foote Whyte (1943) has influenced scholarship and policy since its publication in 1943. The result of four years of participant observation in the area he described as 'Cornerville', Boston, Whyte's aim was to map out the social structure of the community, at a time when many such 'slum' areas were thought to be a 'formidable mass of confusion' (Whyte 1943, xvi). Only by living there, observing and participating in daily activities, could Whyte have found that, in fact, the area was a 'highly organised and integrated social system' (Whyte 1943, xvi). As Whyte became assimilated into the society, learning the local Italian language and participating in activities, he won the confidence of the majority of the social actors. The cost, to him, was to lose some of his 'outsider' status, but the trade was worthwhile. He writes: 'I began as a non-participating observer. As I became accepted into the community, I found myself becoming almost a non-observing participant' (Whyte 1943, 321).

Graham Harvey (2017) is credited with reviving the study of 'animism', a spiritual tradition connected to his own beliefs and practices, but the early study of which was marked by colonial endeavours. As he re-examined it, he formulated the conception of this as 'New Animism', meaning the communion of the 'pan-spirits' amongst humans and non-humans, living and dead. His work is important for all scholars as he is trying to upset the historical balance which was long tipped in favour of the visiting scholar deemed to be an impartial, detached, observing 'outsider' in the regions and lives of indigenous peoples. The 'outsider', apparently neutral, position therefore carries the weight of the scholar-colonial relationship.

Another 'upset' to the outsider-insider relationship is the recognition that people in the 'south' have a role to play in the religious lives of people in the 'north'. This has been forcefully felt in the reshaping of the Anglican communion (Day 2015) with continuing contests over whose leadership and preferred theological directions should dominate. Another example is the phenomenon of 'reverse mission'. While Christian mission-aries from Euro American countries still go to Africa, for example, arguably the most

Christianized continent on earth, the comparative irreligiosity of the West has become a concern for Christians elsewhere. Rebecca Catto's (2008) study on 'reverse mission' examines the practice where, starting in the 1980s, churches in the 'global south' sent missionaries to the 'global north', in a practice described by Matthews Ojo (2007) as: '[t]he sending of missionaries to Europe and North America by churches and Christians from the non-Western world, particularly Africa, Asia and Latin America, which were at the receiving end of Catholic and Protestant missions as mission fields from the sixteenth century to the late twentieth century'.

Case example: music and identity

Pauline Muir, an academic based at Goldsmiths, University of London, wanted to study musical repertoires and the relationship to congregational racial and religious identity musical styles and congregational interaction in churches known as 'Black Majority'. These churches, abundant in London, attract mainly Pentecostal worshippers originating from West African countries such as Ghana and Nigeria, as well as the Caribbean. They are the main growing form of Christianity in London. Muir, a classically trained musician and expert in arts management, wanted to know more about their music and the engagement with congregations. She initially thought that her 'insider' position as someone who had worshipped with her family in the same church for 20 years would work in her favour. In practice, it did not, as church leaders rejected her request to study the congregation, saying that they had experienced too many negative representations from researchers in the past.

In her thesis, she often uses musical language to explain her position and experience. In her discussion of methodology, she begins with 'Playing Outside' (Muir 2018, 95). This, she explains, is 'a technique used in jazz improvisation where a player plays notes that are distant from the original harmonic location'. That reminded her of the insider/outsider debates whereby, she explains:

> The two emic and etic historically pitched as dichotomous opposites, encapsulated the colonial mindset, characterised by the intrepid bespectacled Westerner venturing into 'darkest' Africa armed with his tape recorder and type-writer sifting the deep, unknowable secrets of the native.

As Muir reflected on this during her study, she noted that her insider/outsider status was ambiguous. Although she would describe herself as a Pentecostal Christian who knows the moods, moves, words and what many would describe as manifestations of a holy spirit (speaking in tongues, being 'slain by the spirit'), she was neither raised initially in that faith nor expert in the particular style of music common in such Black Majority Churches. Also, being originally from the Caribbean, she was ethnically 'other' to the West Africans and, theologically, was distant from some of the more fundamentalist positions she encountered. Ultimately, she wanted in that case to study her church environment where, she realized, her 'analytical lens brought to bear on the worship arena would be unwelcome in some circles'. In what way could we now define her as an outsider or insider?

Drawing on warnings about how critical distance might be lost if a researcher becomes too much at home in the environments they studied (Hammersley and Atkinson 1995, 115), she was also aware that her familiarity gave her an advantage of perspective in what was, she mused (Muir 2018, 101), a classic case of 'playing outside' or, as Neitz (2002. 2) described it: taking a 'walk between two worlds'.

Moving to another musical term, Muir then considered the possibility of 'transposition' – the process of moving a series of notes up or down at the same distance. She found the process of moving between her role as a researcher and a worshipper progressively more difficult. As the research continued, she found that, even while trying to immerse herself in a church service as a worshipper, her research questions continued to pop into her mind and distort the experience: 'the environment could no longer fulfil a spiritual function for me. The process of research "transposed" me' (Muir 2018, 102). She writes that most of her concerns and possible ethical dilemmas were resolved through considering another musical concept, harmony: 'the simultaneous sounding of notes together to create a pleasing effect'. Drawing on Thornton (1997, 214), she worked with the idea that ethical dilemmas arise and differ according to where on the insider/outsider continuum she found herself. She decided to always operate on the principle of duty of care, putting the interests of her research participants as the highest priority at all times. On some occasions this included *not* gathering data at a funeral and related events.

Her main finding was that, while music in BMC fulfils an important liturgical role, there are also wider theological, economic and artistic tensions and sites of conflict. The hegemonic nature of contemporary Christian music (CCM) influences and informs the musical repertoires of BMCs, resulting in a denial of black musical authorship and a privileging of white musical forms with its concomitant economic benefits.

Situating the research participants in their wider social contexts would help explain much of what they their believe and practise. Weber argued that social, economic contexts were the main drivers of types of religiosity. Someone living a desperately poor or precarious existence is more likely to be drawn to religions of salvation that promise health, happiness and prosperity in an afterlife; someone who may be described as an elite in society, whose material needs are met and who does not have to worry about their existence every day, would more likely be drawn to more esoteric religions. He argued that there was an affinity between a certain type of religiosity and modern capitalism. As discussed in Chapter 1, his work is highly gendered, through looking at occupations mainly conducted by men.

Sociologist C. Wright Mills (1959) described the 'sociological imagination' as one that examined an individual within wider social structures, attempting to account for the relationship between personal biography and social history. A sociologist of religion tries to take a similar approach, not asking, 'does God exist', but why do these people, in this time and place, believe God exists when other people, in the same time and place, do not believe that? A sociologist of religion will point out that the gods someone envisages will appear in culturally consistent forms: French Roman Catholics may see visions of the Virgin Mary, but they will most likely not see a vision of Buddha.

A sociologist who says she is 'bracketing out' the possibility that God exist may be slightly disingenuous. If she really believed that God had an independent existence, why study why people would believe in such an entity, when the answer 'because he revealed himself' would be most obvious? Few sociologists study why people believe in gravity or whether Rome exists. As Bethamie Horowitz suggests in her studies of contemporary Judaism, the right question is not 'Are you Jewish?', but '*How* are you Jewish?' (Horowitz 2002).

In work on 'religious experience', for example, the sociologist would be more likely to look at how a group facilitates and mediates such experience. How are group members taught to hear what they will describe as the words of God? What disciplines, or regimes, does the group create? What boundaries are enforced? Is everyone assumed to hear God equally, or is there a difference in the experiences of men and women? Of young people and old? Of people from different social classes? Those are good sociological questions that can ground such research in social science. In practice, there is much blurring of disciplines and overlap, but as a generalization it can be assumed that disciplines may vary according to their scales. Psychology is interested in the individual unit, set in a social context; anthropology tends to be more focused on a small group, and sociology tends to look at wider, societal structures and influences. Methods, therefore, will be perfected within each discipline to suit that enquiry.

Sociology of religion and ethnography

Some sociologists use the qualitative method of ethnography to study how and why people believe and behave in religious ways (for an excellent overview, see Stringer, 2008). Although the word 'ethnography' means 'writing' about people, most researchers in practice mean that it is a way of studying people. It usually entails becoming immersed in a specific context with a selected group of people for a significant amount of time. Its history is problematic, mainly because, as discussed above, early ethnographers were often the male, white employees of a European colonial power, or were missionaries. They did not set out to neutrally study a people, but usually had an agenda, usually to save or to trade. Sometimes, they wrestled with their own sets of stereotypes and discriminatory frames, as the posthumous published diaries of Bronislaw Malinowski (1967) attest. He had requested that the diaries never be published, possibly because they contained denigrating, racist comments about the people he had studied, but after his death, his widow, Valetta Malinowski, took the opposite view. Although the person most often cited as the inventor of ethnography, who offered fascinating and enduring ideas about how a society 'functions', his work is now often discredited or, at least, treated with caution.

The recent campaigns to 'liberate' or 'decolonize' the curriculum have further drawn attention to anthropological (and, to a lesser extent, sociological) colonial history (see e.g. Day et al. 2021). This movement was accelerated in 2020 when millions of people around the world marched as part of #Black Lives Matter (https://blacklivesmatter. com/) to protest against police brutality and wider forms of current and historical oppression.

One of the first contributions to the anthropological conversation about its colonial past was Diane Lewis (1973, 581):

> Disillusionment with the discipline from outside is paralleled by growing criticism from within. Most of this criticism, appearing increasingly in the United States since the second half of the 1960s, has focused on the failure of anthropologists to come to terms with and accept responsibility for the political implications of their work.

Some of those implications are material as well as intellectual. As Lewis points out, the anthropological practice of visiting distant places with tax-free research grants, to study indigenous people as 'others' who do not benefit from the research and thereby further the scholar's position and remuneration, has deep ethical problems, as discussed earlier.

Nevertheless, many sociologists will still look to earlier founders of ethnography for inspiration. One of the most celebrated, and consistently respected, of such studies influenced anthropologists and sociologists of religion for generations, primarily because it broke through a fondly held and deeply disturbing assumption: do so-called 'primitive' people operate cognitively with the same sort of thinking that 'we' do? Evans Pritchard (1976) overturned the assumption that people neatly evolved from an early version of mystical and superstitious into a more contemporary, rational modern figure. He showed that the people he studied held strong witchcraft beliefs because they made good sense. Those beliefs helped regulate their communities, as people who believed they had been bewitched needed to look into their own behaviours to find how they might have caused such bewitching through offending or harming someone else. Once those relationships were put right, the bewitching ended and social cohesion was restored. Christians today may call such an action 'forgiveness', a state which usually follows 'repentance'. It took Evans Pritchard time to get to know the people of the Azande in order to explore the practice and function of witchcraft. A social survey at the time, were it possible, might have resulted in the majority of the population ticking a box to affirm that they believed in witchcraft, but it would not reveal the depth of the troubled relationships that needed healing, or the extent to which the so-called witches mirrored their social strata. As later studies of witchcraft continued to show, a society's propensity to identify certain people as troublesome witches is linked to that society's stability. Historical accusations of witchcraft are tied to upheaval and dis-ease.

More contemporary ethnographic studies continue to follow that tradition of immersion and gaining a sympathetic understanding of a group, what Weber called *verstehen,* while, as discussed earlier, creating more collaborative dialogues with their research participants.

Asking questions

Two main ways are available to directly ask research participants questions: the interview or the survey. While the scale will matter, both methods share a central concern: how can researchers ask questions without prompting the answer they want? It is a common issue in all sociological research, with the same problems facing a researcher of religion as a researcher of, say, social class.

Robert Towler (1974, 15) picked up that point by saying that:

> the moment a researcher uses the word 'religion' a ready-made set of attitudes will be thrust at him. As a rule these will be attitudes to 'the church', and any attempt to break through to the respondent's own beliefs will be impossibly hampered.

Nonetheless, most research about religion uses terms like 'religion' or 'belief' or 'sacred' as if everyone shares the same sense of their meaning and, invariably, this begins to skew responses accordingly. One of the first scholars of contemporary religion who tried to break that pattern was Edward Bailey (1998), whose research in 1969 used open questions, such as 'what do you enjoy most in life?' and other conversation-starters such as: 'Supposing you had a minute, just time to say a sentence or two, in which to pass on your philosophy of life to a fifteen year old, what would you say?' A well-known sociologist, Nick Abercrombie, devised with fellow students a research project for their master's degree wherein they tried to form open questions about religion (Abercrombie al. 1970, 106). When it came to asking questions about god-belief, they tried to qualify the question by asking if respondents believed in a God who could change the events on earth. One person replied: 'No, just the ordinary one.' Eileen Barker (1989) whose work transformed the discipline by showing that members of a new religious movement were not brainwashed, passive followers of a 'cult', also tried to avoid leading her research participants by not introducing the topic of religion until they did.

Surveys

Many scholars use large, quantitative studies to support their arguments both for and against enduring religiosity and/or inevitable secularization of society. Although it is easy to criticize surveys for, inevitably, not producing nuance of meaning, it would be naïve to dismiss them. Sociologists are interested in large-scale, demographic trends and changes. A survey may be the best way to capture and compare religious changes over time.

It is important to remember that no method is value-neutral and that some people may choose one over the other in order to support a certain stance. Steve Bruce (2011), for example, is outspoken on why he prefers some sort of data over another and is frustrated with what he sees as the subversion of sociology by other disciplines, such as media studies (and see, for the counter-argument, Chapter 10 in this volume). It is useful to compare his defence of positivist social science with reasons why, for example, Hammersley and Atkinson (1995) rejected it in their defence of ethnography. Referring to its gendered nature, Grace Davie (2011) has summarized the UK field of the sociology of religion as divided between the 'boys', Steve Bruce and David Voas, who prefer positivist, quantitative work, and the 'girls', Grace Davie, Linda Woodhead, and increasingly Abby Day, who prefer qualitative, more interpretivist methods. The above discussion on feminist epistemology can be usefully recalled here.

As we will discuss more in the next chapter, competing theories over religion, change and transformation have deep roots of subjective beliefs, disciplinary preferences and epistemologies.

The debate reminds me of a man I interviewed some years ago (Day 2011) who talked about how his small village was changing, and how many people had different views about what was required. The community association to which he belonged had decided to assess local needs for community facilities through creating and distributing a questionnaire. They were, he told me, aware that in designing questions they might inadvertently influence the outcome:

> if you're trying to draw things out from people but without putting ideas into their mind. I mean, one of the things we wanted in the village was better village hall facilities, and everybody on the community association wants better village hall facilities. But you can't put 'would you like a new village hall' cuz you're leading, you're feeding them the answer you want them to give you.

Nevertheless, scholars seeking to support secularization theories, particularly those attending to Euro American societies, will use often use surveys to support their cases (and see Chapter 3 for more discussion of those theories).

The main problem with surveys is language, particularly in cross-cultural research, but the language itself reflects a culture, whether defined nationally, ethnically or both. Language presupposes a shared understanding. What, for example, is a religious adherent's understanding of 'belief'? As Charles Kadushin (2007) pointed out, social surveys may be theologically incorrect. A Protestant Christian may privilege belief, or 'the word' (Keane 2007), in ways others will not. Jews, Kadushin explained, will understand God more through experience than belief.

Case example: how religious is the UK?

Many countries conduct a census of population every five to ten years to determine demographic characteristics that might influence resource allocations, such as where and how many schools and hospitals will be required in the future. The decennial census in the UK began in 1801 and from then until 2001 no question about religious affiliation had been included in the sections for England, Wales and Scotland. The political implications and impact are discussed in more detail in Chapter 4, but here the variance in wording and options are described to show how choices about these important factors contradicted many basic conventions in survey design. The census question was posed differently amongst the countries of the UK. The England and Wales version of the question was 'What is your religion?', which seemed to presuppose that the respondent had a religion: 72 per cent said Christian. The Scottish census question asked 'What religion, religious denomination or body do you belong to?': 65.1 per cent said Christian. The Northern Ireland census asked 'Do you regard yourself as belonging to any particular religion?' and 85.8 per cent selected 'Christian'. The high Northern Ireland 'Christian' response is likely a feature of the intensely politicized environment, where religion takes on more ethno-nationalized meanings, with Catholics and Protestants vying for recognition, legitimacy and power. It is also worth considering the impact of wording, where questions about 'belonging' to a religion result in considerably lower affirmative responses than that posed for England and Wales on the census. For example, around the same time the UK Christian charity Tearfund (Ashworth and Farthing 2007) question 'Do you regard yourself as belonging to any particular religion?' achieved only a 53 per cent result, in line with other large social surveys such as the British Social Attitudes survey or the European Social Survey.

Apart from difference in wording, the questions on the UK census also varied by response options and their order, which may have influenced the result. The percentage who chose 'Christian' in Scotland was significantly lower than England and Wales (65 per cent vs. 72 per cent respectively), possibly because of both the wording and the location. The England and Wales version had tick-box options: 'None; Christian (including Church of England, Catholic, Protestant, and all other Christian denominations); Buddhist; Hindu; Jewish; Muslim; Sikh', followed by an option to answer 'any other religion'. The Scottish question did not offer a general category of 'Christian' but three tick-box options of 'Church of Scotland, Roman Catholic and Other Christian (Please write in)'. Other non-Christian religions were then listed as in the England and Wales version. The Northern Ireland census did not list non-Christian religions specifically, merely offering the option: 'Other, please write in'. Strikingly, none of the three versions of the UK censuses offered sub-categories of other religions, as if, for example, the second-largest religion, Islam, did not require nuance.

The question's location on the form also varied. On the English and Wales version it immediately followed a question on ethnicity and could therefore have been interpreted as a supplementary question. On the Scottish census it was positioned before the ethnicity question.

The Scottish and Northern Ireland versions asked an additional question: 'what religion, religious denomination or body were you brought up in?' repeating the main question's options. This was useful to assess what proportion of people may disaffiliate with religions over time.

The difficulty in making comparisons of religiosity based on such census detail occurs internationally as well as nationally due, again, to differences in wording. For example, some countries list a generous choice to Christians of Catholic, Adventist, Lutheran, Free Baptist, Methodist and so on; the Republic of Ireland offers distinct Christian denominations and also 'Lapsed Roman Catholic', a choice of 'agnostic' but not 'atheist' (although you can have 'no religion'); respondents in Portugal can be atheists but not agnostic.

Reflecting the complexity involved in survey research about religion, demographer and Pew Senior Researcher Conrad Hackett (2014) suggests seven guiding principles:

1 Definitions and measures of religious identity shape knowledge about religious groups.
2 Differences in question wording produce differences in results.
3 Differences in response patterns across surveys need investigation.
4 Incentives shape how respondents report their religious identity.
5 For some, religious identity is liminal.

6   Salient identity categories are often unmeasured.
7   Religious identity and religious practice are less congruent than may be imagined.

Hackett offers several cases to show the difficulty in measuring religious adherence if everyone does not agree about what counts. For example, while Brazil is often seen as one of the most Catholic countries in the world, how is that to be measured? There is a large discrepancy, depending on who decides what counts. According to the 2010 census in Brazil, fewer than 127 million identified as Catholic. The Vatican, however, puts the number of Brazilian Catholics at 163 million. Hackett explains the difference by showing the criteria being used: the census measures contemporary religious self-identification, whereas the Vatican was measuring the numbers of Brazilians who were baptized.

In trying to research religion and non-religion without introducing overtly religious vocabulary, I recommended working on three criteria:

1   Position the study within social science.
2   Focus on creating questions that prompt discussion without forcing closed answers about religious ideas or behaviours, encouraging research participants to digress, ask questions and tell stories to capture their conceptual frameworks and vocabulary. This was described by Yin (2003, 89–90) as 'guided conversations' and by Bellah et al. (1985, 305) as an 'active interview', involving dialogue and digression rather than rapid-fire questions and answers. In her work with people who may describe themselves as spiritual but not religious, Nancy Ammerman (2014) a pioneer of 'everyday' and 'lived' religion approaches, used techniques of narrative interviewing to encourage participants to tell their stories. With Roman Williams (2012), she describes research methods that involve narratives, photo elicitation and keeping diaries.
3   Interpret the data through categories that arise inductively. Rather than begin with an hypothesis, using, no doubt, other people's vocabulary and conceptual frameworks, take a Weberian approach – he set out to study religion without defining what it was, preferring to keep the concept open while he conducted his research. Nancy Ammerman (2014) and her team discussed meanings of religion and spirituality and maintained throughout their decision to not pre-define it. They noticed that their research participants struggled to define spirituality for themselves; this helped inform her and her research team about the extent to which spirituality is both an emergent and contested term.

Thinking with words

Researchers may either approach their study with a clear hypothesis to be proven, or a theme to be explored. The difference is really one of direction. When scholars adopt the first stance, they are taking a 'deductive' route, as they begin with an hypothesis or statement to be proven. Observations are taken and propositions tested until the conclusion is reached: true or false. Researchers taking an inductive route start from the opposite direction, observing and reflecting before any conclusion, and theories, can be created that may explain the observations.

Scholars of religion often use terms such as religion, spiritual or sacred without discussing what they or their research participants may mean by it. In 2013, I conducted an analysis of papers in the *Journal of Contemporary Religion* and found a variety of assorted and mostly untheorized meanings relating to the term 'sacred'. The messiness, interchangeability and slippery nature of the use of such terms show how important it is to question research methods that seem to assume a stable, widely understood, if largely unarticulated, vocabulary that can be measured and compared. This may involve more than simply a tweak of research methods, but a reconsideration of what is meant by 'religion'.

Ethics and method

Finally, a point about ethics and method. As ethics in research about religion do not vary from ethics in research more generally, they will not be elaborated here in detail. It is assumed that all researchers are subject to ethical review processes in their relative institutions, but students who have not yet conducted research may be unaware of some of the most important pillars of those ethical frameworks. The British Sociology Association, to which a Sociology of Religion sub-group belongs (www.britsoc.co.uk/media/24310/bsa_statement_of_ethical_practice.pdf) emphasizes that members must safeguard the interests of those involved in or affected by their work, and report their findings accurately and truthfully.

Researchers often consider the power dynamics of research relationships and discuss research projects, and particularly interviews, as 'collaborative'. That term is helpful in implying ignorance to some degree on both parts. The informant is usually unschooled in sociological theory and practice, and the researcher is uninformed about the specific content which the informant has to offer. The power dynamic also means that the researcher is usually more able to leave the exact location of research than is the informant. The researcher may need to recognize this in terms of security and safeguarding, particularly with children and other vulnerable people. That is likely to include submitting personal data for extensive background checks by the police. Researchers being granted access to vulnerable people might need to give up some of their own rights in order to protect those most vulnerable. They should be willing to undergo not merely all required safety checks but *must be seen* to be doing everything possible to demonstrate their quality of care and protection. While it was possible a few decades ago to conduct covert research without informed consent, that is no longer permissible. Ethics approval processes stress that researchers need to ensure that all participants understand who is conducting the research, why, who finances it and how it will be used.

The researcher must balance her desire to gain 'spontaneous' answers with the informant's right to be aware of the interview theme and some of the personal material that may be discussed. Having given consent once, the informant has the right to withdraw it at any time during the process of data gathering, and the consent forms should clearly state so.

Ultimately, the goal of a researcher is to remain sensitive and self-critical about how their own definitions of methods and standpoint are affecting their approach.

Sample questions for private study

1 What is understood as the 'field' in social research?
2 Give an example of how you might 'follow' a theme, idea or people?

Sample class exercise

3 Create and conduct an interview about a class-mate's life histories related to religion.

Note

1 And see Guest et al. 2013 for their report showing how the gendered nature of those disciplines force many women scholars to leave them.

Indicative reading

Abercrombie, N., J. Baker, S. Brett and J. Foster. 1970. 'Superstition and Religion: The God of the Gaps.' In *A Sociological Yearbook of Religion In Britain*, edited by David Martin and Michael Hill, 93–129. London: SCM.

Ackerly, Brooke, and Jacqui True. 2010. *Doing Feminist Research in Political and Social Science*. New York: Palgrave Macmillan.

Ammerman, Nancy T. 2014. *Sacred Stories, Spiritual Tribes: Finding Religion in Everyday Life*. New York: Oxford University Press.

Ammerman, Nancy T., and Roman R. Williams. 2012. 'Speaking of Methods: Eliciting Religious Narratives through Interviews, Photos, and Oral Diaries.' In *Annual Review of the Sociology of Religion: New Methods in Sociology of Religion*, edited by Luigi Berzano and Ole Riis, 117–134. Leiden: Brill.

Ashworth, J., and I. Farthing. 2007. *Churchgoing in the UK*. Teddington: Tearfund.

Bailey, Edward. 1998. 'Implicit Religion.' In *Encyclopedia of Religion and Society*, edited by William H. Swatos, Jr., 235. Walnut Creek, CA: AltaMira Press.

Barker, Eileen. 1989. 'And What do you Believe? Methods and Perspectives in Investigating Religion.' In *Investigating Society*, edited by R. Burgess, 32–50. London: Longman.

Barylo, William. 2017. 'Appropriating Islam as a Matrix: Young Muslim Volunteers Blurring the Lines between Sacred and Mundane.' *Method and Theory in the Study of Religion* 29. 10.1163/15700682-12341383.

Beckford, James A. 2003. *Social Theory and Religion*. Cambridge: Cambridge University Press.

Bell, Catherine. 2000. 'Acting Ritually.' In *The Blackwell Companion to Sociology of Religion*, edited by Richard Fenn, 371–87. Oxford: Blackwell.

Bellah, Robert, Richard Madsen, William M. Sullivan, Ann Swidler, and Steven M. Tipton. 1985. *Habits of the Heart: Individualism and Commitment in American Life*. Berkeley, CA: University of California Press.

Bender, Courtney, Wendy Cadge, Peggy Levitt and David Smilde. 2013. *Religion on the Edge: De-centering and Re-centering the Sociology of Religion*. Oxford, New York: Oxford University Press.

Berger, Peter L. 1967. *The Sacred Canopy: Elements of a Sociological Theory of Religion*. New York: Doubleday.

Berger, Peter L., and Thomas Luckmann. 1966. *The Social Construction of Reality: A Treatise in the Sociology of Knowledge*. Garden City, NY: Anchor Books.

Bowie, Fiona. 2006. *The Anthropology of Religion: An Introduction.* Malden, MA, and Oxford: Blackwell.

Bruce, Steve. 2011. *Secularization, in Defence of an Unfashionable Theory.* Oxford: Oxford University Press.

Catto, Rebecca. 'From the Rest to the West: Exploring Reversal in Christian Mission in Twenty-First Century Britain' (unpublished PhD thesis: University of Exeter, 2008).

Collins, Patricia Hill. 1998. *Fighting Words: Black Women and the Search for Justice.* Minneapolis, MN: University of Minnesota Press.

Davie, Grace. 2011. 'Celebrating the Last 60 Years of the Sociology of Religion.' Socrel plenary keynote, British Sociological Association, London, 6 April.

Day, Abby. 2011. *Believing in Belonging: Belief and Social Identity in the Modern World.* Oxford: Oxford University Press.

Day, Abby ed., 2015. *Contemporary Issues in the Worldwide Anglican Communion: Powers and Pieties.* Farnham: Ashgate.

Day, Abby. 2017. *The Religious Lives of Older Laywomen: The Last Active Anglican Generation.* Oxford: Oxford University Press.

Day, Abby, Lois Lee, David Thomas and James Spickard. Forthcoming, 2021. *Doing Diversity in Academia: Practice and Pitfalls.* Bristol: Bristol University Press.

Evans-Pritchard, Edward Evan. [1937] 1976. *Witchcraft, Oracles, and Magic among the Azande.* Oxford: Clarendon Press.

Favret-Saada, Jeanne. 1980. *Deadly Words: Witchcraft in the Bocage.* Cambridge: Cambridge University Press.

Geertz, Clifford. 1966. 'Religion as a Cultural System.' In *Anthropological Approaches to the Study of Religion,* edited by Michael Banton, 1–46. London: Tavistock. (ASA Monographs, 3).

Geertz, Clifford. 1973. *The Interpretation of Cultures: Selected Essays.* New York: Basic Books.

Guest, Mathew, Sonya Sharma and Robert Song. 2013. *Gender and Career Progression in Theology and Religious Studies.* Durham: Durham University.

Hackett, Conrad. 2014. 'Seven Things to Consider When Measuring Religious Identity.' In *Making Sense of Surveys and Censuses: Issues in Religious Self-Identification,* special issue of *Religion,* guest edited by Abby Day and Lois Lee, 44, no. 3: 396–413.

Hammersley, Martyn, and Paul Atkinson. 1995. *Ethnography: Principles in Practice.* 2nd edition. London: Routledge.

Harding, Sandra. 1991. *Whose Science? Whose Knowledge? Thinking from Women's Lives.* Milton Keynes: Open University Press.

Harvey, Graham. 2017. *Animism: Respecting the Living World.* London: Hurst & Co.

Horowitz, Bethamie. 2002. 'Reframing the Study of Contemporary American Jewish Identity.' *Contemporary Jewry* 23, no. 14. https://doi.org/10.1007/BF02967927

Kadushin, Charles. 2007. 'Theologically Correct Survey Questions.' Paper delivered to 2007 conference of the Society for the Scientific Study of Religion, Tampa, Florida, 4 November.

Keane, Webb. 2007. *Christian Moderns.* Berkeley-Los Angeles: University of California Press.

Knott, Kim. 2010. 'Insider/Outsider Perspectives,' In *A Routledge Companion to the Study of Religions,* edited by John Hinnells, 259–73. London: Routledge.

Lewis, Diane. 1973. 'Anthropology and Colonialism.' *Current Anthropology* 14, no. 5: 581–602. www.jstor.com/stable/274103

Malinowski, Bronislaw. 1967. *A Diary in the Strict Sense of the Term.* London: Athlone.

McGuire, Meredith B. 1992. *Religion: The Social Context,* 3rd edition. Belmont, CA: Wadsworth.

McCutcheon, Russell. 2003. 'The Ideology of Closure and the Problem with the Insider/Outsider Problem in the Study of Religion.' *Studies in Religion/Sciences Religieuses* 32, no. 3: 337–52. https://doi.org/10.1177/000842980303200306.

Mills, C. Wright. 1959. *The Sociological Imagination.* New York: Oxford University Press.

Muir, Pauline. 2018. 'Sounds Mega: Musical Discourse in Black Majority Churches in London', PhD thesis, Birkbeck College, University of London.

Neitz, Mary Jo. 2002. 'Walking between the Worlds: Permeable Boundaries, Ambiguous Identities.' In *Personal Knowledge and Beyond: Reshaping the Ethnography of Religion,* edited by James Spickard, J. Shawn Landres and Meredith B. McGuire, 33–46. New York and London: New York University Press.

Ojo, Matthews. 2007. 'Reverse Mission,' In *Encyclopedia of Mission and Missionaries,* edited by Jonathan J. Bonk, 380–2. New York: Routledge.

Robbins, Joel. 2006. 'Afterword: On Limits, Ruptures, Meaning and Meaninglessness.' In *The Limits of Meaning: Case Studies in the Anthropology of Christianity*, edited by Matthew Engelke and Matt Tomlinson, 211—24. Oxford: Berghahn Books.

Ryan, Louise. 2015. ' "Inside" and "Outside" of What or Where? Researching Migration through Multi-Positionalities.' *Forum Qualitative Social Research.* DOI: http://dx.doi.org/10.17169/fqs-16.2.2333.

Ryan, Louise, Eleonore Kofman and Pauline Aaron. 2011. 'Insiders and Outsiders: Working with Peer Researchers in Researching Muslim Communities,' *International Journal of Social Research Methodology* 14, no. 1: 49–60. DOI: 10.1080/13645579.2010.481835

Spickard, James, Shawn Landres, and Meredith B McGuire (eds). 2002. *Personal Knowledge and Beyond: Reshaping the Ethnography of Religion.* New York and London: New York University Press.

Stringer, Martin D. 2008. *Contemporary Western Ethnography and the Definition of Religion.* London: Continuum.

Thornton, Sarah. 1997. 'Introduction to Part Four: Ethics and Ethnography.' In *The Subcultures Reader,* edited by Ken Gelder and Sarah Thornton, 213–16. London: Routledge.

Towler, Robert. 1974. *Homo Religious: Sociological problems in the Study of Religion.* New York: St Martin's Press.

Voas, David, and Alasdair Crockett. 2005. 'Religion in Britain: Neither Believing Nor Belonging.' *Sociology* 39, no. 1: 11–28.

Weber, Max. 1922. *The Sociology of Religion.* Boston, MA: Beacon Press.

Whyte, William Foote. 1943. *Street Corner Society: The Social Structure of an Italian Slum.* Chicago, IL: University of Chicago Press.

Yin, Richard K. 2003. *Case Study Research Design and Methods.* Thousand Oaks, CA, and London: Sage.

Chapter 3

The contemporary religious landscape
Retreat, reinvention and resurgence

Introduction

Billions of people around the world are religious, with many adhering to their faith's key tenets and rituals. Many others experience and sometimes explicitly use religion primarily as a social marker to reflect and affect power relations. Growing numbers, at least in Euro-American countries, claim they have no religion, yet they also have a remarkable array of other beliefs, ranging from hard atheism to beliefs in after-death and spirits. The key is context: while certain religions are dying out, other forms are growing. What happens when we shift the sociological gaze from the west to, for example, the east and the global south? This chapter will summarize those varying trends and offer sociological analyses, particularly within a framework of modernity and its contestations.

Secularization theses and their critiques are reviewed, with in-depth explorations (and signposting to future chapters) of related themes. The objective is to familiarize students with key theories related to religious change, and flag some of their most important strengths and weaknesses.

The over-arching theme here is one of context. Ideas and examples have been generated to provide a breadth of material rather than a single narrative, because that narrative will change depending on who is being studied, where, why and how.

Linda Woodhead (2012, 2), director of the UK's largest research programme on religion, Religion and Society, reflected on religion in post-war Britain. 'Britain is now regularly spoken of as a secular country with a secular state, yet it still has an established church, and the majority of Britons still call themselves "Christian".' Her analysis of the period and evidence from the programme's 75 projects strongly suggested that religion had changed from a time when it was influenced largely by its relationship with the state, to one where it became less regulated, more varied and more attached to transnational networks and new forms of organization and identity. It may (see in the same volume Guest et al. 2012) have lost its monopoly.

Globalization and transnational networks have had a profound effect not only on the organizations themselves, but on the academics who study them. The field of enquiry within the social scientific study of religion has become increasingly deterritorialized.

Simon Coleman (2000) discusses this in his work on two Christian churches in Sweden. What began as fairly conventional ethnography – 15 months of fieldwork, regular church attendance, becoming a member of the choir – needed to shift over time. The objective could not be to study each church as self-contained, stable cultural units as they were closely connected to wider, transnational networks.

Peter Beyer (2006) makes the important point that examining religion as a global system entails more than merely accounting for any one religion's global activity, but understanding that any religious system, like other systems, is an important part of contemporary world society.

Retreat

One of the most influential narratives within sociology is that of secularization. That story is still unfolding and will continue to be told long after this book has been written, read and filed onto a library's shelf. Secularization has caught the sociological imagination for a number of reasons, but first, it should be noted that not all academic disciplines have been similarly interested in such an idea: apart from critiquing it, the theme of secularization appears rarely in the anthropology of religion, for example, or in the ethnographies of people or places outside the west and global north. Fenella Cannell (2010, 86) argued that the picture is further complicated by how key terms, such as secular and secularism, are defined differently in the academic literature and the extent to which scholars consider they are real rather than being, she suggests, 'themselves only a fiction of the historical processes we are examining'. Talal Asad (1993, 2003) makes similar points, tying the shifts to specific historic periods.

Discussing processes of secularization, many scholars will begin with a definition of what they mean as 'secular'. Dictionary definitions usually cite the word's Latin root, *saeculum*, meaning a fixed period of time and, therefore, 'worldly' or 'temporal'. Definitions usually also state that it means to be without, or not affiliated to, religion, and possibly that it also entails how individuals cease to engage with religion on a subjective level.

Secularism is a different term, referring to the stance, or ideology, that societies should become less religious. For example, organizations in the UK, such as the National Secular Society and Humanists UK, and in the USA, such as of the American Association for the Advancement of Atheism and the American Humanist Association, actively campaign to keep religion and government separate and to reduce the influence of religious bodies in everyday life. This will be discussed more in Chapter 12.

As Larry Shiner (1967) pointed out, scholars shift between definitions of secular that range from a decrease in religious beliefs, religious practices or in related ideas like immortality. He traces (Shiner 1967, 208) the first use of the term to G. J. Holyoake, who in the 19th century used it to describe a philosophy to 'interpret and organise life without recourse to the supernatural'. As Peter Berger described it, a secular society would mean that people regard their world 'without the benefit of religious interpretations' (Berger 1967, 107–8).

Secularization theses do not assume that religion will inevitably disappear. Countries one might assume are 'non-religious' also contain religions. For example, China, Russia and France all have religions, but religion does not officially drive their politics or operations. Charles Taylor (2007, 1) described a secular country as one where 'you can fully engage in politics without ever encountering God', apart from, he continues, 'a few moments of vestigial ritual or prayer'. On that basis, the UK and many other 'modern' countries would not be 'secular' nations. The examples are revealing. For example, in the UK's governance structure, the second tier of government is the House of Lords which maintains 26 seats guaranteed for Church of England bishops; worldwide, only the UK and Iran have places for religious leaders reserved permanently in their governments (discussed more in Chapter 4). The UK head of state, the Queen, is also the head of the Church of England. Christian prayers are said each day in Parliament, and also in many state schools where about one-third are 'faith schools', the vast majority being Church of England or Roman Catholic. A similar proportion exists in Australian state schools. In Canada, most public schools are non-religious, apart from Catholic schools which receive government funding; most private schools have a religious affiliation. While the US constitution forbids public schools indoctrinating children into religion, there are thousands of privately funded religious-affiliated schools. Most people in apparently secular Nordic countries are automatically members of their national churches and pay taxes to pay for their upkeep.

Considering mainly the evidence from post-war Britain, Linda Woodhead (2012, 3) concluded that the evidence supports neither a narrative of straightforward secularization nor one of desecularization:

> This only seems puzzling if existing frameworks are retained, because they assume not only that 'religion' and 'secularity' are clear and distinct entities, but that they are elements in a zero sum equation, such that modern history can only be told as a simple evolutionary tale: either from the religious to the secular, or from the secular to the religious.

The complexity does not only exist in regions like the UK and Europe. Although African nations are usually seen as 'religious' due to the high numbers of people professing a faith, the larger story is more complicated. Jon Abbink (2014, 84) notes that 'while we see continued strong religious adherence among people in Africa, most are living in "secular states". How do these two phenomena coalesce, and will the secular model last?' He suggests that earlier, colonizing governments preferred a 'secular' model for states, assuming that this would result in a less divisive society, but in practice many regimes then and now resort to encouraging more religions based on a goal to 'divide and conquer'.

Mirjam Künkler, John Madeley, and Shylashri Shankar (2018) examine 11 countries without a history of being dominated by Christianity: Japan, China, Indonesia, India, Pakistan, Iran, Russia, Turkey, Israel, Egypt and Morocco. They sought to explore areas where religion might not be easily comparable to the monotheistic, exclusive religions of the west, or countries where religion is imposed by the state. The volume interplays the work of Charles Taylor (2007), with contributions from authors engaging with non-western regions. They begin (Künkler et al. 2018, 1–32) by pointing out that Taylor's account specifically considers secularity in 'the North Atlantic world', thereby inspiring the editors and authors to explore religion and non religion 'in countries outside the heartland of Latin Christendom' (Künkler et al. 2018, 2). They take as their first point of analysis what Taylor suggested were the three notions of secularity – differentiation, where most domains of societal life, from politics to education are separated from religious control and authority (see also Chaves 1994); the decline of religious belief and practice, a Euro-American 1960s trend that sociologists assumed would spread globally; and a notion of a 'buffered self' where belief in God, previously prescribed is now an option, amongst many. The chapters broadly demonstrated that levels of differentiation tended to be low, as was religious decline, and that state regulation of religion continues, often as a legacy of colonial and imperial periods.

More assertive, often identity-based, religious groups vie for influence in many multi-faith, multi-ethnic countries (Abbink (2014, 92):

> We saw this pressure in Kenya around both the adoption of the new 2010 consti-tution and the recent family and marriage bills, in Mali in the resistance to the new family law (withdrawn from the parliamentary vote) – not to mention the 2013–14 revolts in the north in the name of religion and ethnicity – and in South Africa, where religious interest groups pressured the state leadership and blamed the high rates of crime and violence on the 'immoral secular order'.

At stake in understanding these events is the much quoted, but possibly fictional, apparent divide between so-called public and private spheres, particularly where, Abbink argues, religion is manifest in many public spheres through media, constitutional forms and human rights.

José Casanova (1994) argued in a similar way that religion has returned to and become more visible in the realm of politics as a medium for ethnic and social iden-tities. Casanova argued that four events in particular shunted religion from a private to public sphere: the 1979 Iranian revolution; the rise of the anti-communist and Catholic-inflected Solidarity movement in Poland; the rise of Catholic political activism in Latin America; and the influence of the Christian right in American politics.

While religion had been pushed from the 'public sphere' and many states act as if God does not exist, in practice people continue to believe in gods and religions continue to thrive. As Titus Hjelm (2015, 15) argued, 'visibility, vitality and social influence (of reli-gion) are different things'. Those are the sorts of things this book hopes to address in the following chapters.

Jurgen Habermas (1989) that the 'public sphere' consisted of largely informal spaces such as coffee houses where 'bourgeois' citizens would contribute to debate and create formations of politics and democracy:

> However much the Tischgesellschaften, salons and coffee houses may have differed in the size and composition of their publics, the style of their proceedings, the cli-mate of their debates, and their topical orientations, they all organised discussion among private people that tended to be ongoing; hence, they had a number of insti-tutional criteria in common.
>
> (Habermas 1989, 36)

The demise of the public sphere occurred as people moved from being 'a culture-debating to a culture-consuming public', with their media attention focused on television and radio (Habermas 1989, 159).

Other scholars, particularly feminists, ask questions about such theories relative to gender and inequalities. In response mainly to Habermas, Nancy Fraser (1990, 77) argued that 'an adequate conception of the public sphere requires not merely bracketing, but rather the elimination, of social inequality'. She proposed that scholars engage with the notion of 'counter-publics', being the marginalized, subaltern groups excluded from an otherwise male and privileged 'public sphere'.

James Beckford (2012) contributed to that debate by pointing out that the binary of public/private was itself problematic as in many cases, such as the UK, so-called secular states did not have such a division. In the UK, for example, the government has been relying increasingly on faith-based groups to supply public services. This has occurred, as Adam Dinham (2009) writes, both because government recognized the value of the community role faith-based organizations can provide, and also because the turn to austerity and visions of a Big Society reduced the government's ability to provide more extensive social services. Such religion-state partnerships further complicate an apparent secular-religious divide.

As definitions and concepts of 'secular' vary widely, so therefore does the term 'secularization', referring to a process of societies becoming more 'secular', and often referred to as one of sociology's 'grand narratives'. There are, however, mini narratives within the discussion and therefore it is advisable to discuss not 'the secularization thesis', but secularization theses.

In considering these, it is advisable to note that secularization theorists do not forecast that increasing modernity will lead to the end of religion. As Detlef Pollack writes (2008, 2–3): 'Neither Weber, Durkheim, nor contemporary secularization theorists such as Bryan Wilson, Steve Bruce, Pippa Norris, or Karel Dobbelaere advance such notions.' What they do argue, as he summarizes, is that: 'the processes of modernization will eventually have a negative effect on the stability and vitality of religious communities, practices, and convictions'.

Bryan Wilson (1966) conceived of secularization as the process by which religion loses its social significance, mainly through institutional decline. The causal variable for Wilson and most advocates of secularization theory was modernity, whereby, Wilson argued, a Christian aesthetic ethic became incompatible with a growing desire for personal happiness and gratification through consumerism. Wilson predicted that the process would accelerate as religious beliefs declined, matched by a decline in religious practice. Steve Bruce, in several works (e.g. see 2002) argued in a similar way that, as practice declined, so would belief and affiliation. He was convinced that secularized contemporary societies were often not so much vociferously opposed to religion as indifferent. Wilson assumed the process was global, a point countered by David Martin (1978) who provided international examples to support his argument that secularization is neither linear nor uniform but depends on degrees of pluralism and differentiation in different societies.

Bruce (2016) reviewed Wilson's original work and concluded that his arguments were as pertinent then as when originally written (Wilson and Bruce 2016). As reviewed in Chapter 1, their accounts are significantly gendered and miss the role that women have played in churches, dismissing such social and community activities as secular, not religious.

In 1990, the field was radically changed by Grace Davie's work questioning the validity of a secularization thesis which may have overlooked the ways in which people may 'believe' without 'belonging'. Davie (1994, 6) was worried that scholars' concepts of the religious state in Euro-American countries may be skewed because while good, but small, studies of the 'exotic edges' of religion in Britain exist, 'the picture in the middle remains alarmingly blurred' with very little known about 'the beliefs of ordinary British people in everyday life'.

Her paper ' "An Ordinary God": The Paradox of Religion in Contemporary Britain' was first published in 1990 in the *British Journal of Sociology* while a complementary paper was published in *Social Compass*. The two papers were quickly woven and updated into her best-known text which, arguably, has had the most impact on the field in generations: *Religion in Britain since 1945: Believing without Belonging* (1994), the updated, second edition of which was published in 2015 (Davie 2015).

The significance of her publications has not simply been to challenge empirical and theoretical works on religion, but to rescue the study of religion from the backwater into which a secular academy, largely assuming religion was over, had pushed it. Suddenly, 'religion' was back, and a thesis had emerged to which future scholars, whether they agreed with her or not, would need to respond. Here, the main arguments and evidence are paraphrased or reproduced verbatim as many are as relevant at the time of writing as they were in 1990 (Davie 1994, 2–37):

1   The majority of British people persist in believing in God but 'see no need to participate with even minimal regularity in their religious institutions'.
2   It is more accurate to describe them as 'unchurched' rather than secular.
3   Few people have opted out altogether – atheists are rare. The churches attract an audience which is disproportionately elderly, female and conservative.
4   The 'nature of family life, including the traditional codes of morality, are altering rapidly'.
5   Changes in gender roles have 'for better or for worse, penetrated the churches and influenced theological thinking'.
6   An 'influx of immigrants in the post-war period, not all of them from Christian countries, has introduced significant other-faith communities'. This represents a trend towards greater religious diversity and has had a 'lasting effect on many aspects of British religious life'.
7   British Christianity is a variant of a common culture of European Christianity quite distinct from immigrant cultures.
8   Relationship with belief and practice was different in the past.
9   Significantn age contrasts will affect the future of religion.
10   Patterns of employment and residence have changed – 'the larger industrial conurbations characteristic of industrial Britain are declining rapidly'. This has reduced those areas of society 'most hostile to religious practice – large cities with high-density working-class populations'.
11   Subtle but significant changes in 'mood' since 1945 are generational. The 1960s, for example, produced a demand for the churches to be more 'relevant', whereas the dominant mood of the 1990s would be more 'new age' or responses to it.
12   'An approach based on the concept of secularization is getting harder and harder to sustain'.
13   There is a 'prevalence of Christian nominalism alongside the hardening of religious boundaries associated with the growth of evangelical (even fundamentalist) tendencies within Christianity and with the increase of other-faith communities'.
14   There is 'disturbing evidence of fundamentalism worldwide'.

David Voas and Alasdair Crockett published a riposte to Davie, arguing (Voas and Crockett 2005, 14) that it was not whether people held certain beliefs but whether those beliefs were important to them and influenced their behaviour that mattered. Davie later created another term for what she latterly felt characterized better the British, but not American, religious landscape: 'vicarious religion', described below.

The retreat of religion in some contexts has opened spaces for different kinds of beliefs that are not religious. The contemporary religious landscape in the global north and south is becoming increasingly marked by growing numbers of people who specifically position themselves away from religion and self-identify as having no religion and also, in many cases, as being spiritual but not religious. Scholars apply a variety of theories to explain this, to be discussed in detail in Chapter 12.

Reinvention

During the last three or four decades, thinking sociologically about religion has shifted attention away from an emphasis on 'progress', functionalism, and binaries to everyday, lived religion and its complexities. Religious rituals, and symbolic meaning, retain significant power for many people, even those who may be described as nominally religious, but for others, their beliefs and practices fall outside a narrow scope of what may be defined, or what qualifies, as religious. The tendency discussed in the previous chapter as an 'obsession' about ritual and meaning that influenced many scholars from Weber onwards has lost its singular hold on the study of religion and may now be regarded as a symptom of the writer's thinking, rather than the researched. Beckford (2003, 29) referred to that obsession as something outside the scope of the sociological book he was writing, describing it as an assumption that all people need to 'fend off chaos by socially constructing sacred frames of meaning. It posits a phenomenology of mental categories that are supposedly constitutive of all human meaning. These issues fall outside the scope of this book.'

A turn towards the 'everyday' occurred first in France where *la religion veçue* 'has long been current in the sociology of religion' (Hall 1997, vii). This edited volume, which arose from a research strand at Harvard University, became influential in the sociology of religion by shifting a focus from the institutional and theological to the ordinary practices of (predominantly Protestant) lay people. In particular, lived religion as studied then was built on several distinct lines, including congregational studies, ritual studies and cultural anthropology (Hall 1997, ix), and found its methodological home in a variety of places, such as sociology, anthropology and history.

Case example: religion in the American mainstream

Nancy Ammerman begins with a light critique of a study (Hoge et al. 1994) which explored the practices of 'baby-boomers' who were confirmed, as teenagers, in churches in the 1950s and 1960s. That study described those who attended church irregularly and did not believe in core doctrinal tenets as 'lay liberals'. Ammerman says (1997, 196) that those people 'did not get ringing endorsements from Hoge, Johnson and Luidens, nor from the many other sociologists and theologians who have recognized similar categories of non-orthodox church-goers'. She suggests that, rather than demoting those people to a lower league of Christians or seeing them as 'a paler reflection of evangelical fervor' (Ammerman, 1997, 197), they need to be understood on their own terms. That meant, she proposed, not describing them in terms of categories relating to what they did or did not believe, but rather how they measured Christianity by 'right living more than right believing' (Ammerman, 1997, 197). This was an orientation she described as 'Golden Rule' morality: compassion for those in need. She analysed survey responses of 1,995 people from 23 congregations, observations in those congregations and 103 interviews. Her findings describe, she said, middle-class suburban Americans who on, on average, were university graduates on comfortable incomes – in contrast with evangelical Christians who tended to be less well-educated with lower earnings: 'They are people with the social resources for making their own choices rather than following a single orthodoxy or narrow institutional commitment' (Ammerman, 1997, 200). Ammerman also found a fairly equal distribution of men and women of all ages. There was not, therefore, a distinct 'baby-boomer' religion, but rather a set of practices shared by parents and their offspring, similar to the religion of the 1950s which favoured practice over belief.

When analysing the sample to identify their beliefs, Ammerman found that the Bible was important to the 'Golden Rule' Christians, not as an unerring source of truth, but through its useful ideas about morality and social activism. Ammerman pointed to how the Hoge et al. (1994) study concluded that the respondents were not very interested in 'the meaning of life'. Ammerman argued that the Golden Rule Christians were interested in meaning insofar as it affected how they would be good people, leading good lives. In practice, this meant 'care for relationships, doing good deeds, and looking for opportunities to provide care and comfort for people in need' (Ammerman 1997, 203), with the most important relationship being between parent and child (Ammerman 1997, 204; see also Day 2011 and discussion of nominal Christians and their 'believing in belonging', Chapter 12). They also carry their values into the workplace, treating co-workers with care and respect. Although they do not believe they can change the world, they frequently carry out small acts of volunteering and donations of food or clothing.

Turning to some of the wider implications of her study, Ammerman considers whether such Christians are really Christians at all, and are instead examples of a secularizing trend in society: 'Could they not be members of a lodge or community club just as easily as of a church?' (Ammerman 1997, 207). Ammerman disagrees, partly because the Golden Rule Christians she studied still find even occasional church attendance important to them, but mostly because 'Golden Rule Christians have not given up on transcendence' (Ammerman 1997, 207). They attest to sensing God's presence, often at church, and feel that the church's 'sacred time' is a way to 'feed the soul' (Ammerman 1997, 208). Many also discussed feeling close to nature and, in other ways, feeling connected so something larger than themselves. Turning to the congregations in which Golden Rule Christians are involved, she found they have three essential qualities: 'opportunities to serve (or contribute to serving) people in need, dynamic worship, and attractive activities for children' (Ammerman 1997, 209).

Ammerman's conclusion speaks to all of us involved in studying religion. While the people she has studied may 'have no coherent theology, and evangelists might worry about their eternal souls, sociologists cannot afford to dismiss a form of lived religion just because it does not measure up to orthodox theological standards' (Ammerman 1997, 210). Further, she points to a history and a tradition of unorthodox, yet spiritual, American religiosity (and, she adds, they rarely talked about 'spirituality': Ammerman 1997, 216). In later work, Ammerman (2013) returns to the idea of lived religion in order to understand 'spirituality'. Her research and analysis will be discussed in more detail in Chapter 12.

Just as Ammerman suggests that people do not often experience everyday religion in ways that match existing theological standards or categories, Meredith McGuire (2008) argued that how people 'live' religion often differs from how scholars suppose they do. Researching religion as it is lived requires more diverse research methods than a survey or questionnaire. She explored how researchers should consider more fine-grained methods to understand lived diverse experiences of religion and spirituality as everyday, embodied, material and often gendered (an important theme of hers that is revisited in later chapters concerning the body and healing). A turn to the 'lived' approach has widened the study of religion.

New religious movements

Popular media reports, often sensationalistic, created a public imaginary in the 1970s of new religious movements (NRMs) as crazed cults, threatening to society at large and abusive to those who joined. These reports claimed that the new, typically young, recruits were troubled and vulnerable, and subsequently brainwashed and often held captive by malicious leaders. Worried parents hired professional 'cult-busters' to kidnap their young, adult children and return them home for 'de-programming'. And yet, a key question remained unanswered: why would young people choose their new groups, and how different were those groups from existing 'old' religions?

The academic, interdisciplinary field of studying NRMs is itself new and lacks a consensus of how to define precisely a 'new religious movement' (but, also, recall that scholars vary in their definition of 'religion' more generally). One of the discipline's founders, sociologist Eileen Barker (2004, 99), reflected on how scholars have struggled to define new religious movements, and while she suggested that they all should not be lumped together, their common characteristic was they are 'new':

> In the first century, Christianity was new, in the seventh century Islam was new, in the eighteenth century Methodism was new, in the nineteenth century the Seventh-day Adventists, Christadelphians and Jehovah's Witnesses were new; in the twenty-first century the Unification Church, ISKCON and Scientology are beginning to look old.

Barker settles on a time period of post-World War II, and a loose definition that an NRM would include both a supernatural or transcendent element and a philosophy that would help practitioners answer ultimate, ontological, questions about, for example, the nature of God or meaning of life.

Thinking with words: ontology and epistemology

Philosophers study 'ontology' as a branch of metaphysics concerned with the nature of being and existence. It is an important term for sociologists as well, because we are often concerned with 'meaning' and whether something exists as an independent, objective reality, or as a 'social fact', depending on people's definitions and experiences in the social world. The difficulties in answering those questions can lead quickly into subsidiary questions, such as 'if I claim to know this exists' (like, for example, 'racism'), 'how do I know?'. This is an 'epistemological' question, relating to the sources and production of knowledge. It is often used in a value-driven, political sense, particularly in feminist discourse where questions often arise as to the taken-for-granted 'common sense' ideas and theories which, on critical inspection, arise from patriarchal forms of power and knowledge. It is also an important term for academic study and writing, when students are often challenged to account for their ideas and distinguish between opinion and evidence-based argument.

Gordon Melton (2004, 79) proposed that new religions could be defined by the way existing religions discussed them because one of their common characteristics was that they were not seen just as different, but 'unacceptably different'. Marat Shterin (2012, 295), for example, cites the response of the Moscow Patriarchate (MP), the leadership of the Russian Orthodox Church, to the growth of NRMs in post-Soviet Russia. While it may have appeared that the church would welcome a new era of religious freedom, its attitude soon became critical of such new freedoms which threatened its own claim as the guardian of national identity.

One common way to discredit NRMs is by creating moral panics through circulating conspiracy theories about them. David Robertson[1] (2019, 5, and see the complete publication Dyrendal et al. 2019) writes:

> Religious minority groups can draw on conspiratorial elements to demonise schematic groups, or to target religious minorities; minorities, on their part may demonise majority institutions as part of a cosmic conspiracy connected to metaphysical evil.

Examples he discusses in his chapter include how the Buddhist majorities in Myanmar and Sri Lanka, supported by other powerful interest groups, justified persecution of Muslim minorities on the basis that they posed existential threats. Robertson is careful to point out that adopting conspiracy theories and targeting minorities are also features of non-religious institutions and movements.

Difficulties often arise regarding who is entitled to say whether a new movement should be classified as 'religious'. A celebrated example was the 2001 international internet campaign encouraging people to add 'Jedi' (popularized in the *Star Wars* movies) to the list of recognized religions. Following the tick-box list of main religions, respondents could choose to write in an option. In the UK a total of 390,127 people – or 0.7 per cent of the population, added Jedi. Seventy thousand Australians and 20,000 Canadians also chose that option. A decade later, the figures had declined, perhaps as a result of an ageing population. In 2016, the UK Charity Commission rejected an application by the Temple of the Jedi Order to register for charitable status as a religion, ruling that it failed to meet requirements to show that it promoted moral or ethical improvement. While many people dismissed the campaign as a satirical hoax, others suggest there was a core of people who aligned themselves to what they felt was a legitimate religion (see e.g. Beth Singler https://bvlsingler.com/2015/08/04/make-a-religion-check/ last accessed June 2020 and and Debra McCormick 2006).

A common theme has emerged in NRM scholarship relating to the impact of 'modernity'. For example, in his work on NRMs in post-Soviet Russia, Marat Shterin (2012) suggests that a simple, binary analysis of modern/pre-modern is insufficient to explain the emergence of NRMs, and that it is more accurate to refer to the *transformation* of religion when new forms of belief, practice and affiliation emerged. During decades when the state enforced secularism and atheism, religion became an unintentionally modernized concept, where choosing to be religious 'lends itself to becoming a basis for reconstructing individual and group identities and to programs of personal and societal transformation' (Shterin 2012, 287). Transnational NRMs, such as the International Society for Krishna Consciousness (ISKCON), the Unification Church and the Church of Scientology became popular in the 1990s, and although their popularity did not grow as quickly or was sustained, as some expected, their ideas and practices 'become part and parcel of the post- Soviet cultural milieu' (Shterin 2012, 291). Home-grown NRMs that developed during the same period tended to be structured around charismatic leaders, responding to local anxieties about change and potential insecurities.

Roy Wallis (1984) suggested a three-part typology to help analyze NRMs: world rejecting, world affirming and world accommodating. One can see that the same kind of categorization could also apply to older, established religions. The world-rejecting group abhors the values they see in 'the world', be they consumerist, focused on success or rejecting 'family values'. They revere their leaders, who often have Christ-like qualities, and favour a physical withdrawal from mainstream society while awaiting a new epoch they feel is imminent. An example is the Unification Church, or 'Moonies' as they are more popularly known, founded in 1954 by South Korean Sun Myung Moon. One of their practices that achieved widespread interest, and often vilification, was their mass weddings. When Eileen Barker (1984) studied them, through detailed observations, interviews, questionnaires and wider data analysis, she found that characteristics like age, class or gender did not help explain why people joined the movement. Rather, the 'Moonies' shared complex experiences, attitudes and desires. They came mainly from conventionally religious families, held the same values as they did during their religious upbringing and often simply wanted to return to and recreate a sense of a warm family.

On the other hand, members of a world-affirming NRM do not reject society outright or hold it to blame for people's unhappiness. They believe the way forward, to truth and perhaps eternal life, lies within individuals and requires a complete acceptance of often difficult and arduous programmes to unlock their potential for happiness, prosperity and the ability to help solve the world's problems. Examples may (subject to definitions) include the Transcendental Meditation movement, created by Maharishi Mahesh Yogi in the 1950s. This was brought to wider fame through his world tours in the 1960s and 1970s, and his endorsement by celebrities, including the Beatles. Adherents practise a form of meditation, focusing on a 'mantra', and seek through that to find internal peace and harmony. The movement is often classed as a religion, against the wishes of many of its members, most famously by the United States courts whose ruling that it was a religion prevented it from being taught in public schools. Scientology, a movement founded in 1952 by author L. Ron Hubbard, welcomed a decision by the UK court in 2013 that it was a religion. This was a landmark case for Scientology and, potentially, other new religious movements because the judges overturned a 1970 case that had rejected Scientology's request to be classed as a religion. The court had ruled then that because the movement did not include worshipping a personal god, it did not fit the correct definition of a religion.[2] Scientology's principles include a belief in an immortal soul whose traumas can be healed, thereby freeing individuals from repeating harmful behaviours and helping them work together to solve wider societal problems.

World-accommodating new religious movements are typically new branches of existing religions, whose members want to restore what they see as the religion's original core, pure, most authentic teachings. Their emphasis is not, as world-affirming movements, typically on personal growth and happiness, but on a deeper, more authentic, relationship with their religion and their god. One example may be the violent jihadi movement within Islam, described by Reuven Firestone (2012, 263–4) as:

> a transnational movement of militant Sunni Muslim activists, often called jihadis who feel that they must be engaged in a prolonged and perhaps even endless war with the forces of evil defined vaguely as the West, or the 'Judeo-Christian' or 'Crusader-Zionist' enemy. It arises out of a Muslim religious and cultural context in response to the combination of contemporary Western economic, political, and cultural developments that have tended to be lumped together and defined over the last decade by the term globalism.

While jihadis see themselves as Muslims, Firestone (2012, 265) suggests that they strive to return to a more fundamental aspect of Islam that Muslims have been neglecting in their process of adapting to Western modernity. The movement has, like revivalist Jewish and Christian movements, a strong anti-intellectualist quality. In considering how Al-Qa'ida acts as a new religious movement, Firestone (2012, 272) notes that it has been positioned as anti an existing form of (corrupt) leadership and authority: Osama bin Laden's 'claim as an untrained (and therefore untainted) authority reflects the modern, Western trend toward individuation and the authority of personal autonomy to confront scripture and tradition'.

Although most NRMs are not violent, those which are have been given disproportionate publicity. Further, as Ian Reader points out (see Chapter 5), violent acts are usually framed by NRM adherents as religious and honourable, just as they are framed when committed by more established religions.

Resurgence

Religion may, indeed, be 'back', but in new and different forms. Indeed, one of the difficulties is establishing if it ever left, and therefore it is important to clarify in what context one might make that claim. In what country? And by whose definition of religion?

Following the 2001 UK census, the Scottish Pagan Federation commissioned data from the Office for National Statistics and found that there were enough Pagans to register Paganism as the seventh largest religious affiliation. Pagans believe that everything, human and other-than-human, has spirits. A definition of religion could encompass not the traditionally theological, but also the more relational, nominal and spiritual.

Grace Davie drew attention to this possibility with her important sociological question. What if, she asked, the smaller population of committed, faithful people were to have a disproportionately high impact on the wider population? And what if, I would add, those who were religious mainly through a nationalistic, ethnicized imaginary also had a growing impact? Given that identities are produced (rather than inherently *a priori* in existence) a minority or a majority is a function of discourse and power relations, as well as statistics. A group that is small numerically can be a majority in terms of power, voice and impact. What they do is often vicariously appreciated and perhaps even required by a larger, more passive population.

Davie (2007) suggested that an 'unchurched' European population may be experiencing religion vicariously through those religious adherents. Peter Berger (1999), with not quite a withdrawal from his previous assumptions that secularization would continue unabated, acknowledged that in many parts of the world Christian Pentecostalism and Islam are growing. Further, Berger, Grace Davie and Effie Fokas (2008) explored how it would be more accurate to consider Christian decline in Europe as an exception, and scholars need to account for how religion may be a device to bolster national and international claims. This theme is explored more extensively in further chapters here, particularly amongst discussions of politics and identity.

Reflecting on the work of scholars who had argued religion would decline as modernity increased, Adam Possamai (2015, 132) cited the same events as did Casanova (1994) and added to the list the attacks of 9/11: 'Religion was not only back, it had been reincarnated and far from rejecting modernisation, it had adopted its creed of progress and emancipation in its many forms'.

In her summary of the UK's multi-project research programme, Religion and Society, Linda Woodhead (2012, 27) concluded that 'There is no question of a "return" of religion. For one thing, it never really went away, and for another, it emerged after the 1980s in significantly different forms.' She found (2012, 27) that

> The new entrants to the spiritual marketplace are more focused on supporting individuals in their everyday lives, fostering new kinds of identity and lifestyle, and linking the likeminded and like-hearted to one another in a vast plurality of different forms of religious alliance. Religions and non-religious spiritual or 'wellbeing' movements have less strong relationships with the State, which has increasingly tried to regulate them, and more connections with consumer capitalism, media, and networks.

A theory that contests secularization, and one more widely accepted in the United States, is the market or economic model. This suggests that the more pluralistic societies become, the more a demand for religion is stimulated (see e.g. Stark and Finke 2000).

Detlef Pollack (2008, 1–22) considers the viability of the idea, and points out that, unlike secularization theory, the concept does not analyse religious change on a macro-societal scale but rather according to the individual activities of various religious providers. Further, it contains a problematic underlying assumption that people's religious desires are fairly constant, in line with an apparently ever-present need for religion. This makes the idea of religious decline and disappearance impossible.

Eisenstadt (2000, 2, see also Hervieu-Léger 2003,) introduced the idea of 'multiple modernities' as presuming that:

> the best way to understand the contemporary world – indeed to explain the history of modernity – is to see it as a story of continual constitution and reconstitution of a multiplicity of cultural programs. These ongoing reconstructions of multiple institutional and ideological patterns are carried forward by specific social actors in close connection with social, political, and intellectual activists, and also by social movements pursuing different programs of modernity, holding very different views of what makes societies modern.

Grace Davie (2002) considered the idea of different trajectories of modernity in order to explain how 'modern' Europe, and particularly the highly secularized France, could differ so much from the 'modern', more religious, United States, Although interesting, and tempting to adopt in post-secular augmentation, others have criticized the concept of multiple modernities and urged scholars not to accept it without qualification. Later, with Peter Berger and Effie Fokas (2008, 3), she identified seven differences that may help explain it, such as

> differences in church-state relationships: questions of pluralism; different understandings of the Enlightenment; different types of intellectuals; variations in culture and how this is understood; institutional contrasts (how in concrete terms the Enlightenment and associated cultures are sustained); and differences in the ways that religious organizations relate to indices of social difference (notably class and ethnicity).

Possamai (2015, 141) warns that, while useful, and important to lead into a post-secular thesis, that does not make multiple modernities theory 'a panacea. When analysing the relationship between religion and the state, for example, how do we deal with religious groups that have such radically different outlooks on what their modernity should be and on what post-secularism entails?'

The phrase 'post-secular' is often used to discuss what may appear to be resurgent religion or, perhaps, retrenchment and re-enchantment. Jürgen Habermas (2006, 19) argued that society has to 'adjust itself to the continued existence of religious communities in an increasingly secularised environment'. The term 'post-secular' was embraced quickly by many scholars, often uncritically, prompting others (Gorski et al. 2012, 1) to warn that 'we should be wary of its deployment simply to signal a contested claim about the resurgence of religion' and suggest scholars differentiate between two questions: has religion resurged or has scholarly attention increased? In the same volume, Michele Dillon (2012, 139–56) drew attention to the overly rational-cognitive frame provided by Habermas and questioned its application to a richer understanding of what religion is, marginalizing its aspects of spirituality, tradition and emotion.

James Beckford (2012) suggested that there are a variety of meanings related to the 'post-secular', and tensions amongst them. He identified six (Beckford 2012, 6–12) that arise in different disciplines and range from the philosophical to the normative. He (Beckford 2012, 13) argued that meanings of post-secular 'are so varied and, in some cases, incompatible with each other that it would make little sense to try to assess whether any particular country or region of the world had actually entered a Postsecular age'. Referring to the contested nature of secularization theses, Beckford cites geographer Lily Kong (2010, 764), who wrote that theories of and evidence for secularization require more analysis before drawing conclusions about any re-emergence of religion. Engagement between the sacred and secular was not, she concluded, re-emerging but continuing.

Indeed, religion, or 'the sacred', has a disconcerting habit of popping up when and where least expected. Paul-Francois Tremlett (2015) studied the anti-capitalist 'Occupy' movement in Hong Kong in 2011, noting that, at first glance, Hong Kong appears to conform to an old, colonial-inflected image of indifferent, successful capitalism. And yet, during the global Occupy protest movement, it was the occupation of space below Hong Kong's global bank HSBC that proved to be the longest of all occupations at the time. Tremlett argues that this represents an eruption of the sacred, an explosion of emotions and frustrations.

Following an extensive discussion of religion within the UK, Beckford concludes that the combination of increased social diversity, equalities legislation and long-standing partnerships between government and religious institutions better explains the contemporary religious landscape than a nebulous term such as 'post-secular'.

Helping to unravel this complexity, Peter Nynäs directed a two-year Centre of Excellence in Research at Åbo Akademi University in Finland titled 'Post-Secular Culture and a Changing Religious Landscape'. Using qualitative and ethnographic methods, the project began with the assumption that secularization theses are becoming increasingly questioned, particularly when framed as a current and inevitable decline of religion's social and cultural relevance. One of their conclusions (Nynäs et al. 2012) was a warning not to dismiss the explanatory potential of a secularization thesis, but to continue to explore a multi-dimensional and contested relationship between religious and secular categories (and see also Nynäs et al. 2015; Day et al. 2013).

Sample questions for private study

1. Reflecting particularly on Habermas and Beckford, how convincing is the idea of 'post-secular' to signal an apparent resurgence of religion?
2. Suggest at least three sociological explanations for the rise of new religious movements.

Sample class exercise

Arrange a visit from a member of a new or alternative religion.

Notes

1   Robertson also leads, with Christopher R. Cotter, a valuable and vibrant resource showcasing some of the latest research in contemporary religion. Most items are free to download, with appropriate citation: The Religious Studies Project www.religiousstudiesproject.com/.
2   In their edited collection, James T. Richardson and François Bellange (2016) showcase several legal cases involving New Religious Movements, instigated by a number of parties, including governments, former members and NRM leaders.

Indicative reading

Abbink, Jon. 2014. 'Religion and Politics in Africa: The Future of "The Secular".' *Africa Spectrum* 49, no. 3: 83–106. https://doi.org/10.1177/000203971404900304

Ammerman, Nancy. 1997. 'Golden Rule Christianity: Lived Religion in the American Mainstream.' In *Lived Religion in America*, edited by David Hall, 196–216. Princeton, NJ: Princeton University Press.

Ammerman, Nancy. 2007. *Everyday Religion: Observing Modern Religious Lives*. Oxford and New York: Oxford University Press.

Ammerman, Nancy. 2013. 'Spiritual But Not Religious? Beyond Binary Choices in the Study of Religion.' *Journal for the Scientific Study of Religion* 52: 258–78. https://doi.org/10.1111/jssr.12024

Asad, Talal. 1993. *Genealogies of Religion: Discipline and Reasons of Power in Christianity and Islam*. Baltimore, MD: Johns Hopkins University Press.

Asad, Talal. 2003. *Formations of the Secular*. Stanford, CA: Stanford University Press.

Barker, Eileen. 1984. *The Making of a Moonie: Choice or Brainwashing?* Oxford: Blackwell.

Barker, Eileen. 2004. 'Perspective: What are we Studying?' *Nova Religio: The Journal of Alternative and Emergent Religions* 8, no. 1: 88–102. DOI: 10.1525/nr.2004.8.1.88

Beckford, James A. 2003. *Social Theory and Religion*. Cambridge: Cambridge University Press.

Beckford, James A. 2012. 'SSSR Presidential Address. Public Religions and the Postsecular: Critical Reflections.' *Journal for the Scientific Study of Religion* 12, no. 1: 1–19. https://doi.org/10.1111/j.1468-5906.2011.01625.

Berger, Peter L. 1967. *The Sacred Canopy: Elements of a Sociological Theory of Religion*. New York: Doubleday.

Berger, Peter L. (ed.). 1999. *The Desecularization of the World: Resurgent Religion and World Politics*. Grand Rapids, MI: William Eerdmans Publishing Co.

Berger, Peter L., Grace Davie and Effie Fokas. 2008. *Religious America, Secular Europe? A Theme and Variations*. Aldershot: Ashgate.

Beyer, Peter. 2006. *Religions in Global Society*. London: Routledge.

Bruce, Steve. 2002. *God is Dead: Secularization in the West*. Oxford: Oxford University Press.

Cannell, Fenella. 2010. 'The Anthropology of Secularism.' *Annual Review of Anthropology* 39: 85–100. https://doi.org/10.1146/annurev.anthro.012809.105039.

Casanova, José. 1994. *Public Religions in the Modern World*. Chicago, IL: University of Chicago Press.

Chaves, Mark. 1994. 'Secularization as Declining Religious Authority.' *Social Forces* 72, no. 3: 749–74.

Coleman, Simon. 2000. *The Globalisation of Charismatic Christianity* (Cambridge Studies in Ideology and Religion). Cambridge: Cambridge University Press.

Davie, Grace. 1994. *Religion in Britain since 1945: Believing without Belonging* Oxford: Blackwell.

Davie, Grace. 2002. *Europe: The Exceptional Case: Parameters of Faith in the Modern World*. London: Darton, Longman & Todd.

Davie, Grace. 2007. Vicarious Religion: A Methodological Challenge. In *Everyday Religion: Observing Modern Religious Lives*, edited by Nancy T. Ammerman, 21–36. Oxford and New York: Oxford University Press.

Davie, Grace. 2015. *Religion in Britain*. Chichester: Wiley Blackwell.

Day, Abby, Giselle Vincett and Christopher R. Cotter (eds). 2013. *Social Identities between the Sacred and the Secular*. Farnham, UK, and Burlington, VT: Ashgate.

Dillon, Michele. 2010. '2009 Association for the Sociology of Religion Presidential Address: Can Post-Secular Society Tolerate Religious Differences?' *Sociology of Religion* 71, no. 2: 139–56. www.jstor.org/stable/25681274

Dillon, Michele. 2012. 'Jürgen Habermas and the Post-Secular Appropriation of Religion: A Sociological Critique.' In *the Post-Secular in Question: Religion in Contemporary Societies*, edited by Philip S. Gorski, David Kyuman Kim, John Torpey and Jonathan Van Antwerpen, 139–56. New York: New York University Press. 10.18574/nyu/9780814738726.003.0010.

Dinham, Adam. 2009. *Faith, Public Policy and Civil Society: Policies, Problems and Concepts in Faith-Based Public Action*. Basingstoke: Palgrave Macmillan.

Dyrendal, Asbjørn, David G. Robertson and Egil Asprem (eds). 2019. *Handbook of Conspiracy Theory and Contemporary Religion*. Leiden and Boston, MA: Brill.

Eisenstadt, Shmuel N. 2000. 'Multiple Modernities.' *Daedalus* 129, no. 1: 1–29. https://doi.org/10.1177/0725513615604418

Emerson, Michael O., and David Hartman. 2006. 'The Rise of Religious Fundamentalism.' *Annual Review of Sociology* 32: 127–44. https://doi.org/10.1146/annurev.soc.32.061604.123141

Firestone, Reuven. 2012. '"Jihadism" as a New Religious Movement.' In *The Cambridge Companion to New Religious Movements*, edited by Olav Hammer and Mikael Rothstein, 263–85. Cambridge: Cambridge University Press.

Fraser, Nancy. 1990. 'Rethinking the Public Sphere: A Contribution to the Critique of Actually Existing Democracy.' *Social Text* 25/26: 56–80. DOI: 10.2307/466240.

Gorski, Philip S., David Kyuman Kim, John Torpey and Jonathan Van Antwerpen. 2012. *The Post-Secular in Question: Religion in Contemporary Societies*. New York: New York University Press.

Guest, Mathew, Elizabeth Olson and John Wolffe. 2012. 'Christianity: A Loss of Monopoly.' In *Religion and Change in Modern Britain*, edited by Linda Woodhead and Rebecca Catto, 57–78. London: Routledge.

Habermas, Jürgen. 1989. *The Structural Transformation of the Public Sphere*, translated by T. Burger. Cambridge: Polity Press.

Habermas, Jürgen. 2006. 'Religion in the Public Sphere.' *European Journal of Philosophy* 14, no. 1: 1–25. https://doi.org/10.1111/j.1468-0378.2006.00241.x

Hall, David. 1997. *Lived Religion in America: Toward a History of Practice*. Princeton, NJ: Princeton University Press.

Hervieu-Léger, Danièle 2003. *Catholicisme, la fin d'un monde*. Paris: Bayard.

Hjelm, Titus. 2015. *Is God Back? Reconsidering the New Visibility of Religion*. London: Bloomsbury.

Hoge, Dean, Benton Johnson and Donald A. Luidens. 1994. *Vanishing Boundaries: The Religion of Mainline Protestant Baby Boomers*. Louisville, KY: Westminster/John Knox.

Kong, Lily. 2010. 'Global Shifts, Theoretical Shifts: Changing Geographies of Religion.' *Progress in Human Geography* 34, no. 6: 755–76.

Künkler, Mirjam, John Madeley, and Shylashri Shankar. 2018. *A Secular Age beyond the West: Religion, Law and the State in Asia, the Middle East and North Africa*. Cambridge: Cambridge University Press.

Martin, David. 1978. *A General Theory of Secularization*. Oxford: Blackwell.

McCormick, Debra. 2006. 'From Jesus Christ to Jedi Knight – Validity and Viability of New Religious Movements in Late Modernity.' Conference Paper Social Change in the 21st Century Conference, 27 October, Brisbane, Queensland University of Technology.

McGuire, Meredith. 2008. *Lived Religion: Faith and Practice in Everyday Life.* Oxford: Oxford University Press.

Melton, Gordon J. 2004. 'Toward a Definition of "New Religion".' *Nova Religio: The Journal of Alternative and Emergent Religions* 8, no. 1: 73–87. 10.1525/nr.2004.8.1.73.

Nynäs, Peter, Mika Lassander and Terhi Utriainen (eds). 2012. *Post-Secular Society.* New Brunswick, NJ: Transaction Books.

Nynäs, Peter, Ruth Illman and Tuomas Martikainen. 2015. *On the Outskirts of 'the Church': Diversities, Fluidities and New Spaces of Religion in Finland* Zurich: Lit verlag.

Pollack, Detlef. 2008. *The Role of Religion in Modern Societies.* New York: Routledge.

Pollack, Detlef, and Gergely Rosta. 2017. *Religion and Modernity: An International Comparison.* Oxford: Oxford University Press.

Possamai, Adam. 2015. 'The Gracelands of Multiple Modernities.' In *Modernities, Memory and Mutations: Grace Davie and the Study of Religion,* edited by Abby Day and Mia Lövheim, 131–42. Farnham: Ashgate.

Reisebrod, Martin. 1993. *Pious Passion: The Emergence of Modern Fundamentalism in the United States and Iran.* San Francisco, CA: University of California Press.

Richardson, James T., and François Bellanger. 2016. *Legal Cases, New Religious Movements, and Minority Faiths.* London: Routledge.

Roberts, Keith, and David Yamane. 2016. *Religion in Sociological Perspective.* London: Sage.

Robertson, David. 2019. 'Introducing the Field: Conspiracy Theories in, about, and as Religion' In *Handbook of Conspiracy Theory and Contemporary Religion,* edited by Asbjørn Dyrendal, David G. Robertson and Egil Asprem, 1-20. Leiden and Boston, MA: Brill.

Shiner, Larry. 1967. 'The Concept of Secularization in Empirical Research.' *Journal for the Scientific Study of Religion* 6, no. 2: 207–20.

Stewart, Pamela J., and Andrew Strathern. 2010. *Ritual.* Farnham, UK, Burlington, VT: Ashgate.

Shterin, Marat. 2012. 'New Religious Movements in Changing Russia.' In *The Cambridge Companion to New Religious Movements,* edited by Olav Hammer and Mikael Rothstein, 286–302. Cambridge: Cambridge University Press.

Stark, Rodney. and Roger Finke. 2000. *Acts of Faith: Explaining the Human Side of Religion.* Berkeley, CA: University of California Press.

Taylor, Charles. 2007. *A Secular Age.* Cambridge, MA and London: Belknap Press of Harvard University Press.

Tremlett, Paul-Francois. 2015. 'Affective Dissent in the Heart of the Capitalist Utopia: Occupy Hong Kong and the Sacred.' *Sociology* 50, no. 6: 1156–69. https://doi.org/10.1177/0038038515591943

Vertovec, Steven. 2001. 'Transnationalism and Identity,' *Journal of Ethnic and Migration Studies* 27, no. 4: 573–82. https://doi.org/10.1080/13691830120090386

Voas, David and Alasdair Crockett. 2005. 'Religion in Britain: Neither Believing nor Belonging.' *Sociology* 39, no. 1: 11–28.

Wallis, Roy. 1984. *The Elementary Forms of the New Religious Life.* London and Boston, MA: Routledge & Kegan Paul.

Wilson, Bryan R. 1966. *Religion in Secular Society: A Sociological Comment.* London: Watts.

Wilson, Bryan R., and Steve Bruce. 2016. *Religion in Secular Society: Fifty Years On.* Oxford: Oxford University Press.

Woodhead, Linda. 2012 'Introduction.' In *Religion and Change in Modern Britain,* edited by Linda Woodhead and Rebecca Catto, 1–33. London: Routledge.

Woodhead, Linda, and Rebecca Catto (eds). 2012. *Religion and Change in Modern Britain.* London: Routledge.

Part II

Religion and its publics

Chapter 4

Politics and religion

Introduction

Only a few years ago many people in the 'west' assumed religion and politics were separate: it was common to talk about religion's place in the 'public sphere'. And yet, such discussions rested on particular and peculiar definitions of religion and politics, often seen as neat, impervious containers. The idea of 'public' and 'private' reflects certain often taken-for-granted assumptions. What do we mean by 'public' or 'publics', and who constructs these categories?

Key debates are reviewed here through looking at case examples where religion and politics enmesh and we can see there is no strict separation: the UK's governmental connections between religion and the state, Donald Trump's dependence on conservative Christians, the relationship between Islam and politics and Vladimir Putin's rhetoric of Russian expansionism with Orthodox Christianity.

Locating the study of politics and religion

It is evident that discussions of religion and any emerging theoretical frameworks have been sparse within the discipline of politics or political science. In their review of that issue, Kenneth D. Wald, Adam L. Silverman and Kevin S. Fridy (2005) suggest that the absence of religion may be explained by the background of political scientists, the complex nature of religion and the events-driven nature of political science. A few years later, Daniel Philpott (2009) suggested that at least a few political scientists were taking the study of religion more seriously and paying attention to varieties and distinctiveness rather than subsuming it into a secularization paradigm.

What do we mean here as 'politics'? There are understandings of politics that are perhaps familiar in everyday lives. This represents a distinction people may make between what is sometimes called 'big P' and 'little p' politics: the big P is how we think about government or state relations, and little p is a term people might apply to their workplace dynamics. The idea of office politics, for example, refers to a sometimes daily jostle for status and recognition; in a different context, non-governmental organizations who rely on funding for their activities may recognize the politics of competing national and international interests; sports clubs may bemoan their 'internal politics' that influence decisions over players or venues for international fixtures; religious groups may recognize the shifting relations amongst the laity and their relationship with leaders. Some sociologists, such as Jay Demerath (2001), distinguish between those who seem to be motivated and inspired by their religion, and those who may be using religion to advance a political agenda. Scholars explore that suggestion by asking what is not 'religious' about certain forms of politics and what is not 'political' about religion, and in what context these might be viewed as separate?

Of increasing relevance since the latter half of the twentieth century is 'identity politics', whereby groups may privilege certain aspects of their identities which they feel have been under-represented and recognized. That theme is explored in detail in Chapter 9.

At stake is the state: sharing the load

While there are many, and contested, definitions of politics, most involve a notion of state, a government and a region.[1] State generally refers to a cluster of institutions that are seen as permanent or at least semi-permanent, such as education, law enforcement, security or health care, whereas the government is a temporary body composed of elected politicians who will affect the workings and size of the state. Apart from its governance role of specific states, governments will both cooperate and sometimes oppose other states through inter-state structures such as the United Nations, the African Union and the European Union. What is seen now as a 'state' was a product of modernity within sixteenth-century Europe. The modern 'state', as political theorists discuss (see e.g. Held 2000) is created within an area designated by certain boundaries and they are historical, not 'natural' entities. For the study of religion, it is important to recognize that states are much younger than most religions and what we often see as political/religious conflicts have long historical antecedents. If modernity was characterized by progress, stability and differentiation, post-modernity is usually presented as its opposite: diffuse, antithetical, unstable and fluid.

The government will determine the level of state activities to be provided for the public: some governments reduce spending on education and increase it on security, for example; others may try to reduce the size of the state by shrinking spending on its institutions and hoping non-state actors, like religious organizations, pick up those responsibilities and share the load.

As example, I will turn here to the UK's programme of austerity when public spending was cut by 10 per cent between 2010 and 2018, hitting some sectors and people more than others. Reduction in welfare provision has a disproportionately deleterious effect on women and minority populations, as discussed by European authors brought into conversation by Lina Molokotos Liederman (2018). And yet, such austerity programmes sometimes have an overtly religious tinge.

The phrase 'big society' emerged then, apparently coined by Phillip Blonde, a former theology lecturer who influenced then Prime Minister David Cameron and the governing Conservative Party. The idea was that the 'big state' should shrink its institutions so that non-governmental organizations, most particularly the Church of England, could help create instead a 'big society'. The Church of England has historically played an important part in social provision and to a large extent still does: since the beginning of state education in 1870, England and Wales have granted state funding for some schools with a Christian foundation. In 1944, the Education Act allowed for the provision of state funding to some Jewish schools and the Blair administration in the late 1990s to

2000s extended state funding to Muslim and Sikh schools (Jackson 2003, 89). By 2009, there were 5,000 (including independent Church of England and Church of Wales) religious schools, providing education to a quarter of primary school pupils and 6 per cent of secondary school pupils (Flint 2009,164). At the time of writing, that number has risen to approximately 7,000.

Supporters of state-funded faith schools argue that they provide high-quality education, promote justice and fairness for religious communities, while promoting social cohesion and the integration of minority communities into the life of the state; on the other hand, opponents claim that faith schools use state money to proselytize, disadvantage other schools through selection procedures and do not promote social cohesion because they separate pupils of different religious and non-religious backgrounds (Jackson 2003, 89). For a more recent detailed analysis of the legal frameworks and implications, see Suhraiya Jivraj (2013).

UK and other governments have struggled with the financial burden of the welfare state since it was established in the 1940s. From its creation in 1994, the National Lottery has helped to address a shortfall in some of this welfare funding, with church-affiliated programmes using the lottery's subsidies to work on community projects; this has been said to be one example of the government 'rediscovering' the social capacities of faith sector organizations (Hill 2009, 28). More recently, faith organizations, including the Church of England, have been involved in the provision of foodbanks, tneed for which increased following the Conservative governments' welfare reforms since 2010. With David Cameron's articulation of the 'Big Society' and its ideal of voluntarism, Christian involvement in foodbanks has bolstered this faith group's role as 'active citizens' (Garthwaite 2017, 287). The Church of England also played a historic role in providing health and other care in, for example, almshouses, before supporting the establishment of the National Health Service, with Archbishop William Temple – along with other Christian thinkers in church-led consultations – involved in the creation of the welfare state following World War II (General Synod 2012, 1). Today, the Church of England is one of several faith groups that provide chaplaincy in the healthcare system, employed through NHS Trusts.

Blonde and colleagues formed a think-tank called Respublica which in 2013 launched their 'Holistic Mission Social Action and the Church of England' report.[2] The report argued for more recognition of the Church of England's social work role and called for the government to recognize this through, amongst other things, establishing a specific unit in the Cabinet. That claim and request was somewhat undermined by the report's own data, showing, for example, that the majority of voluntary church activities consisted of 'Promoting Church, e.g. Coffee Mornings'. The report was further weakened by its failure to account for what church leader Justin Welby was to describe as a demographic time-bomb. It is mostly a quiet army of elderly women who carried out the church's coffee morning and related activities. Faithful Church of England supporters in government, bishops who sit in the House of Lords, were not wholly convinced by the Respublica report. A discussion about the report (www.respublica.uk/wp-content/uploads/2014/11/akt_HouseofLordsdebateofHolisticMission-21112013.pdf, last accessed Oct. 2019) was introduced by the Bishop of Leicester whose motion asked the House to take note of the report. His opening comments are worth studying in detail as they portray a certain view of the Church of England. He describes the report as presenting:

> a picture of a church which is present in every community, town, village and city and embedded in its localities. It is a church which baptises, marries and buries a significant proportion of the population, educates some 1 million children in church schools and serves the poor, the homeless, the lonely, the hungry and the distressed in often unnoticed but crucial ways. The report's central argument is that a nation cannot thrive and progress purely as a result of the success or otherwise of the market or the Government. These have both in different ways failed us. The NHS has been implicated in massive scandals of appalling care and resultant cover-ups. Our banking system has been the province of vested and bonus-seeking self-interest. In the United Kingdom, social mobility is stagnating and inequalities are rising and embedding. This debate arises from the conviction that we need to renew, recover and restore the transformative institutions which can make a vital difference. The institution primarily placed to do that is the Church of England.

While he was correct that this was the image presented in the report, several other Lords who responded to his remarks were not so convinced. Lord Phillips of Sudbury, who described himself as a doubting Anglican and occasional Quaker, took exception to the report's sole focus on the Church of England, when other religious institutions have a practical, 'exemplary' role, and doubted that:

> the Church of England, although I love it dearly, is fit for that purpose. It is in a state of extreme inequality within itself. In some parts of the country, some churches and cathedrals are vibrant and thriving, but many are not. They are very much on the back foot and struggling.

The idea that the Church of England should have a special unit in government was also not welcomed. Lord Griffiths of Burry Port, for example, asked why there should be a special office to centre all that work, when: 'The Department for Communities and Local Government already has a base there, and it has accomplished a great deal in bringing faith groups together as one means of helping to build an integrated society in Britain.'

This example provokes another question beyond state and church cooperation in social issues: why are there bishops in the House of Lords at all, and does this reflect a sometimes less visible but possibly significant role that institutional Christianity still plays, despite diminishing numbers of adherents in Euro-American countries? The UK and Iran share the peculiar distinction of being the only two countries in the world with permanent places for religious leaders in their houses of government.

The Lords Spiritual, as the 26 bishops[3] that sit in the House of Lords are known, are 'as much a part of the English Establishment as barons, big businessmen and bureaucrats' (Drewry and Brock 1971, 222). They constitute 3 per cent of the total number of Lords. Many people defend their place in government on the basis that the Church of England is synonymous with English identity. Respondents to recent surveys of beliefs and values in Great Britain and evangelical Christians in the UK regard the Church of England as 'integral to English culture', 'an ethical voice in society' and 'part of our heritage'. Greg Smith and Linda Woodhead note: 'The C of E is inseparable from the development of the English nation, monarchy, language, people, culture and mores: they have coevolved for five centuries' (Smith and Woodhead 2018, 216).

In 2006, the UCL Constitution Unit published *Church and State – A Mapping Exercise*, part of a broader study of church establishment. It showed that, although the church and state relationship has 'changed greatly' over the years, current arrangements 'span something more than a merely vestigial residue of the former partnership, especially in the relationship with the sovereign' (Cranmer et al. 2006, 6). The UK's constitutional arrangements have an 'especial complexity'; faith has a high profile, with the monarch acting as both head of state and as head of the established church (Dinham et al. 2009, 1). Even in an era of increased secularization, the Church of England enjoys 'more institutional opportunities than other religious bodies to shape the cultural landscape of the nation', with state-funded Church of England schools as one example (Guest et al. 2012, 68).

The Church of England's special relationship with the state carries with it certain rights and privileges, along with accompanying restrictions and limitations: 'the benefits that have accrued to the Church of England by virtue of establishment have come, and continue to come, at a price [such as] the intrusion of political authority into matters that in other churches would be the preserve of internal authorities' (Partington and Bickley 2007, 16).

The Church of England Parliamentary Unit (2018) https://churchinparliament.org/about-the-lords-spiritual/ last accessed Oct. 2019) considers the 'continuing place of Anglican bishops in the Lords [to reflect] our enduring constitutional arrangement, with an established Church of England and its Supreme Governor as Monarch and Head of State'. Rodger (2017, 12) contends that the Lords Spiritual occupy 'a place of unique ecclesiastical and political significance' at the juncture between the established church, British politics and the state.

Religions and states have a lot in common, observed Phillip Hammond and David Machacek (2009), who pointed out that all religions have a strong idea of how to live a good life, and all states are invested in policing and to some extent often enabling that life. Further, writes José Casanova (1994, 5), each has a set of concepts and practices that serve to organize and structure the social reality of a society. Questions will arise about the legitimacy of the authority of those who organize the state; typically politicians. Sometimes, in attempts to resolve those conflicts, a dichotomy is presented between so-called public and private spheres of life: the state being public and religion apparently being private. Such a division, argued Jürgen Habermas (2006, 2–3), is spurious. He writes of interlocking conflicts in the Middle East and narratives in the 'west' that seek to explain those conflicts, drawing on motifs of a clash of civilizations or an axis of evil. And yet, the 'west' often ignores the impact of colonization, decolonialization and capitalism it generated and imposed, and its own revitalization of religious rhetoric, particularly in the United States, which fosters and encourages cultural divisions on familiar fault lines of 'God, gays, guns'. One of the reasons that religion cannot be shunted away into a private, separate sphere, he argues, is that 'true belief is not only a doctrine, believed content, but a source of energy that the person who has a faith taps performatively and thus nurtures his or her entire life'. He posits a conflict between religion and modernity[4] and asks, rhetorically, whether (Habermas (2006, 3) the 'cognitive burden' of adapting to modernity should not be equally shared between religious and secular people, with each required to behave self-reflexively in the public sphere. Habermas acknowledges the view of political theorist John Rawls that a civil state requires reason, civility and respect, but presses the point further by asking (Habermas 2006, 3) whether it is reasonable for the state to insist on actions that contrast with a citizen's 'devout life'.

As American sociologist Jay Demerath (2001) travelled the world for more than a decade, visiting 14 countries, and explored religions in their national and international contexts. He was particularly interested in the ways in which religious actors experience their religions and often collaborate and compete with secular interests.

Demerath points out that such interactions had been largely ignored by scholars in the 1970s who were so swayed by secularization theses that they thought religions were anachronistic, declining and therefore irrelevant. But then came the rise of the hard-right religious conservatism, the visits and blessings of a Pope to Latin America and Poland with their strong, anti-government political agendas, and crises in the Middle East fuelled by religious sentiments and identities. What can be seen as a new wave of populist sentiments at the time of writing may be tied to conservative, nationalistic agendas that make comfortable allegiances with conservative religion (see e.g. Claire Blencowe 2020; Greg Smith and Linda Woodhead 2018).

Demerath shows how the interests of politicians and religious leaders often merge and overlap. He distinguishes between two types of religion-politics interaction. One is where religious leaders seek to influence politics as part of their wider agenda to change people's behaviours, whereas the other is when religious people become part of a nation's governance. The first, he suggests, may be inevitable and is usually tolerated, whereas the second is usually related to power struggles and is therefore particularly contentious, both for religious and secular publics.

Religion and nationalism

I will turn now to a theme running through that debate, particularly with reference to the kind of religious revitalization taking place in many Euro-American countries that depends on a renewed form of nationalism. Rogers Brubaker (2012, 3) usefully approaches the analysis of religion and nationalism by proposing it be analysed in four ways:

1   Treating religion and nationalism as 'analogous phenomena' (meaning that useful comparisons can be drawn between them to deepen understanding of each and both).
2   Specifying ways in which religion helps explain nationalism.
3   Considering religion as part of nationalism.
4   Proposing a distinctively religious form of nationalism.

He elucidates his first point, that religion and nationalism are analogous, by citing other scholars who would draw such parallels, notably Émile Durkheim, Carlton Hayes and Anthony Smith, who all show that nationalism, like religion, has a set of beliefs, a sense of a collectivism, rituals, sacred books, holy days, the power to inspire great acts, emotions and sacrifices in defence of the collective and, perhaps, as a sense of shared gods in the person of charismatic leaders. While those comparisons are 'fruitful', Brubaker (2012, 4) notes, he suggests that another way of considering the relationship is to see religion, nationalism and ethnicity as 'under more encompassing conceptual rubrics: a mode of identification, a mode of social organisation and a way of framing political claims'. They are all ways of seeing the world, constructing identities, creating sameness and difference, and imagining community. The phrase 'imagined community' was also used by Benedict Anderson (1991) who argued that it was the novel and the newspaper that permitted the rise of nationalism and the promotion of certain values deemed to be English. Anderson argued that imagined moral superiority over others was part of English identity, but he linked that rise to nationalism, classism and colonialism rather than to Protestantism.

That observation leads Brubaker to his second point, that religion, ethnicity and nationalism can all be means of creating social organizations that can exist in parallel with other so-constructed social organizations, and thirdly, of increasing or preserving social segmentation: the most important mechanism for achieving which, he suggests, is 'endogamy' (the practice of marrying only within certain social groups). Finally, he argues that religion, ethnicity and nationalism all can and increasingly do make claims for rights and recognition, as well as resources (Brubaker (2012, 5):

> politicised ethnicity, broadly understood as encompassing claims made on the basis of ethno-religious, ethno-national, ethno-racial, ethno-regional or otherwise ethno-cultural identifications, which have proliferated in both the developed and the developing world in the last half century.

To the extent that religion has been used to produce or cement nationalism, Brubaker cites examples of how religious symbols and narratives have been used to further the claim of what Anthony Smith referred to as chosen-ness: 'that act as "deep cultural resources" that continue to provide the "basic cultural and ideological building blocks for nationalists"' (Smith 2003, 254–5, in Brubaker 2012, 6). Brubaker slows the rhetoric down a little by making the important point that not all religious-derived language is necessarily religious in intent or content. Referring to something as 'sacred', for example, may be a way to signal its special quality without trying to reduce it to religion: 'can it be considered simply one of many ways in which originally religious language can be used metaphorically in other domains?' (Brubaker 2012, 10). There is a long and rich tradition of biblical language and metaphors in English literature and language, for example, but this does not mean all English literature is religious.

The nationalistic drive towards having a state contains within it the idea that a state is one amongst many other states, he argues, referring to Anderson's (1991) notion of the 'imagined community' being essentially pluralistic and not the same as a call for fellow Muslims to recognize their true identity and live in a place and manner that would allow them to conduct their daily lives in an authentic, Islamic form. Such claims for recognition, respect, rights and resources are better understood, he concludes, as a form of politicized ethnicity.

One strand of argument Brubaker (2012, 13) touches on is Roger Friedland's (2002) thesis that possibilities for nationalistic ambitions are afforded through exploiting the power and resources of family, gender and sexuality because the 'traditional' family structure is the prime site for generating and reproducing social hierarchies and morals. The family can therefore be used against those economic or cultural forces that threaten a normative entity of nation, by 'upholding traditional gendered divisions of labour within and outside the family; and by promoting restrictive regulation of sexuality, seeking to contain sexuality within the family'. Brubaker does not wholly accept that argument,[5] particularly when it cites contemporary Islam as an example of a national-istic religion because it seeks an *umma,* a community of Muslims that should have its own state, or a Caliphate. He cautions against taking the idea of nationalism too far (Brubaker 2012, 14):

> Nationalism is a useful concept only if it is not overstretched. If the concept is not to lose its discriminating power, it must be limited to forms of politics, ideology or discourse that involve a central orientation to 'the nation'; it cannot be extended to encompass all forms of politics that work in and through nation-states.

Michael Billig (1995) focuses on less extreme and obvious forms of nationalism by drawing attention to its sly, everyday, banal forms that reinforce national identity and belonging. He (Billig 1995, 6) suggests that 'these habits are not removed from everyday life, as some observers have supposed. Daily, the nation is indicated, or "flagged," in the lives of its citizenry'. To imagine one belongs to a nation requires, he argues, 'a whole complex of beliefs, assumptions, habits, representations and practices'. These rely on foundational myths and institutions that reinforce them: one can think of the monarchy, the Church of 'England', faces printed on money or casual references to 'our team'. Although not as 'hot' as more apparent nationalisms, banal nationalism may be more dangerous mainly through its unremarkable, less visible forms.

Another significant idea emerging here is the idea of the 'imaginary'. Influenced ini-tially by Anderson, Charles Taylor (2002, 92) considered ideas of a 'social imaginary'[6] which, for him, extended beyond ideas and beliefs to social practices reflecting a new moral order:

> My hypothesis is that central to Western modernity is a new conception of the moral order of society. At first this moral order was just an idea in the minds of some influential thinkers, but later it came to shape the social imaginary of large strata, and then eventually whole societies. It has now become so self-evident to us, we have trouble seeing it as one possible conception among others. The mutation of this view of moral order into our social imaginary is the development of certain social forms that characterize Western modernity: the market economy, the public sphere, the self-governing people, among others.

Aligning himself to a particular form of moral order, American President Donald Trump owed much of his electoral success to evangelical, fundamentalist Christians. In his 2016 election victory, he was supported by nearly 90 per cent of self-identified Evangelical Christians. What these Christians share is both a religious and political belief. Most of them believe that the Bible is the word of God and must be taken literally. Professor Martyn Percy, an Anglican priest and Dean of Christ Church College, Oxford, argued that Trump's electoral support by American Christians was made possible by the statement made by Franklin Graham, son of Billy Graham (a much revered figure often seen as a spiritual guide to American political leaders). He encouraged evangelists to back Trump because he would enforce the kinds of regulations in domestic and foreign policy that they wanted. He was, Graham claimed, a kind of modern 'Cyrus' – the biblical figure styled as a messiah (www.theguardian.com/commentisfree/2018/feb/06/donald-trump-faith-politics-religious-presidency). It was not his character as a moral, god-fearing Christian that was important in this case, but his ability to wield power in the right direction. True to his promise, Trump backed changes to abortion laws after his election, ranging from how the US government would curtail funding to organizations that advised on family planning, including birth control and abortion, to appointing conservative and anti-abortion Justice Brett Kavanaugh to the Supreme Court.

It is not the first time in the last few decades that popular American power has swung towards enforcing more conservative actions regarding gender and sexuality. In the 1970s, American political power shifted far to the right, with top agenda items concerning gender and sexuality. Sociologists studying this period of American history observe a general upsurge in conservatism in both politics and religion, described as the 'New Right' and 'New Christian Right'. The two forces combined during the late 1970s and 1980s with the Moral Majority, a well-organized network of mainly fundamentalist Christians credited with helping Ronald Reagan become president. This may be seen as a response to and backlash against the liberalizing forces of the 1960s and an attempt by religious actors to resist and relegitimize themselves. In such cases these religious practitioners may feel pushed to establish themselves within a particular political allegiance as an act of resistance (see e.g. Levi et al. 2012).

On the other side of the globe, Russian Leader Vladimir Putin has appealed to people who have at least a residual connection to the Orthodox Church. Visiting one of eastern Europe's most sensitive hot spots in 2013, Putin marked the anniversary of the conversion of Slavic Grand Prince Vladimir to Orthodox Christianity more than one thousand years earlier in what is now Ukraine. His announcement, in a country which has struggled to maintain its independence from Russia, could be seen as intensely provocative: 'We are all spiritual heirs of what happened here . . . and in this sense we are, without a doubt, one people' (www.nytimes.com/2013/07/28/world/europe/putin-in-ukraine-to-celebrate-a-christian-anniversary.html). One year later, Russia annexed Crimea from Ukraine and Putin visited the site of an old monastery to proclaim the event as a reunification of Russian people on a pensinsula with important strategic and religious significance. Putin portrayed an image of himself as a national saviour, a near-mythic figure almost singlehandedly saving an old monastery: (www.bbc.co.uk/news/world-europe-42707957). He likened the region to the contested holy site in Jerusalem, 'Temple Mount' (www.washingtonpost.com/news/worldviews/wp/2014/12/04/why-putin-says-crimea-is-russias-temple-mount/?utm_term=.eb16ee192193).

> because Crimea is where our people live, and the peninsula is of strategic importance for Russia as the spiritual source of the development of a multifaceted but solid Russian nation and a centralised Russian state [. . .] Crimea, the ancient Korsun

or Chersoness, and Sevastopol have invaluable civilizational and even sacral importance for Russia, like the Temple Mount in Jerusalem for the followers of Islam and
Judaism.

Crimea in general and Sevastopol in particular are militarily significant as the base
of the Russian Black Sea Fleet. Historian and retired Major-General Mungo Melvin
(2017)   observed   (https://theconversation.com/vladimir-putin-and-donald-trumps-
great-success-in-exploiting-the-rise-of-nationalist-christianity-92963) that 'many in the
Kremlin now, and perhaps long into the future, would argue that Russia's honour was at
stake in Sevastopol as much as its national interests'. Melvin adds: 'Rather than being an
opportunistic tactician as some suppose, he is following a deliberate strategy of making
Russia great again, backed by increasing military spending.'

   The religious composition of Russia is complicated. The number of people claiming to
be 'Orthodox' increased from 31 to 72 per cent between 1991 and 2008 (www.pewforum.
org/2014/02/10/russians-return-to-religion-but-not-to-church), and yet regular church
attendance only grew marginally, from 2 to 7 per cent. This phenomenon of 'nominal
Christianity' or 'believing in belonging' is familiar: most people who self-identify as
Christian on the decennial UK census do not attend church or participate in important
rituals, such as confirmation or communion. A similar pattern can be seen across
western Europe and increasingly in the United States. Such self-identification arises at
certain times when people may use religion as a cultural, nationalistic marker that both
includes and excludes. That phenomenon also raises the question about how 'political'
the act of counting may be.

Religion and politics by census

As first described in Chapter 2, many countries conduct a census of population every
five to ten years to determine demographic characteristics that might influence resource
allocations, such as where and how many schools and hospitals will be required in
the future. The decennial census in the UK began in 1801 and from then until 2001
no question about religion had been included in the sections for England, Wales and
Scotland.[7] The move to include a question about religion was initiated by the Muslim
Council of Britain which argued that there needed to be a better understanding of
how many Muslims there were in the UK and where they were living (Hussain and
Sherif 2014).

   As Muslims define themselves in terms of their religion, not ethnicity (already covered
on the census), a census religious question would give government necessary information about the Muslim community:

> The allocation of resources and the monitoring of discrimination on the basis of
> ethnicity alone are therefore no longer adequate. An objective of the 2001 census
> is to provide essential statistics for the more equitable allocation of public services
> and better planning on matters such as community relations, health care, education,
> employment and housing. Without a religious affiliation question, the 2001 census
> will lose a valuable data collection opportunity.
>
> (www.salaam.co.uk/knowledge/ukcensus.php)

Intense lobbying by other religious groups followed (see e.g. accounts from two of its members, Francis 2003 and Weller 2004; for further detailed examination and historical review, see Southworth 2005). The final wording and placement of the question was decided by the Office for National Statistics, in consultation with government. Variations made comparisons difficult, if not impossible, as discussed in Chapter 2, but the Christian result of 72 per cent triggered a triumphalist, if sometimes inaccurate, response from Christian leaders and others to reinforce their claims for a Christian religious and cultural identity.

When MP Evan Harris complained in the House of Commons that religious groups were exempt from human rights legislation (which prohibits discrimination on grounds of, for example, sexual orientation and gender|) and yet were engaged in delivering publicly funded services, MP Jack Straw replied for the government, making explicit reference to the census:

> the hon. Gentleman is a secularist, and I respect his views, but his is not the position of the vast majority of this country, 70 per cent of whom declared themselves to be Christian in the 2001 census, and there are many who subscribe to other religions.
>
> (Hansard, 25 January 2007)

Shortly after the census results were published, the Bishop of Manchester said in the House of Lords that the BBC should increase its religious broadcasting because the census figures 'support broadcasters who are seeking peak time for high-quality religious and spiritual content' (Hansard, 22 May 2003). In another census-related move, the Archbishops' Council, representing the Church of England, suggested that the country's broadcasting company, the BBC, should change its programming policy (Archbishops' Council, 2006) because 'The 2001 Census finds that a higher proportion, 80%, associates with a faith community.'

When Revd Barry Morgan was inaugurated as the new Archbishop of the Church in Wales on 12 July 2003, he commented (Morgan 2003) that he had been 'heartened by the 2001 Census results, which show most people in Wales believe in God'.

The Bishop of St Albans also referred to the census:

> the most recent census figures would indicate that, yes, of course fewer people attend and practise their belief in specific religious buildings, but the levels of belief and spirituality in our nation are huge. To describe us as secular is simply not accurate.
>
> (Hansard, 6 June 2003)

This was a point explicitly raised by the then British Humanists Association (now Humanists UK) which campaigned against the inclusion of a religious question on the census[8] and its impacts on public policy, particularly public broadcasting:

> This representation of the data as implying the population in England and Wales as strongly religious and spiritual is used to influence the direction of legislation passing through Parliament (and sometimes with success), despite the fact that the Census 2001 data on religion attempts to measure religious affiliation/identity and does not even attempt to measure feeling, belief or faith.

The above examples are provided as a case study to illustrate how something like a census can be both political and discursive, and how statistics can be used in a variety of ways. The questions on the censuses only asked about *religious* self-identification, and yet the quotes range much more widely, claiming that census findings prove something about belief, spirituality and theism. Measured against all the usual metrics of church attendance, participation in rituals and membership, mainstream Christianity is in steep decline in the UK, Europe. Australia and Canada. Several scholars argue that many, particular older, people may continue to self-identify as Christians as a form of belonging to a nostalgic vision of their country's past 'culture'. This is a form of 'nominal' Christianity that reflects deeply held social allegiances.[9] In this sense, nominal belief is not neutral or insignificant, but, in the UK context, may be a form of resistance performed by, largely, older, white, English people striving to retain and even reimpose their version of English 'culture' by marking boundaries.

Case example: being Marshallese and Christian

An apparent contradiction between two forms of identity struck anthropologist Peter Rudiak-Gould (2010) as a puzzle. He explored why it was that Marshall Islanders presented two distinct forms of their previous identities, depending on whether they were seeing those through a cultural or religious lens. Gould spent 15 months in the Marshall Islands, part of Micronesia in the Pacific Ocean, first as a teacher and translator and then as an ethnographer. He begins his report with a brief history of the Marshall Islands, when, for about 2,000 years the Islanders, adept in sea-faring skills, remained in frequent contact with each other throughout the archipelago and maintained a uniform language. Despite this, there was almost certainly no pan-Marshallese identity before the arrival of Westerners. In the mid-19th century, American missionaries arrived and Germany took control of the territory. In just a few generations, he writes, the entire population was converted to Christianity. Japan took over the islands after World War I, and after World War II the islands became administered by the United States, whose military tested nuclear weapons on two atolls from the 1940s to the late 1950s. Hundreds of people were displaced and thousands more exposed to radiation. The country achieved political independence in 1986 but, he writes, remains heavily dependent on American subsidies.

Rudiak-Gould became fascinated with the way the Islanders responded to his questions about their histories. When he asked them to describe their past, most spoke longingly about a time before consumerism and individualism, when the Islanders helped each other and lived in harmony. One of his interlocutors described this eloquently (Rudiak-Gould 2010, 71):

> There's no question that life was better in the past. Everyone worked together, helped each other, fed each other, and made food. No one was hungry. Everyone worked and ate and respected their chief. Nowadays, you see crime, theft and fighting. None of these things existed before because they were

against Marshallese custom … There wasn't any money or things like that yet. It's harder nowadays because of the economic reality. People need money for all kinds of things. Once Westernization, Western culture and all of those things came, people were influenced by it. They need money, and they need things that aren't in their community.

Their stories changed abruptly, however, when Rudiak-Gould (2010, 71) asked them more specifically about their pre-Christian past. The quoted material describes a time of chaos and disorder:

Rather than contrasting the past with present-day decline, they contrasted the past with present-day progress, and Western influence was praised rather than denigrated. 'Marshall Islanders killed each other then,' informants typically said. 'Life was dark. Now we have received the light of God from the missionaries, and we love each other.' 'People hadn't learned to pray and fear God yet.' 'You would say hello to a person by spearing them.' 'People slept unsoundly, for fear of being ambushed.' 'They would bury their chiefs alive, because they were not yet enlightened by Christianity.' 'The islands used to be overrun by spirits sent by the Devil. Now there are fewer, because people learned from the missionaries to pray to God. The only good spirit is the Holy Spirit.' 'For this change we are grateful to *your* people.'

While it would be tempting for a visiting anthropologist to describe those apparent contradictions as a visitor's misapprehension about the complexity of religious belief, the Islanders themselves saw a contradiction and were not able to reconcile it. In his discussion about how to analyse that puzzle, Rudiak-Gould (2010, 75) suggests that 'Often unknown or dimly remembered, the past can function as a blank slate upon which people inscribe ideologically appropriate stories.' This means, he argues, that both accounts are best understood as ideology, where the past is rewritten to suit a contemporary narrative of decline. Rudiak-Gould argues that the versions he heard arose from two distinct identities: one Christian, one indigenous. In conclusion, he suggests (Rudiak-Gould (2010, 83): 'Even at the same point in history, within the same individual, regarding the same sort of belief, there can exist inconsistency. Paradox penetrates all the way down; the ability of people to compartmentalise, to hold multiple frames without realizing or minding, may have no bounds.'

The above discussion and examples demonstrate the interplay of dynamics such as nationalism, new formations of states, consequences of globalization, the role of religion in society, the rise of new religious movements, religion and social policy, the role of faith-based organizations, and religion and national memory and, perhaps above all else: power.

Sample questions for private study

1 Discuss 'the state' and its problematic in relation to religion.
2 Relate current examples of far-right populism to the key themes of this chapter.

Sample class exercise

Ask students to bring an example of a news item that shows the relationship between religion and politics.

Notes

1 A journal that publishes work exploring just this intersection, *Religion, State and Society,* is a helpful resource: www.tandfonline.com/toc/crss20/current
2 www.respublica.org.uk/our-work/publications/holistic-mission-socialaction-church-england/>, last accessed Jan. 2016.
3 There are 46 bishops and archbishops eligible to sit in the House of Lords, but only 26 may sit at any one time.
4 Students of the sociology of religion will likely recognize his religion/modernity binary as problematic, given the debates in this volume and elsewhere about the contested relationship between modernity and religion.
5 Friedland's (2001, 2002) arguments are, nonetheless, significant for illuminating what often seems mysterious: the concentration in nationalist movements of discussion about the dangers of sexual and gendered identities. His ideas will be elaborated further in Chapter 7.
6 And for further discussion see Calhoun et al. 2015.
7 In 1851 a separate survey called the *Accommodation and Attendance at Worship* census was taken on the same day, asking questions about church attendance. Questions about religious affiliation had been covered in the Northern Irish census since 1861.
8 I am grateful to the BHA for providing convenient access to the Hansard excerpts used in this chapter.
9 For further discussion of censuses and their impact on a range of countries, see Day and Lee 2014.

Indicative reading

Anderson, Benedict. 1991. *Imagined Communities.* London: Verso.
Billig, Michael. 1995. *Banal Nationalism.* London: SAGE.
Blencowe, Claire. 2020. 'Disenchanting Secularism (or the Cultivation of Soul) as Pedagogy in Resistance to Populist Racism and Colonial Structures in the Academy.' *British Educational Research Journal.* https://doi.org/10.1002/berj.3665.
Brubaker, Rogers. 2012. 'Religion and Nationalism: Four Approaches.' *Nations and Nationalism* 18, no. 1: 2–20. https://doi.org/10.1111/j.1469-8129.2011.00486.x
Calhoun, Craig, Dilip P. Gaonkar, Benjamin Lee, Charles Taylor and Michael Warner. 2015. 'Modern Social Imaginaries Revisited: A Conversation.' *Social Imaginaries* 1, no. 1.

Casanova, José. 1994. *Public Religions in the Modern World*. Chicago, IL: University of Chicago Press.

Cranmer, Frank, John Lucas, and Bob Morris. 2006. *Church and State: A Mapping Exercise*. London: UCL, Constitution Unit.

Day, Abby, and Lois Lee (eds). 2014. 'Making Sense of Surveys and Censuses: Issues in Religious Self-Identification.' *Religion*, 44, no. 3: 345–356, DOI: 10.1080/0048721X.2014.929833

Demerath, N. Jay, III. 2001. *Crossing the Gods: World Religions and Worldly Politics*. New Brunswick, NJ: Rutgers University Press.

Dinham, Adam, Robert Furbey and Vivien Lowndes (eds). 2009. *Faith in the Public Realm: Controversies, Policies and Practices*. Bristol: Policy Press.

Drewry, Gavid, and Jenny Brock. 1971. 'Prelates in Parliament.' *Parliamentary Affairs* 24, no. 3: 222–50.

Flint, John. 2009. 'Faith-Based Schools: Institutionalising Parallel Lives?' In *Faith in the Public Realm: Controversies, Policies and Practices,* edited by Adam Dinham, Robert Furbey and Vivien Lowndes, 163–82. Bristol: Policy Press.

Francis, Leslie. 2003. 'The Flaw in the 2001 Census in England and Wales.' In *Public Faith? The State of Religious Practice in Britain,* edited by Paul Avis, 45–64. London: Society for Promoting Christian Knowledge.

Friedland, Roger. 2001. 'Religious Nationalism and the Problem of Collective Representation.' *Annual Review of Sociology* 27: 125–52. https://doi.org/10.1146/annurev.soc.27.1.125

Friedland, Roger. 2002. 'Money, Sex and God: The Erotic Logic of Religious Nationalism.' *Sociological Theory* 20, no. 3: 381–425. ttps://doi.org/10.1111/0735-2751.00169.

Garthwaite, Kayleigh. 2017. '"I Feel I'm Giving Something Back to Society": Constructing the "Active Citizen" and Responsibilising Foodbank Use.' *Social Policy and Society* 16, no. 2: 283–92.

General Synod. 2012. *Health Care and the Church's Mission: Report by the Mission and Public Affairs Council.* www.churchofengland.org/sites/default/files/2018-01/gs%201857%20 health%20care%20and%20churchs%20mission%20%28web%20version%29_Feb12.pdf.

Grzymala-Busse, Anna. 2012. 'Why Comparative Politics Should Take Religion (More) Seriously,' *Annual Review of Political Science* 15: 421–2. 10.1146/annurev-polisci-033110-130442

Guest, Mathew, Elizabeth Olson, and John Wolffe. 2012. 'Christianity: Loss of Monopoly,' In *Religion and Change in Modern Britain*, edited by Linda Woodhead and Rebecca Catto, 57-78. London: Routledge.

Habermas, Jürgen. 2006. 'Religion in the Public Sphere,' *European Journal of Philosophy* 14, no. 1: 1–25. https://doi.org/10.1111/j.1468-0378.2006.00241.x

Hammond, Phillip, and David Machacek. 2009. 'Religion and the State.' In *The Oxford Handbook of the Sociology of Religion*, edited by Peter Clark, 391–405. Oxford: Oxford University Press.

Held, David. 2000. *Political Theory and the Modern State: Essays on State, Power, and Democracy*. Cambridge: Polity Press,

Hill, Mark (2009). 'Voices in the Wilderness: The Established Church of England and the European Union.' *Religion, State and Society* 37, no. 1: 167–80

Hussain, Serena, and Jamil Sherif. 2014. 'Minority Religions in the Census: The Case of British Muslims'. In *Making Sense of Surveys and Censuses: Issues in Religious Self-Identification,* special issue of *Religion,* guest edited by Abby Day and Lois Lee, 44, no. 3: 414–433, DOI: 10.1080/0048721X.2014.927049

Jackson, Robert. 2003. 'Should the State Fund Faith Based Schools? A Review of the Arguments.' *British Journal of Religious Education* 25, no. 2: 89–102. https://doi.org/10.1080/0141620030250202

Jivraj, Suhraiya. 2013. *The Religion of Law: Race, Citizenship and Children's Belonging,* Basingstoke: Palgrave Macmillan.

Kenney, Jeffrey T., and Ebrahim Moosa. 2014. *Islam in the Modern World*. Abingdon, Oxon: Routledge.

Liederman, Lina Molokotos, with Anders Backström and Grace Davie (eds). 2018. *Religion and Welfare in Europe: Gendered and Minority Perspectives*. Bristol: Policy Press.

Lever, John. 2013. 'The Postliberal Politics of Halal: New Directions in the Civilizing Process.' *Human Figurations* 2, no. 3. http://hdl.handle.net/2027/spo.11217607.0002.306.

Levi, Margaret, Simon Jackman and Nancy Rosenblum. 2012. *Annual Review of Political Science*. Palo Alto, CA: Annual Reviews.

Melvin, Mungo. 2017. *Sevastopol's Wars: Crimea from Potemkin to Putin*. London: Osprey Publishing.

Modood, Tariq. 2005. *Multicultural Politics: Racism, Ethnicity, and Muslims in Britain*. Minneapolis, MN: University of Minnesota Press.

Morgan, Barry. 2003. 'Church enthrones new archbishop'. http://news.bbc.co.uk/1/hi/wales/3060347.stm, last accessed Mar. 2008.

Nussbaum, Martha C. 1999. *Sex and Social Justice*. Oxford, New York: Oxford University Press.

Partington, Andrew, and Paul Bickley. 2007. *Coming off the Bench: The Past, Present and Future of Religious Representation in the House Of Lords*. London: Theos. www.theosthinktank.co.uk/cmsfiles/archive/files/Reports/TheostheBench.pdf.

Philpott, Daniel. 2009. 'Has the Study of Global Politics Found Religion?' *Annual Review of Political Science* 12: 183–202. https://doi.org/10.1146/annurev.polisci.12.053006.125448

Rodger, Thomas Matthew. 2017. *Bishops in Parliament: the Lords Spiritual, c. 1903-1974*. http://etheses.dur.ac.uk/12036/.

Rudiak-Gould, Peter. 2010. 'Being Marshallese and Christian: A Case of Multiple Identities and Contradictory Beliefs.' In special issue of *Culture and Religion* guest edited by Abby Day and Simon Coleman, 11, no. 1: 68–87.

Smith, Greg, and Linda Woodhead. 2018. 'Religion and Brexit: Populism and the Church of England.' *Religion, State and Society* 46, no. 3: 206–23, DOI: 10.1080/09637494.2018.1483861

Southworth, Joanna R. 2005 ' "Religion" in the 2001 Census for England and Wales.' *Population, Space and Place* 11: 75–88. https://doi.org/10.1080/09637494.2018.1483861

Taylor, Charles. 2002. 'Modern Social Imaginaries.' *Public Culture* 14, no. 1: 91–124.

Wald, Kenneth D., Adam L. Silverman and Kevin S. Fridy. 2005. 'Making Sense of Religion in Political Life.' *Annual Review of Political Science* 8: 183–202. https://doi.org/10.1146/annurev.polisci.8.083104.163853

Weller, Paul. 2004. 'Identity, Politics and the Future(s) of Religion in the UK: The Case of the Religion Questions in the 2001 Decennial Census.' *Journal of Contemporary Religion* 19, no. 1: 3–21. https://doi.org/10.1080/1353790032000165096

Chapter 5

Violence and crime

Introduction

Most literature on religion and crime speaks to the normative, taken-for-grantedness that religious people are 'good'. Such assumptions ignore the way religion actually 'works' on the ground. Research that explores how religious people imagine crime helps orient the reader to the symbolic, structural nature of assigning criminality and sometimes justifying religious persecution. These claims often lead to processes of labelling and 'othering'. What people define as 'violence' and 'religion' will differ according to context, but this chapter proposes conceptual maps and theoretical frameworks that can help us navigate such complex terrain.

Globally, conflicts and war crimes are often driven by ethno-religious claims and aspirations. When is conflict over land religious, secular or both? This chapter explores the importance of tangible, material properties of land and resources to religious conflicts.

The topic of terrorism is fraught with difficulties in concepts and terminology. When is a terrorist a freedom fighter? Why would someone kill in the name of their religion? This chapter considers the kinds of people who commit such acts, the justifications they use and the societal response. The chapter ends with a brief discussion of violations against children, often perpetrated by religious people and institutions.

Defining religious violence

Religious violence is a loose term that suggests a violent act committed in the name of religion. And yet, many people who conduct acts do not consider themselves to be violent, just as those who perceive those acts may label and discuss them in different ways. Readers will know by now that the term religious can be defined differently according to time and place; what is also evident, but may not yet be so clear, is that 'violence' is also an unstable and multiply construed term.

Violence may refer to a physical act of harm, such as rape or killing, and to an intangible act, such as invoking terror or revoking human rights. While a standard dictionary definition may mention physical force resulting in injury, abuse, damage or destruction, a more sociological treatment will stress the unequal use of power to damage people in both physical and non-physical ways, with causal influences ranging from tangible motives for land and resources, to intangible struggles for dominance, belonging, exclusion and authority.

For example, decades of conflict in Somalia, combined with a drought, have led to the displacement and starvation of hundreds of thousands of people. Although drought may be seen as a natural disaster due to lack of rain, the effects can be compounded by conflicts which impede efforts to provide water. Such obstacles to aid efforts can in themselves constitute acts of violence. As the UK Refugee Agency UNHCR describes it (www.unhcr.org/uk/somalia.html, last accessed July 2019):

> The impact of nearly two and a half decades of armed conflict in Somalia, compounded by drought and other natural hazards, challenges the resilience and the coping mechanisms of Somalia's most vulnerable citizens. Over 870,000 Somalis are registered as refugees in the Horn of Africa and Yemen, while an estimated 2.1 million men, women and children are displaced within the country itself.

What was once widely described as a war of clans against clans has now been reshaped to one more aligned to struggles for religious legitimacy amongst the Sufi 'moderates' and Al Shabab 'extremists' who espouse a strict form of Wahhabi Islam. Even the idea of 'clan' needs to broaden to encompass a religious influence, as Nyamwaya writes (2014, 77):

> It should be noted also that clannism, which has been the foundation of identification in Somalia, has also been quite predominant to Islamism. As earlier explained, no organization seems to operate without the consent from clan leaders. However one can observe also that the Islamist movements also engaged the clans in that they also manipulated the use of these clans for their own benefit.

While religion may not always be the obvious source of violence, it often affects violent confliction through collusion, expressions of support and silences (Nyamwaya 2014, viii):

> Religion has been used in the conflict in Somalia not only to manage violence but also to escalate it. The emergence of Islamist movements also had led to further inclusion of the country in the global jihadist list [...] The use of religion in the Somali conflict has further shown how radicalization can further escalate a conflict [...] The study concludes that religion is not necessarily the cause of conflict in Somalia, currently. But rather it has been used as an instrument of conflict and as such it can also be used for the management of the same conflict to attain sustainable peace.

Another example is the religious aspect of the Rwanda genocide of 1994, when 800,000 Tutsis were systematically murdered by Hutu. Although it may not have appeared so at the time, religion was deeply implicated in the way the conflict developed, with Catholic nuns and priests being accused of assisting the Hutu and allowing churches to be used to retain Tutsis for extermination (www.theguardian.com/commentisfree/2014/apr/08/catholic –church –apologise –failure –rwanda –genocide –vatican, last accessed July 2019).

The Organization for African Unity's report on the genocide described the church in Rwanda as carrying a 'heavy responsibility' for failing to oppose, and even promoting, ethnic discrimination. It said the church offered 'indispensable support' to the Hutu regime during the killing and described church leaders as playing 'a conspicuously scandalous role' in the genocide by failing to take a moral stand against it.

The Rwanda conflict had deep roots in colonial history and the shifting relationship of the Catholic Church with minority and majority populations, writes Gerard van't Spijker (2006, 344–5):

> the Hutu regime that came to power after independence continued to construct a society based on the racial divisions that had been introduced by the colonial powers in the twentieth century.
>
> The racist interpretation of Rwandan society is seen as the most fundamental cause of the genocide. It was the Roman Catholic Church that had promoted these ideas and, through its quasi-monopoly of the educational system, it had exposed the population to these ideas, which were then internalised during the course of the century. For this reason, the Catholic Church is ultimately responsible for the genocide. This view is held by Paul Kagame.
>
> (2002)

The example shifts the question from 'is the violence strategically and intentionally religious because the actors say it is' to other, related questions such as 'is the violence religious because it was promoted and assisted by religious institutions' and 'is the violence religious because onlookers or analysts say it is' to, even, 'is the violence religious because there are religious aspects that are, perhaps deliberately, not overt'.

Religious genocide

Scholars broadly agree that the term 'genocide' was coined by a legal expert, Ralph Lemkin in the 1940s (Lemkin 1944), but acts which are now commonly referred to as genocide certainly preceded its linguistic and legal formulation. There has not been, since then, consensus in defining genocide, or the formulation being used in this chapter of religious genocide. The definition of genocide proposed by Helen Fein (1993, 24) is a sociological rendering:

> Genocide is sustained, purposeful action by a perpetrator to physically destroy a collectively directly or indirectly, through interdiction of the biological and social reproduction of group members, sustained regardless of the surrender or lack of threat offered by the victim.

It is also often difficult to define 'religious' genocide because of how religion is sometimes not foregrounded. For example, in 1995, Serb forces commanded by General Ratko Mladić separated approximately 7,000 Bosnian Muslim men and boys from the rest of the population in the supposedly 'safe haven' of Srebrenica and killed them. Tens of thousands of people were also abused, killed and raped by the soldiers, and yet the religious affiliation of the perpetrators as Orthodox Christians is rarely, if ever, mentioned. We know that at least 6 million Jews were killed in the Holocaust, yet the perpetrators are rarely, if ever, defined by their Lutheran Christian religion.

James Hughes (2016) provides an excellent, critical overview. He begins by pointing out (Hughes 2016, 119) that, although there is likely to be universal revulsion when considering the ideas of mass killings, sometimes leading to the annihilation of an entire group, there is 'in fact no consensus over the definition of what acts are covered, which groups are protected, nor of what causes it'. Hughes describes scholarship divided over two main approaches to genocide: is it caused by historical rivalries, events, hatred and racisms, or by more social structural issues such as pluralism and unequal access to power and resources? The picture is further clouded by political motives, such as the international community's choices not to intervene in some humanitarian crises mainly because, Hughes continues, such interventions might have threatened American interests. Hughes points out that the Nuremberg trials of 1945, when senior Nazi officials were tried for 'crimes against humanity', did not use the term genocide but described acts that would fit its later applications: the deliberate attempts to exterminate groups of people based on their ethnicity, nationality or religion. Hughes (2016, 124) notes that the later definitions used by the UN on genocide stress the physical destruction of a group, wholly or partly, and does not include the, often brutal, events where populations are forcibly expelled, massacred or experience other atrocities.

As for the causes of genocide, Hughes (2016, 128) concludes that scholars generally agree that there is no single cause or trigger. He points out that the conditions for genocide, which may include rivalry between groups, economic insecurity, tensions and inequalities, are fairly ubiquitous throughout history and yet, genocide acts are comparatively rare. While scholars may also identify the importance of charismatic leaders who can influence groups and may even direct acts of violence, 'there is little agreement on why certain contexts or triggers turn mass violence into genocide in some cases and not others'.

While there may not be agreement on exact causes, an eight-stage schema designed by Gregory Stanton (http://genocidewatch.net/genocide-2/8-stages-of-genocide/ last accessed Mar. 2020) in 1996 for the United States State Department has considerable utility for analysing acts of genocide and, he suggests, preventing them by identifying early warning symptoms:

1   Classification – where populations become differently described by, for example, race or religion.
2   Symbolization – through naming or dress: the yellow star for Jews mandated by the Nazis, for example.
3   Dehumanization – where the target groups are described in animal or insect terms, thus making it easier to murder a 'non-human'.
4   Organization – genocide is a group crime and therefore must be organized, usually by the state.
5   Polarization – the target group is blamed for violent acts, usually staged by the state, and their cultural and religious centres are attacked.
6   Preparation – forced separation occurs, weapons are stockpiled and extermination sites and centres prepared.

Once those stages are passed, it will be easier for the state to carry out killings with overt or covert civilian collusion. The population is by then complicit in viewing the target population as non-human and their obliteration seen as 'extermination' or 'ethnic cleansing'. A final act in the genocidal process, Stanton argues, is denial. Perpetrators will claim the numbers have been exaggerated, will destroy evidence and claim the violence was in self-defence.

Religious terrorism

In providing a social scientific analysis of terrorism, discussion in this chapter will address predominantly two aspects: the acts of terrorism and the responses to it, both academic and lay. Terrorism is usually defined as acts against civilians, or 'non-combatants', created or threatened by a group, usually to achieve political change. A useful version of this idea is Paul Wilkinson's (2001, 15):

> The systematic use of coercive intimidation, usually to service political ends. It is used to create and exploit a climate of fear among a wider target group than the immediate victims of the violence and to publicize a cause, as well as to coerce a target to acceding to the terrorists' aims.

In the UK, the government's Crown Prosecution Service (CPS) describes terrorism in a similar way, but adds the specific nature of the 'cause': (www.cps.gov.uk/terrorism, last accessed Dec. 2019):

> Terrorism is the use or threat of action, both in and outside of the UK, designed to influence any international government organization or to intimidate the public. It must also be for the purpose of advancing a political, religious, racial or ideological cause.

The CPS also stresses in the same note that a person does not have to actually commit a terrorist act to be convicted of a terrorism offence: 'Planning, assisting and even collecting information on how to commit terrorist acts are all crimes under British terrorism legislation.'

Scholars are divided on what 'makes' a terrorist. Most research stresses the ordinary nature of terrorists. They are shown not to possess unusual psychological traits and, in fact, must possess reasonably good social and cognitive attributes as their activities require detailed planning and good social skills within cell groups. For example, Mohammed Emwazi, called 'Jihadi John' by the popular UK media, was raised in the UK from the age of 6, attended good schools and graduated with a degree in IT from London's Westminster University. He became an IT salesman before joining ISIS, where he personally carried out or led the executions (often by beheading) of 32 victims: soldiers, aid workers, journalists and other civilians.

How does someone change from a conscientious student and employee to a sadistic murderer? What motivated him to carry out such barbaric and cruel acts? Louise Richardson (2006) describes the process of turning from an otherwise apparently unexceptional and non-violent person into a homicidal terrorist as a 'lethal cocktail'. She suggests that several factors are usually present: a disaffected individual supported by an enabling community with a legitimizing ideology. Such a community is one that gives open or tacit support, allowing the 'terrorist' to then act. Researchers stress that terrorists are not brainwashed or programmed, but rather experience a 'cognitive opening' that may include a job loss, bereavement or alienation. This 'opening' permits processes of radicalization through adopting certain beliefs and values, often then leading them to join groups and develop practical skills. Sometimes those beliefs are cohered into collective motivations, fuelled by anger at, for example, how members of their religion or ethnic group have been treated in parts of the world. Research also shows the importance of existing social ties.

Case example: Aum Shinriky and the Sarin subway attacks

Ian Reader (2000) documented the case of Aum Shinriky, a religious group responsible for a poison gas attack on the Tokyo subway in 1995, asking how an organization founded in 1984 by a partially blind leader, Asahara Shōkō, apparently dedicated to spiritual practices such as yoga and meditation, could turn to acts of mass murder. Although the Tokyo sarin attack may have brought the organization into the public eye for the first time, members had been involved in violent acts since 1988. Reader (2000, 2) asks: 'How did the movement's leaders get to this seemingly contradictory position of killing in the name of salvation?' Reader (2000, 7) suggests that his work can be of value to scholars outside the field of Japanese studies because the core of Aum's violence was not nation or ethnicity but religion. Reader describes the group as a significant organization with more than 10,000 followers and numerous activities carried out at sites throughout Japan. About 10 per cent of adherents had turned from the outside world, renouncing ties with families and friends, to become full-time practitioners. The violence committed by the group began within the organization itself and against its own members, many of whom were abducted if they left the group and subsequently incarcerated and beaten. The severe ascetic practices of members, designed apparently to purify their polluted bodies, were physically difficult and painful. These were sometimes forced upon unwilling members through 'coercive asceticism' (Reader 2000, 15). Thus, what may be described by outsiders as terrible acts of torture and suffering were, for members, paths to eventual salvation. On 20 March 1995, members released poison gas on five subway trains, killing 12 people and injuring others both physically and psychologically. It later transpired that the group has been manufacturing poison, biological and chemical material, for several years and the 20 March attack was an effort to distract police attention from what the group had heard was to be an imminent raid on its sites. Reader (2000, 25) describes the nature of the group's activities as so horrific that they might only be understood initially through the lenses of either political terrorism or organized crime. Such an interpretation would be incorrect, Reader argues, because the criminal activities were not the primary motive but, rather, arose from their religious nature. Further, it was not a political organization characterized by a belief in its own agenda for society in contrast to other political groups' agendas but, rather, by a belief in its own unique way of ensuring good triumphed over evil. The leader, Aum, did not see himself as a future political leader but, rather, 'a sacred hero and messiah with a mission to save the world' (Reader 2000, 26). The site of the attacks, near the main government buildings, was not an accidental choice but a deliberate and symbolic act. The group saw itself as above mere worldly, temporal structures and institutions. While some, Reader (2000, 39–44) notes, tried to argue that the group should not be described as religious because it was not 'good', religion is an inclusive, value-neutral, multi-dimensional institution with the ability to be both 'good' and 'bad'. Aum, Reader discusses (2000, 68), became increasingly associated with Christian imagery of sacrifice and atonement, within millenarian grand narratives of the world's ending.

Researchers need to be wary of overgeneralization and to consider their own ontological and epistemological stances. Why, for example, is so much written about so-called Islamic terrorism and, comparatively, so little about Christian terrorists?

Sometimes, news media and other mediators shape public understandings of religious violence in the way such activities are described and defined. For example, although the Norwegian killer Anders Breivik is often described as a mass killer or right-wing terrorist, he is rarely described as a Christian extremist, although, through his own writings, he admitted being primarily motivated by ideas about Christianity and Islam. On 22 July 2011, the 33-year-old Breivik detonated a car bomb in Oslo, killing eight people, wounding many more and distracting police attention from what was to be the intended target: a summer camp of young people on the island of Utøya 25 miles away. He killed 79 people there, mostly teenagers who were members of a left-wing Norwegian political movement Breivik claimed was responsible for allowing so many Muslim immigrants into Norway that they were diluting the country's Christian heritage and identity. At his trial, Breivik claimed he was part of a Christian militia and refuted claims that he was a violent criminal, saying he was carrying out acts of moral goodness that would ensure the country did not descend into civil war.

Media and most scholarly analysis of school shootings ignore Christian connections. Birgit Pfeifer and Ruard R. Ganzevoort (2014) wrote about how most shootings occur in areas with strong conservative religious populations, and several shooters were active participants in churches. They analysed the writings of seven shooters, five American, one German and one Finn, and found shared elements of their profiles included being male, most of them were white and they were keenly interested in weapons and violence. While those characteristics tended to be well-covered in media, less publicized were their religious connections. Although several shooters were self-declared atheists, the authors' analysis concluded that there was a strong underpinning throughout of implicit religion, understood as a concern with existential issues framed in religious language, in most of their narratives.

In another example of suppressed attention, Gordon Lynch (2012) asks why the abuse of children in Irish Catholic residential schools was both rife and ignored. He suggests that the 'sacred' concept of Ireland as Catholic nation suppressed criticism of the 'sacred' state. His work on UK forced child migration in the early 20th century, when 100,000 children were sent to countries of the British Commonwealth and former Empire, revealed harrowing stories of abuse and neglect committed by the host parents.

The Catholic Church, he argued, was complicit in that knowledge, as were many sectors of the wider population who ignored the problem (Lynch 2016).

Further, one might ask why little is written about everyday domestic violence that kills far more people than terrorism. On average in the UK, two women a week are killed by their male current or former partners. As most violence and crime is committed by men, why do scholars not devote more time to interrogating masculinity, rather than ethnicity or religiosity, as the prime cause of both religious and non-religious violence? One answer may be to look at the role of the state, and the way that acts of terrorism threaten the state's prime role and source of legitimacy: the need to protect its citizens.

Sociologist Max Weber (1946,1918) wrote extensively about the state and its right to violence, arguing that the state can be understood as a human community with a monopoly on the legitimate use of physical force, in a specific territory. If the state is the only social actor with a monopoly on 'legitimate' violence, the question then arises as to what is meant by 'legitimate' and who decides that it is legitimate? Weber suggests that there are several forces at work, including a notion of the 'eternal yesterday' which insinuates a habitual inclination to conform. There is also the authority of 'charisma', inspiring in people a sense of trust in personal leadership, often underpinned by a 'virtue of legality' where people will show loyalty and trust in rule and laws – often spontaneously and not always with the benefit of usual mechanisms of governance. Talal Asad (2007, 14-38) problematizes the twin, related concepts of state-sanctioned war and terrorism to show that they are not so different, although the discourse about them may be. War, carried out by the state, can instil levels of fear and vulnerability just as terrorism does. A public whose country is at war may not be as traumatized by horrific violence and cruelty as they would be if such acts occurred in their own neighbourhoods, but such distinction is spatial rather than ethical.

Case example: state-sanctioned settler violence

Given that a condition of modernity is differentiation, it will be likely that most modern states are complex, with no one agent acting alone. Some agencies – such as police, prisons and counter-terrorism agencies are seen as 'legitimately' violent. Sometimes, a civilian population, in collusion with the state, commits violent acts that mostly go unpunished. For example, Nir Gazit (2015) discussed the phenomenon of Jewish settler violence in Palestine as a case of state collusion with vigilantism. Acts of Jewish settler violence against Palestinians and Palestinian property in the Occupied Palestinian Territories increased as Israeli army attacks decreased. This was because, Gazit argued, settlers had become 'informal agents of the state'. They welcome the army and treat them as guests or family. One woman said (Gazit 2015, 448): 'They [the soldiers] should feel they are one of us. We treat them as our own biological sons'. They also justify their violence with the excuse that the 'army can't be everywhere at once'. Gazit argues that settler violence strengthens the Israeli state through providing *ad hoc* Israeli control in the Occupied Territories area through 'permanent temporariness' and 'political ambiguity'. The state's role is further strengthened and reproduced by interfering occasionally to protect Palestinians.

Suicide bombing

The 20th century saw a new form of terrorism frequently linked to religion: suicide bombing. Malise Ruthven (2002, 26–7) shows that suicide bombing began in the 20th century, arguably first with Japanese kamikaze pilots in World War II who flew their planes into American naval ships. The Hindu Tamils in Sri Lanka fought against the Buddhist majority government through inventing the first human suicide bomb, and other groups swiftly followed with the same technique, she wrote, citing as examples an Indian woman who hid a bomb under her dress in order to kill the Indian prime minister in 1991, Hezbollah fighters in Lebanon using the same tactics in the 1980s and a Palestinian suicide bomber wreaked death and injury in a restaurant in Jerusalem in 2001.

Greater attention to this phenomenon was prompted by the suicide airplane attacks of September 11, 2001. It was a novel idea both to the public and security officials that planes would be hijacked as flying bombs rather than, as previously had often happened, hijacked in order to land and negotiate for sums of money, release of political prisoners. Ruthven (2002, 30) suggests that a major difference between the September 11 attacks and previous suicide acts was their religious nature: 'Religious violence differs from violence in the "secular" world by shifting the plane of action from what is mundane, and hence negotiable, to the arena of cosmic struggle, beyond the political realm. Targets of religious terror are symbolic as much as strategic.'

Talal Asad (2007, 41) challenges his readers to question why the motives of a suicide bomber invite such intense scrutiny, suggesting that such analysis may reveal some assumptions of those who are scrutinizing. He asks why people in the west respond to reports of suicide bombing with such horror, given that other atrocities and cruelties that occur more often in prisons, through enforcing immigration rules and participating in ethnic cleansing, do not prompt such an intense reaction. Asad (2007, 65–6) draws on the work of psychologist Jacqueline Rose (2004), who notes that suicide bombings kill fewer people than conventional warfare, and yet the suicide bomber provokes more revulsion. This may be, she suggests, because the suicide bomber, unlike the pilot of a bomber jet, is locked in close, dying connection with their victims. Asad argues there must be more to explain such horror, such as the attacker being *in cognito*, appearing as an ordinary citizen before the attack and because of the taboo in Abrahamic religions against suicide. He refers to Mary Douglas's work on purity and danger, and her analysis of anomaly, or how something without form (in this case, the bomber's body) is realized as 'matter out of place', and therefore taboo. Asad (2007, 86) refers to the crucifixion of Jesus Christ, who offered himself willingly as a sacrifice, as 'the most famous suicide in Judeo-Christian history'. Asad: 'In short, in Christian civilization, the gift of life for humanity is possible only through a suicidal death; redemption is dependent on cruelty or at least on the sin of disregarding human life.'

Asad (2007, 88–90) suggests that a mix of violence and tenderness is part of the genealogy of modern secular liberalism, despite and perhaps because of its apparent contradiction. He points to Durkheim's formulation that legal punishment expresses a collective outrage and is therefore tied strongly to vengeance. He concludes that suicide bombing poses, for those steeped in Christian tradition, a horrific act without the possibility of redemption for the bomber, the victim or the witnesses.

In their review of suicide terrorism theories, Susanne Martin and Ami Pedahzur (2017) observe that academic research into the field of terrorism grew rapidly after the 9/11 attacks. Where there were only some 1,200 papers on the topic before the event, at the time of their writing there were more than 9,000. It was also notable, they add, that 11 per cent of the research was externally funded, compared to 0.3 per cent previously.[1] They point out (Martin and Pedahzur 2017, 2) that an understanding of suicide terrorism is blurred with definitional issues: following a common definition of terrorism to effect political change, what does it mean when a suicide bomber targets a military installation? Further, while most understanding of terrorism stresses its intentionality and voluntary commitment, how do we understand a suicide bombing as 'terrorism' that may be coerced?

A citation analysis conducted by the authors showed that most research papers on the topic of suicide terrorism were published in political science or international relations journals. This inevitably affects how suicide terrorism is explained, the authors write, with researchers in political science and international relations seeking explanations within theories of instrumental rationalism, group processes and strategy. The latter, a strategic logic, has been by far the most widely accepted, they say. According to this theory, groups may adopt strategic objectives, such as seeking to oppose foreign powers, attract attention to a specific group, distinguish one group from another or to demonstrate commitment.

Religious response to crime

Religious people may express their responses to terrorism and other crimes in specific ways that symbolize their beliefs. For example, after the 9/11 attacks, leaders of American far-right movements initially greeted the attacks with something coming close to glee, writes Ruthven (2002, 31).

Jerry Falwell, leader of the Moral Majority religious campaign group, blamed 'the pagans, and the abortionists, and the feminists, and the gays and the lesbians' for creating an environment which might have 'caused God to lift the veil of protection which has allowed no one to attack America on our soil since 1812'.

Pat Robertson, a prominent televangelist, agreed, as did several other fundamentalist leaders. It was not, however, only the feminists and pagans who needed to worry about wider society's scapegoating response to the events. As Asad (2007, 1) noted, for many American Muslims 9/11 'was the beginning of a long period of anxiety, during which they found themselves associated, occasionally explicitly but more often implicitly, with terrorism'. Asad began to contemplate a number of questions such as: is there something different about religiously motived terrorism compared to non-religious acts; what might it be to determine the act 'religious and how do Christians and post-Christians address the image of the suicide bomber?' Asad critiques some responses to religious terrorism which presume a 'clash of civilisations' – as if a so-called civilization is static, universal and understood by everyone equally: 'sociologically, the people who are said to belong to that civilisation are highly differentiated by class and region and gender' (Asad 2007, 10). He points out the apparent difficulty people had in understanding the events of 9/11 as a particular, Islamic form of terrorism when those same people would have no difficulty in understanding the violence of other groups in history who were, apparently, aligned to 'progress'. In contrast, Asad argued, there is another paradigm which does not imagine a clash of civilizations but recognizes the centuries of Muslim-Christian-Jewish peaceable coexistence, followed by division. Christian Crusaders, motivated by an ideology, were 'the first militant incursions of European Christians into Muslim lands' (Asad 2007, 9 –10).

Creating the criminal subject

Empirical MA research conducted by Charles Stubblefield (2015) amongst evangel-ical Protestant Baptist church members in Salt Lake County, Utah, USA, explored how criminal subjects are created through a religious lens. Based on semi-structured interviews and analysis, and adopting an intersectional approach, he analysed how new religious identities are often created when intertwined with other categories, principally race, gender, political orientation and social class. His study showed how criminalized religious categories were mixed with negative 'out-group' identity categories, with positive in-group identities regularly assigning innocence to the in-group. One signifi-cant strategy used by participants was the claim their Christian faith would prevent them from acting in a criminal or violent manner. For example (Stubblefield 2015, 39), Mary, aged 35, said that God would stop her from stealing food even if her family was starving: 'I believe God would keep me from that. Not to say that it would not be a battle but that's an inherent sign of a Christian person, is fighting the battle and not just going with whatever we feel like.'

Nathan, aged 29, said that Christians are unique in being protected from committing wrong acts because they 'are not simply avoiding punishment but they are actively seeking to do what's right because they want to please God' (Stubblefield 2015, 40).

Mark, 30, claimed that all non-Christian religions are 'incited and empowered and blessed by Satan himself to cause destruction and disturbance and evil in the world'. He added that Muslims were more likely than Christians to be criminals: 'I'm not being racist here but, because I'm not racist. I don't have any problems with Muslims but I would say that just as a whole that maybe they, um, tend more … to crime then say a Baptist' (Stubblefield 2015, 34).

The Christians interviewed identified other criminalized identity categories besides Muslims, such as atheists, feminists and non-heterosexuals. Mark said that atheists' beliefs in evolution would diminish their value of human life:

> If you don't have any value for human life because we just evolved out of some soup that, that kinda puts your value at zero or nothing. And, so if I kill someone else then what's, you know, no value has been lost right it's just like killing another animal.
>
> (Stubblefield 2015, 43)

Stubblefield (2015, 33) observes:

> The category women does not in itself confer criminality, rather deviance arises from its relation to feminism. The category 'man' was never problematized in the same manner, as the male identity was subsumed into gender neutral categories of religion, race, and gangs.

There is a long history of conflating women with witchcraft. Christina Larner (1984), in her review of Scottish witchcraft trials in the 18th, 17th and 16th centuries, argues that witch-hunts were not isolated events but coincided with wider social movements, such as the rise of the Christian nation-state. The category of witchcraft was not random, but generally included only older women. Alan Macfarlane (1970) also demonstrates links between witch-hunts and social tensions.

Women have been labelled as evil for centuries, with Christians, Jews and Muslims often relying on scriptural narratives about Eve, responsible for the fall of Adam and, consequently, humankind. Scholars (see e.g. Douglas 2004; Larner 1984; Macfarlane 1970) have argued that witch-hunts have occurred during times of heightened social tensions and uncertainties, where the apparently unseen power and malevolence of witches could be blamed.

In another study of crime perception, I found that (Day 2011) Christian English research participants also often identified women as responsible for witchcraft, and the general moral decline of society. While they usually shared broad social norms of honour, fairness and what was often described as the 'ten commandments' (without, notably, reference to the first four governing one's relationship with God), research participants often claimed that criminal behaviour was a problem created by 'others': people who lived in other towns or villages, or immigrants. The tendency to identify others as problematic has been widely discussed in the sociological literature, notably by Stanley Cohen (1972), who discussed the process of scapegoating and creating moral panics through the creation of 'folk-devils', deemed to be responsible for crime and other unacceptable behaviour. David Mason (1995, 112) also discussed 'moral panics' incited by media-supported stereotypes about crime, immigration and certain categories of people. Ralph Grillo's (2005) study of a town's reaction against asylum-seekers drew attention to scapegoating and stereotyping, pointing out that sometimes the discourse is coded and oblique.

Sample questions for private study

1   How can a 'turn' to more orthodox religions help explain the rise of religious violence?
2   Suggest at least three sociological explanations for recent 'religious' contestations over land.

Sample class exercise

A visit from a prison chaplain.

Note

1   This is important, I suggest, as it demonstrates how much of academic research relies on, and is shaped by, funding arrangements and agendas.

Indicative reading

Ammerman, Nancy Tatom. 1998. *Bible Believers: Fundamentalists in the Modern World.* New Brunswick, NJ: Rutgers.

Asad, Talal. 2007. *On Suicide Bombing.* New York: Columbia University Press.

Barak, Gregg. 1990. 'Crime, Criminology and Human Rights: Towards an Understanding of State Criminality.' *Journal of Human Justice* 2, no. 1: 11–28.

Bloxham, Donald, and Dirk Moses (ed.). 2010. *The Oxford Handbook of Genocide Studies.* New York: Oxford University Press.

Cohen, Stanley. 1972. *Folk Devils and Moral Panics: The Creation of the Mods and Rockers.* London: Macgibbon & Kee.

Day, Abby. 2011. *Believing in Belonging: Belief and Social Identity in the Modern World.* Oxford: Oxford University Press.

Dilulio, John J. Jr. 2009. 'More Religion, Less Crime? Science, Felonies, and the Three Faith Factors.' *Annual Review of Law and Social Science* 5, no. 1: 115–33. https://doi.org/10.1146/annurev.lawsocsci.093008.131603

Douglas, Mary (ed.). 2004. *Witchcraft Confessions and Accusations.* London: Routledge.

Dubler, Joshua, and Vincent Lloyd. 2019. *Break Every Yoke: Religion, Justice, and the End of Mass Incarceration.* New York: Oxford University Press.

Fein, Helen. 1993. *Genocide: A Sociological Perspective.* London: Sage.

Gazit, Nir. 2015. 'State-Sponsored Vigilantism: Jewish Settlers' Violence in the Occupied Palestinian Territories.' *Sociology* 49, no. 3: 438–54. https://doi.org/10.1177/0038038514526648.

Gerges, Fawaz A. 2009. *The Far Enemy: Why Jihad went Global.* Cambridge: Cambridge University Press.

Grillo, Ralph. 2005. 'Saltdean Can't Cope: Protests Against Asylum-Seekers in an English Seaside Suburb.' *Ethnic and Racial Studies* 28, no. 2: 235–60. https://doi.org/10.1080/01419870420000315834.

Gutkowski, Stacey. 2014. *Secular War: Myths of Religion, Politics and Violence.* London: I. B. Tauris.

Hall, Stuart. 1978. *Policing the Crisis: Mugging, the State, and Law and Order.* London: Macmillan.

Hirschi, Travis, and Rodney Stark. 1969. 'Hellfire and Delinquency.' *Social Problems* 17, no. 2: 202–21. DOI: 10.2307/1384608.

Horowitz, Michael. 2014. 'The Rise and Spread of Suicide Bombing.' *Annual Review of Political Science* 18: 69–84. https://doi.org/10.1146/annurev-polisci-062813-051049.

Hughes, James. 2016. 'Genocide.' In *Routledge Handbook of Ethnic Conflict,* edited by Karl Cordell and Stefan Wolff, 119–37. Abingdon, Oxon: Routledge.

Innes, Martin, and Michael Levi. 2012. 'Terrorism and Counter-Terrorism'. in *The Oxford Handbook of Criminology,* 5th edition, edited by Mike Maguire, Rod Morgan and Robert Reiner, 660–86. Oxford: Oxford University Press.

Larner, Christina. 1984. *Witchcraft and Religion: The Politics of Popular Belief.* Oxford: Blackwell.

Lemkin, Raphael. 1944. *Axis Rule in Occupied Europe: Laws of Occupation – Analysis of Government – Proposals for Redress.* Washington, DC: Carnegie Endowment for International Peace.

Lynch, Gordon. 2012. *The Sacred in the Modern World.* Oxford: Oxford University Press.

Lynch, Gordon. 2016. *Remembering Child Migration: Faith, Nation-Building and the Wounds of Charity.* London: Bloomsbury.

Macfarlane, Alan. 1970. *Witchcraft in Tudor and Stuart England: A Regional and Comparative Study.* London: Routledge & Kegan Paul.

Martin, Susanne, and Ami Pedahzur. 2017. 'Suicide Terrorism Theories.' In *Oxford Research Encyclopedia.* Oxford: Oxford University Press. DOI: 10.1093/acrefore/9780190228637.013.579

Mason, David. 1995. *Race and Ethnicity in Modern Britain.* Oxford: Oxford University Press.

Nyamwaya, Priya. 2014. 'The Role of Religion in Conflict and Management: The Case of Somalia, 1999–2012.' Unpublished master's dissertation, Nairobi: University of Nairobi.

Pfeifer, Birgit, and R. Ganzevoort. 2014. 'The Implicit Religion of School Shootings: Existential Concerns of Perpetrators Prior to their Crime.' *Journal of Religion and Violence* 2, no. 3: 447–59.

Reader, Ian. 2000. *Religious Violence in Contemporary Japan.* Honolulu: University of Hawaii Press.

Richardson, Louise. 2006. *What Terrorists Want: Understanding the Terrorist Threat.* London: John Murray.

Rose, Jacqueline. 2004. 'Deadly Embrace.' *London Review of Books* 26, no. 21.

Ruthven, Malise. 2002. *Islam in the World,* 2nd edition. London: Penguin.

Salas-Wright, Christopher P., Michael G., Vaughn, David R. Hodge and Brian E. Perron. 2012. 'Religiosity Profiles of American Youth in Relation to Substance Use, Violence, and Delinquency.' *Journal of Youth and Adolescence* 41, no. 1: 1560–75.

Stubblefield, Charles. 2015. 'The Construction of the Criminal Subject through the Religious Lens.' Unpublished master's dissertation, Goldsmiths, University of London.

Sullivan, Winnifred Fallers. 2014. *A Ministry of Presence: Chaplaincy, Spiritual Care, and the Law.* Chicago, IL, London: University of Chicago Press.

van't Spijker, Gerard. 2006. 'Religion and the Rwandan Genocide.' *Scripta Instituti Donneriani Aboensis* 19: 339–57.

Weber, Max. 1946 (1918). 'Politics as a Vocation.' In *Max Weber: Essays in Sociology,* translated and edited by H. H. Gerth and C. Wright Mills, 77–128. New York: Oxford University Press.

Wessinger, Catherine. 2000. *Millennialism, Persecution, and Violence: Historical Cases.* Syracuse, NY: Syracuse University Press.

Wilkinson, Paul. 2001. *Terrorism versus Democracy: The Liberal State Response.* Abingdon, Oxon: Frank Cass.

Chapter 6

Policing religion

Religious equality, social justice and the law

What is meant by religious equality, and how does this impact on human rights and social justice? Do religious people have the 'right' to follow their religion's teaching if it affects the rights of other people, and who decides? This chapter examines the creation of laws affecting rights to religion and belief, and the effects of social inequality and injustice. For instance, we examine several cases brought before the European Court of Human Rights to show how religious individuals and groups have campaigned against what they see as a threat to their rights in multi-faith societies. We also look at how 'secular' courts and the United Nations operate to show how religion is regulated and represented.

Introduction

At the beginning of his book on the freedom of religion, Paul Taylor (2005) discusses a number of trends which he thinks are producing more critical and more publicized attention on the issue of religious freedom, several of which will be explored in this chapter. One of the most significant was the public reaction to the attacks of 9/11, which produced widespread 'xenophobia, intolerance and discrimination towards Muslims' (Taylor 2005, 3). This led many states to conflate 'Islam' with 'extremism' and pass legislation banning, for example, Islamic headwear. At the same time, some political parties were calling for stricter laws based on their religion. A rise in intolerance towards some religious people has increased the state's involvement in protecting religious rights and freedoms, 'and it is expected that this principle will see greater practical recognition in future years' (Taylor 2005, 4).

What are 'human rights'?

Twentieth-century understandings and implementation of 'human rights' generally relate to declarations and conventions created by the United Nations and drawn upon by other nations ever since. The first treaty adopted by the UN was, in 1948, The Convention on the Prevention and Punishment of the Crime of Genocide (Genocide Convention). It codified for the first time the crime of genocide, demonstrating the commitment of the international community to ensure that the horrors of the Holocaust would never happen again. While, as reviewed in Chapter 5, academics agree there is no single accepted definition of genocide, the UN is quite specific and significant in terms of international law and enforcement: the UN will only intervene in mass killings and other atrocities if its definition of genocide is met (www.un.org/en/genocideprevention/genocide.shtml).

Article II
In the present Convention, genocide means any of the following acts committed with intent to destroy, in whole or in part, a national, ethnical, racial or religious group, as such:

a. *Killing members of the group;*
b. *Causing serious bodily or mental harm to members of the group;*
c. *Deliberately inflicting on the group conditions of life calculated to bring about its physical destruction in whole or in part;*
d. *Imposing measures intended to prevent births within the group;*
e. *Forcibly transferring children of the group to another group.*

The next major step the UN took was to codify 'human rights'. There are various definitions of human rights, as Mark Goodale explains (2013, 4), as a force emerging after World War II: 'human rights system of law, international political organisations and (later) transnational non-governmental organisations created as a response to the great evils of our time'. Such 'evils' include colonialism, structural inequalities and mass atrocities. Although laudable on paper, the critique of human rights points to the contradiction that human rights as a movement is usually associated with the west, while the west is also a major perpetrator of those 'evils'. While it is usually unproblematic to insist such evils be corrected, scholars also point out that such claims are intrinsically 'moral' (see e.g. Nash 2015; Goodhart 2013).

Human rights are socially constructed, drawing on political, social and cultural forms, within which also emerge legal mechanisms. This means that they shift, both in construction and practice, often through the mobilization of advocacy and grassroots movements, many of which are religious. Human rights depend on certain forms of moral, legal and political authority. While one might say that human rights are socially constructed, their presentation is usually couched in terms that suggest an inherent, even 'god-given', source. The preamble to the United Nations Declaration of Human Rights (UDHR) (1948) refers, for example, to the inherent dignity of all people; the American Declaration of Independence (1776) refers to all men being given by 'their Creator' unalienable rights; the Magna Carta (1215) declaration referred to the rights of 'free' men; the French Declaration of the Rights of Man and the Citizen (1789) referred to men's 'natural inalienable, and sacred rights'. The idea of a natural set of rights was central to prominent European philosophers who presumed that people were naturally free and would consent to be governed for so long as those rights were respected, and, further, retained the right to overturn the government by revolution if those rights were threatened. An inherent difficulty in invoking what may seem as 'natural' law is its likely incompatibility in pluralist societies. Such societies are characterized by people having different claims on what is 'truth' and 'natural', usually with regard to some higher power, which, itself, is subject to difference.

Such pluralism may create divisions over which claim, often couched via religion, is right and should be respected. To address that, the United Nations in 1948 adopted the view that every human being on the planet has the right to hold a religion or belief, or not. As the United Nations website explains (www.un.org/en/universal-declaration-human-rights/ last accessed Feb. 2020):

> The Universal Declaration of Human Rights (UDHR) is a milestone document in the history of human rights. Drafted by representatives with different legal and cultural backgrounds from all regions of the world, the Declaration was proclaimed by the United Nations General Assembly in Paris on 10 December 1948 (General Assembly resolution 217 A) as a common standard of achievements for all peoples and all nations. It sets out, for the first time, fundamental human rights to be universally protected and it has been translated into over 500 languages.

Of its 30 articles, several are of particularly of interest for scholars of religion:

> Article 2. Everyone is entitled to all the rights and freedoms set forth in this Declaration, without distinction of any kind, such as race, colour, sex, language, religion, political or other opinion, national or social origin, property, birth or other status. Furthermore, no distinction shall be made on the basis of the political, jurisdictional or international status of the country or territory to which a person belongs, whether it be independent, trust, non-self-governing or under any other limitation of sovereignty.
>
> Article 16. (1) Men and women of full age, without any limitation due to race, nationality or religion, have the right to marry and to found a family. They are entitled to equal rights as to marriage, during marriage and at its dissolution. (2) Marriage shall be entered into only with the free and full consent of the intending spouses. (3) The family is the natural and fundamental group unit of society and is entitled to protection by society and the State
>
> Article 18. Everyone has the right to freedom of thought, conscience and religion; this right includes freedom to change his religion or belief, and freedom, either alone or in community with others and in public or private, to manifest his religion or belief in teaching, practice, worship and observance.
>
> Article 26. (1) Everyone has the right to education. Education shall be free, at least in the elementary and fundamental stages. Elementary education shall be compulsory. Technical and professional education shall be made generally available and higher education shall be equally accessible to all on the basis of merit. (2) Education shall be directed to the full development of the human personality and to the strengthening of respect for human rights and fundamental freedoms. It shall promote understanding, tolerance and friendship among all nations, racial or religious groups, and shall further the activities of the United Nations for the maintenance of peace. (3) Parents have a prior right to choose the kind of education that shall be given to their children.

A significant shift occurred that had a lasting impact on religion: Article 18 in particular produced that shift by defining religion not in terms of minority rights, but as a general human right (Evans 1997) and, additionally, one that was seen as an individual as well as collective right. Karl Marx, a century earlier, critiqued what he saw was the individualistic, property-based basis for the rights enshrined in the French Revolution. Kate Nash (2015, 3) summarized more recent critiques which argue that human rights

> are depoliticizing, individualising: they are enabling the world to be made secure for neo-liberal global elites rather than ending the suffering of ordinary people … [but] Human rights also represent a language in which a variety of claims for justice are articulated against imperialism and neoliberalism.

Much of the debate that has emerged about religious rights will centre on the definition of religion. As Russel Sandberg (2008) discusses, this can be seen in sociological terms by tracing how religion has been defined by the discipline. While, famously, Max Weber never defined religion, Émile Durkheim had been clear that it was a collective phenomenon.

Most countries voted in favour of the UDHR when it was drawn up in 1948, as a response to the horrors of war and the Holocaust, in particular, when six million Jews were killed because of their religion. The Declaration has had its critics over the years, including the American Anthropological Association which argued that it was western-centric, Saudi Arabia which refused to sign up to it because it violated sharia law, and many Christian groups and sects which argued that it set secular rights over God-given rights and rules.

While such rights may seem non-contentious, freedom of religion is still curtailed in significant ways. New religious movements specialist Eileen Barker (2020) writes that religious freedom is contentious and curtailed, chiefly amongst countries that consider themselves to be non-religious, such as China (see also Pitman 2003) and France. In China, for example, the government list of 'heretical organizations' include the Church of Almighty God, the Unification Church and Falun Gong. France compiled a list in 1995 of 173 apparently dangerous 'cults'. People who were on the list were discriminated against in numerous ways, including not being able to work, rent accommodation or send their children to local schools.

While not legally binding, the UDHR has influenced international human rights legislation and the manner in which human rights are understood and enforced. For example, the European Convention on Human Rights, signed in 1953, makes binding certain of those rights. Since the Council of Europe was extended in the 1990s to cover 22 former communist countries, the Convention has been used to help enforce rights in central and eastern Europe and more widely (see Johnson and Falcetta 2018, 2019; Falcetta and Johnson 2018).

Other international treaties and conventions include the International Convention on Civil and Political Rights (ICCPR); International Convention on Economic, Social and Cultural Rights (ICESCR); Convention Against Torture (CAT), American Convention on Human Rights (Organization of American States – OAS), European Charter of Fundamental Rights, African Charter on Human and People's Rights (African Union – AU), Arab Charter on Human Rights (League of Arab States).

As will be reviewed later in this chapter, the articles of the European Convention on Human Rights match the UDHR and are referred to and either upheld or found not applicable in cases brought before the European Court of Human Rights. One of the most important relating to religion is Article 9, which states that:

9.1 Everyone has the right to freedom of thought, conscience and religion; this right includes freedom to change his religion or belief, and freedom, either alone or in community with others and in public or private, to manifest his religion or belief, in worship, teaching, practice and observance.

9.2 Freedom to manifest one's religion or beliefs shall be subject only to such limitations as are prescribed by law and are necessary in a democratic society in the interests of public safety, for the protection of public order, health or morals, or the protection of the rights and freedoms of others.

As Gladys Ganiel, and Peter Jones observe (2012, 303), while the freedom to hold a belief is seen as absolute, the freedom to manifest it is conditional.

In the UK, the Equality Act 2010 was created to be consistent with Article 9 of the Universal Declaration of Human Rights. The Act covers discrimination against anyone on the grounds of religion or belief (www.legislation.gov.uk/ukpga/2010/15/contents, last accessed Mar. 2020).

The Act further defines what it means by religion or belief. This refers to 'organised' religions with a clear structure and belief system. such as Christianity, Judaism, Islam or Buddhism, or 'smaller' religions such as Rastafarianism or Paganism. People with no religion or belief are also protected. (This raises some contentious points, as readers will by now realize, with the religion-centred idea of 'no belief'.) The UK Equality and Human Rights Commission further sets out the criteria for a philosophical belief to qualify for protection. Any such belief must be genuinely held as a belief and not just an opinion, related to a 'weighty and substantial aspect of human life and behaviour', be cogent, serious, important and coherent, be respectable in a democratic society, be compatible with human dignity and not conflict with the fundamental rights of others.

The Act prohibits discrimination against people because they are, or are not, a member of a particular religion, or because they hold (or do not hold) a particular philosophical belief. It also protects people against 'discrimination by perception', whereby a person is discriminated against because someone thinks they are members of a particular religion or they hold a particular belief. The Act also protects someone against 'discrimination by association', or for associating with someone who holds a particular religion or belief (www.equalityhumanrights.com/en/advice-and-guidance/religion-or-belief-discrimination).

Despite such legislation, religious organizations are permitted exemptions in certain cases, mainly related to employment. As Ganiel and Jones observe (2012, 304), 'religious organizations often want to discriminate on religious grounds, in, for example, employment and the use they allow others to make of their premises'. That means, for example, religious schools can discriminate in the appointment of teachers or admissions of students. Nevertheless, Ganiel and Jones add (2012, 304) that 'this is an area of law where there is scope for different judgments on how generously the domain of permitted discrimination should be understood'.

Such exemptions do not, however, occur without consistent effort, campaigning and influencing processes of legislation. For a detailed case examination of how the Church of England succeeded in their goal to have the Act amended to allow exemptions relating to homosexuality, see Paul James Johnson and Robert M. Vanderbeck (2017).

Case examples: climate change and veganism

In November 2009, a UK judge ruled that someone's deeply held beliefs about human-generated, catastrophic climate change were as worthy of protection under the 2010 Equality Act as a religious or philosophical belief. The ruling concerned an employee, Tim Nicholson, who had claimed that his employer, Grainger, had made him redundant because of his philosophical beliefs. His argument was based on the idea that beliefs about climate change, while based on science, also had a philosophical and therefore 'protected' dimension.

A decade later, in January 2020, Jordi Casamitjana achieved a significant victory when a UK Employment Tribunal agreed with him that 'ethical veganism' is a philosophical belief that should be a 'protected characteristic' in terms of the 2010 Equality Act. An 'ethical' vegan is someone who not only eats a plant-based diet, but avoids anything that involves animal exploitation, including products that are tested on animals. He had brought his case to the tribunal following his dismissal by his employer, the League Against Cruel Sports. The League had dismissed him for sharing amongst colleagues his concerns, deeply held as a vegan, that the organization's pension fund investments included companies which participated in testing on animals. The tribunal then did not rule on the issue of unfair dismissal, but first established the principle that ethical veganism was a protected characteristic.

The public, the private: are human rights sacred?

What does it mean to consider the role of religion in the 'public sphere', particularly when it intersects with politics, practices, policies, and human rights – areas both 'public' as well as private. Answering those questions requires taking a close look at what is meant by 'religion', the 'sacred' and the 'secular', as religion does not arise in public debates as an homogeneous pre-formed entity, but rather as fragment, a shard, pointed at a particularity whose identity is most often linked to values and anxieties about 'purity' and power. Further, for the most part in Euro-American contexts in recent years, the debate is not about religion with a big R, as if it is a generic entity, but most often as Islam, sometimes as Christian, and usually as a contest between what are still conceived as separate spheres as religious or secular.

This contest is often a fight between competing powers over who claims and controls the seemingly indisputable ground of what is pure. The battle presents problems. Do all religions follow public/private divide? Do men and women observe this divide equally? Do new or 'eco'/pagan spiritualties fit in the public or the private as a religion? As a hobby? As an opinion?

Feminist and eco-theologians and practitioners have argued that such a split is implicitly gendered, prioritizes the 'spirit' over the material and devalues the natural world and the here and now. Those involved in alternative spiritualities often claim that such a split is not typical of all religions, but only certain ones (in particular, Christianity), and that many other spiritual traditions, as Graham Harvey (1996) argued, involve no such either/or compartmentalization of the world. Peter Berger's (1999) theory that the west, having moved through decades of secularization, then saw a resurgence of religion – or resacralization – chimes with many of the observations that there is an 'in between', where the practice of intellectually creating in-between spaces has allowed academics to better understand the limitations of the binary and to question its utility (see the varied collection of such accounts in Day et al. 2013).

The categories of the 'religious' and the 'secular' have been subject to increasing scrutiny in recent decades, with scholars (see e.g. Day and Coleman 2013; Cannell 2010; Asad 2003; Fitzgerald (2000, 2007) exploring the 'religious' and 'secular' not only to destabilize the categories but to expose their mutual dependency. The categories can also reveal uncritical tropes and unquestioned assumptions, as research on non-governmental organizations (NGO) within the UN by Jeremy Carrette and Sophie-Hélène Trigeaud described (2013, 7–22). They discussed 'modern myths' based on the false assumption that there is a separation between religion and politics, between the individual and collective and between the individual and society. The UN is an important site for a case study about human rights, with its formational charter of 1945 describing its purpose as protecting human rights and fundamental freedoms, which are without distinctions as to race, sex, language or religion. The research they describe was a three-year study of the United Nations in New York and Geneva, the UN's major sites. The research team studied texts, processes, organizations and practices of non-governmental organizations (NGOs) at the UN in order to discern and analyse the confusion of the religion/secular binary. When they studied (Carrette and Trigeaud 2013, 10) the founding document of the UN, they discovered that 'religion' appeared three times in the context of peace-building and freedom while the term 'secular' never appeared. They also found that there are no 'religious' NGOs at the UN because it only recognizes religion as something held by individuals, not groups. This made it difficult to identify which NGOs could be classified as religious and thus an object for their research. Even those that might have seemed at first glance to be religious, such as an NGO for Jews and an NGO for Quakers, refused the term 'religion' in favour of 'faith-based'. An example of the researchers' methodological innovation was a questionnaire they developed which offered NGOs a spectrum of classifications from which they could choose their preferred marker, such as 'secular with religious roots, religious, spiritual, faith-based, ethnic-cultural or other' (Carrette and Trigeaud 2013, 12). The questionnaire also asked about any of the NGOs' institutional and organizational affiliations. On that basis, they selected 58 out of 192 NGOs which indicated they were on the religion-spiritual-faith part of the spectrum. From analysing the questionnaire and other texts the researchers concluded that 7.29 per cent of the total of 3,275 consultative status NGOs at the UN are within the spectrum of religious language. Significantly, interviews with diplomats who might engage with such NGOs revealed that most were unaware of whether they were religious or not, and those western diplomats who were aware expressed concern. The researchers concluded that this was evidence of how the 'modern myth' of a secular-religious binary operated at the UN.

Part of the impact of religion on international development may have been underestimated by many international aid organizations' reluctance to engage with religion. Nora Khalaf-Elledge (2020) found in her research that such organizations often find religion confusing, problematic and too 'tricky'. Their hesitance stemmed from, she argued, an 'Orientalist' idea that religions were dated, a lack of religious literacy (see e.g.

Dinham 2017) and a lack of confidence (see for wider discussion of religion and development, Tomalin 2015).

The role of the state in human rights

The state is the body, through its judicial processes, which is positioned to protect and enforce its citizens' human rights. It sometimes fails to do so when it is itself the violator. Gregg Barak's (1990) work explores the relationships between crime, human rights and the state, arguing that criminologists have failed to engage sufficiently to research such acts and actors. One of the reasons might be for personal safety, but also due to the definitional complexity and lack of 'official' statistics, and a resistance within the discipline of criminology to recognize the state as a perpetrator of terrorist acts. Barak calls for social science and critical criminology to interrogate the issue of state terrorism as it reflects so many themes already present within the social sciences: order, authority, power, legitimization, hegemony, organization and change. To accomplish such analysis, it will be necessary to shift thinking away from individualistic, psychological models to other acts outside those defined legally as crime. This will mean, he argued, calling on 'higher' frameworks, such as international treaties, covenants, laws and to consider social structures, ideologies, cultural production and political economies.

The state's violations of human rights take many forms, including state killing, systematic theft, corruption, collusion, genocide and torture. Daily media reports highlight such acts and events occurring in many nations, such as Sudan's Darfur, Zimbabwe, Israel, Palestine, Egypt, Syria and Libya. As the police are the agent of the state, many people argue that the state's practices of racialized arrests, incarcerations and lengthy sentences constitute human rights violations. Barak points out that that, while the state can commit 'obvious' crimes such as theft, kidnapping, murder, torture, rape, espionage and drug trafficking, he calls for attention to the systematic violations of a ruling elite.

The question may then rise, why treat the state differently than any other social actor who may be considered substantially and morally the same as a criminal or terrorist? To understand that, it may be necessary to consider the hegemonic nature of state violations, by which they are received as and even discussed as normal, or 'common sense', when they are, in fact, acts or assumptions that serve the interests of the elite and powerful and ascribe criminality to the powerless.

Human rights and religion: case examples

As illustrations, I will turn now to cases that have caught the public imagination as applicants have tried to gain recognition or enforcement of rights.

Right to education

The case of case of *Folgerø and others v. Norway* (http://hudoc.echr.coe.int/eng?i=001-81356, last accessed Feb. 2020) arose following a change in the Norwegian education syllabus in 1997 when two previous subjects about religion were merged into one, covering Christian philosophy, scriptures and cultures. When three sets of parents, members of the Norwegian Humanist Association, were refused permission to exempt their children from the class, they appealed to the ECHR, citing an article of the Convention that said that 'the State shall respect the rights of parents to ensure such education and teaching in conformity with their own religious and philosophical convictions'. The parents argued that the curriculum was not objectively or critically written or pluralistic, giving undue weight to Christianity as both a historical and moral category. The Court found in their favour, stating that the state should not engage in indoctrination and had violated Article 2 Protocol 1, covering the right to education.

Right to work with religious beliefs

An application made by four British nationals to the ECHR, known as *Eweida and Others v. the United Kingdom* (http://hudoc.echr.coe.int/eng?i=001-115881, last accessed Feb. 2020), were heard together in 2012 as they all claimed similar rights in relation to their Christian religion. Two related to employment and two to religious symbols being worn.

Lillian Ladele worked as a registrar for Islington Council in north London. She had been dismissed for refusing to conduct same-sex civil partnership ceremonies on the grounds of her religious beliefs which construed same-sex relationships as sinful. She took her case to an Employment Tribunal and won, both in terms of unfair dismissal and harassment. She lost, however, on appeal by Islington Council to the ECHR which found that she was employed to perform purely secular, public work and her refusal constituted discrimination against gay people in the course of her job. Someone's religious freedom cannot be defended if it includes discrimination against others.

In a similar case, Gary McFarlane was employed by Relate, a counselling charity. In March 2008 he told his managers that, as a Christian, he would be unwilling to comply with Relate's policy to provide counselling to people regardless of their sexual orientation. He was dismissed, and lost his case, and subsequent appeal, claiming discrimination and wrongful dismissal before the Employment Tribunal. His case was later heard by the European Courts of Human Rights which ruled against him.

Two other cases in *Eweida and Others v. the United Kingdom* were related to the material representations of religion. Nadia Eweida, a 60-year-old British Airways employee who wanted to wear her cross visibly above her uniform in defiance of BA policy won her case. Shirley Chaplin, a 57-year-old nurse employed by Devon and Exeter NHS hospital, who wanted to wear her cross on a chain around her neck above her uniform, in defiance of hospital policy, lost.

Ms Eweida, quoted in the *Guardian* newspaper (www.theguardian.com/business/2006/oct/15/theairlineindustry.religion, last accessed Feb. 2020) claimed that: 'I was forced to take unpaid leave because I have refused to remove my cross or put it under my cravat. A cross is a cross, when you explain the reason is your belief in the Lord Jesus Christ. That's the end of it. Muslims wear their hijabs.'

In 2004 BA had changed the female uniform to include an open-necked blouse with a cravat. According to their regulations, any piece of jewellery or other accessory that the employee is required to wear as part of their religion must be covered up. In cases where employees refused to cover up, they would be sent home without pay to change their clothes, as indeed happened in the case of Ms Eweida. In recognition of some religions' mandatory rules, British Airways allowed male Sikh staff to wear turbans and female Muslims to wear the hijab. Although BA subsequently revised its policy on religious symbols and agreed they would be permitted, BA refused to compensate Ms Eweida her for loss of earnings. She took her case to an Employment Tribunal but lost. When her case was heard by the ECHR, they found in favour of her argument that wearing a cross was an example covered by the Convention and ruled in her favour. There had been no evidence, the judges observed, that BA customers had been offended by others wearing religious clothing and it was therefore unreasonable that Eweida was singled out.

In what seemed to be a similar situation of a Christian's right to wear a cross, Shirley Chaplin, a 57-year-old nurse employed by Devon and Exeter NHS hospital, lost her case in Strasbourg. She was prevented from wearing her crucifix on a necklace due to rules about health and safety, her employer argued: no one was permitted to wear necklaces of any kind as they could get caught up in equipment. She was told she could wear it under her clothing or pinned to her clothing, but she refused and took her case first to an Employment Tribunal, and lost, and then to Strasbourg, which she also lost. The right to freedom of religion cannot overturn other people's rights to health and safety.

The four cases above generated considerable media interest, which will be reviewed in more detail in Chapter 10. They also appeared to be part of a growing trend, as Méadhbh McIvor found in her paper summarizing her doctoral research concerning UK Christians' propensity to be litigious. McIvor (2019, 861) wrote:

> Funded by conservative lobby groups and influenced by the legal strategies of their American peers, increasing numbers of English Christians – including nurses and teachers disciplined for praying for patients and students, registrars and hoteliers unwilling to serve LGBTQ+ clients or customers, and uniformed employees who had been asked to remove cross necklaces that went against their employers' dress codes – were using the courts to claim a violation of their right to religious freedom.

Courts compared: the ECHR and Supreme Court (USA)

In her discussion of two different courts in two different continents, Effie Fokas is careful to first describe the courts' separate histories, contexts and purposes: the United States Supreme Court was established in 1789, the European in 1959. The American court serves to be the ultimate judge on a wide range of matters relating to the legal system laid down with the formation of a country while the European court hears only human rights cases, and those are brought by citizens and governments of 47 countries. Despite these and many other more trivial differences, the courts are often compared, she suggests (Fokas 2015, 164–5). because of the high-profile and high-impact nature of some of their cases and judgments:

> where some of the most contentious debates around religion have been played out, and to riveting effects [...] the ECtHR and the US S.Ct. grapple with the same per-ennial question: what formal relationship between religion and the state provides sufficiently for both freedom of and freedom from religion, and for equal treatment of all citizens?

Fokas directs her attention to how the court decisions cannot be viewed as either secular or religious, or as any clear-cut evidence of religious/state relations, because they have been influenced and refracted through a lens of 'everyday religion' in primarily three ways: the debates about the role of governments in relation to religion; the relationship between religion and national identity and the role of external, often 'grassroots', response and mobilization as a result of what is perceived as interference with lived religion. While she retreats from offering a definition of;'everyday religion', readers of this text may recall the work of Nancy Ammerman (2007) whose eponymous text emphasized the experiences of the 'everyday' in the lives of those non-professionals or non-experts – those who are not paid to study or lead religion. Further, as Fokas (2015, 166) quotes Winnifred Sullivan: 'Rationalizing religion in the ways proposed by courts and legislatures "fails to capture the nature of people's religious lives at the beginning of the twenty-first century, maybe of any century" (Sullivan 2005, 10).'

One religious issue that has been examined by the Supreme Court concerns controversy over the American Pledge of Allegiance, and whether school children should be required to recite it at the beginning of the school day. As this example so clearly shows the significance, intersection and volatility of nationalism, religion, ethnicity, social justice and human rights, I will give it a longer elucidation here.

The pledge officially adopted by Congress in 1942 was 'I pledge allegiance to the flag of the United States of America, and to the Republic for which it stands, one Nation indivisible, with liberty and justice for all.' In 1954, likely as a response to the then Cold War anxiety with the Soviet Union, an officially atheist state, and the recent conversion of president Dwight Eisenhower to Presbyterianism, the words 'under God' were added, to read: 'I pledge allegiance to the Flag of the United States of America, and to the Republic for which it stands, one Nation under God, indivisible, with liberty and justice for all.'[1] An illustration here will be the case in 2017 when 17-year-old India Landry was expelled from school for refusing to stand during the Pledge of Allegiance as a protest against perceived police brutality and the presidency of Donald Trump. Writing in the *Washington Post* (www.washingtonpost.com/news/made-by-history/wp/2017/11/03/the-ugly-history-of-the-pledge-of-allegiance-and-why-it-matters/ last accessed Feb. 2020; www.washingtonpost.com/news/made-by-history/wp/2017/11/03/the-ugly-history-of-the-pledge-of-allegiance-and-why-it-matters/ last accessed Feb. 2020), American academic Christopher Petrella refers to legal scholars and the Supreme Court's ruling that, according to rights protected in the Constitution, students cannot be forced to recite the pledge, or stand during its recital by others. Petrella goes on to chart what he describes as the pledge's political origins in nativism and white nationalism.

Formulation of the pledge began in 1891, when publishers of the *Youth's Companion* magazine commissioned a former Baptist pastor, Francis Bellamy, to create a programme for schools to commemorate the arrival of Christopher Columbus in America 400 years earlier. The words Bellamy wrote were: 'I pledge allegiance to my Flag and to the Republic for which it stands – one Nation indivisible – with liberty and justice for all.' Petrella notes that, while the words are not explicitly xenophobic, Bellamy was trying to establish 'true Americanism', writing in fear of what he described as waves of unsuitable immigrants from southern and eastern Europe, which would lower what he described as a 'racial standard'. Petrella comments that Bellamy was resonating with an 'ubiquitous turn-of-the-century nativism' that was opposing the Slavs, Jews and Italians who had immigrated in the late 19th century and were seen as different from, and less worthy than, the 'white' immigrants from western and northern Europe.

Congress, Petrella wrote, legalized those sentiments of exclusion through passing immigration laws, such as the Chinese Exclusion Act of 1882. Creating and spreading his pledge allowed Bellamy to help consolidate white Anglo-Saxon Protestant American values that the white mainstream perceived as being 'under siege', wrote Petrella. When the words 'under God' were added to the pledge in 1954, this 'constituted a salvo against another outside menace – godless Communism'. Petrella believes the nativism of the 1890s is still prominent, citing Donald Trump's restrictive policies on immigration, and his promise to build a wall between the United States and Mexico.

Following Petrella, I agree that it is significant that, when signing it into law, the new Presbyterian convert President Dwight Eisenhower stated: (www.todayifoundout. com/index.php/2013/05/the-origin-of-the-u-s-pledge-of-allegience/ last accessed Feb. 2020):

> In this way we are reaffirming the transcendence of religious faith in America's heritage and future; in this way we shall constantly strengthen those spiritual weapons which forever will be our country's most powerful resource in peace and war.

The right to rights

Returning to Fokas, she describes how the pledge reached the Supreme Court in 2004 precisely because of the God clause. In *Elk Grove Unified School District v. Newdow*, a non-custodial parent argued that his daughter should not be subjected to having religion forced on her. While the 9th Circuit, a lower court, agreed, the Supreme Court dismissed the case on the technicality that as a non-custodial parent, Newdow did not have the right to bring the case. What Fokas (2015, 172) then describes is key to understanding the unstable and publicly affected notion of 'human rights'. The day following the decision there was an enormous venting of outrage from politicians: the US Senate and House of Representatives condemned it, the then President George Bush called it 'ridiculous and inconsistent with the traditions and history of America' and there was a credible move, not completed in the end, to strip the courts of its jurisdiction over Pledge of Allegiance cases. Supreme Court Justices issued statements acknowledging that the court could risk becoming a political institution.

Discussing the example of the ECHR, Fokas cites Susanna Mancini (2010, 26), indicating that the court must be aware of their audiences, as their authority depends on the public's confidence and the extent to which the court's decisions reflect citizens' convictions. 'If a court's interpretations deeply differ from the convictions of the people, the people will start resisting judicial decisions.' As Fokas notes, and Petrella above argued, some of those convictions may be intertwined with other convictions, such as nationality. Indeed, Christian Concern, a UK Lobby group, described on its website that it was worried about the ECHR *Eweida and Others v. the United Kingdom* cases explicitly because of the national interest (https://archive.christianconcern.com/our-issues/islam last accessed Feb. 2020):

The influence of radical Islam has grown in the UK and as an ideology it seeks to shape our political and social landscape. From the introduction of sharia law and Islamic finance to the implications on freedom of speech and women's rights, the presence of Islamism in the UK has great repercussions for all of us. At Christian Concern we hope to bring awareness of the impact that this may have on the UK and offer a Christian response.

'Rights' and the conservative/liberal divide

The above examples and extended discussion ruffle the surface of what are deep, diverging views held by religious groups. As mentioned at the beginning of this chapter, many religious actors, from Christians in the United States to Muslims in Saudi Arabia opposed the formation of the UDHR, and the United Nations itself.

Reporting to the UN in March 2020 (https://news.un.org/en/story/2020/03/1058411), its Special Rapporteur on freedom of religion or belief, Ahmed Shaheed, urged the UN to overturn religious rights and practices if they contravene human rights, stating: 'I firmly reject any claim that religious beliefs can be invoked as a legitimate "justification" for violence or discrimination against women, girls or LGBT+ people.' He urged United Nations countries to repeal gender-based discrimination laws that were created and upheld because of religious convictions, referring to laws that criminalize adultery, forms of sexual orientation or gender identity, abortion and religious practices that violate human rights. Shaheed also criticized what he saw as increasing actions in politics by religious institutions and their followers who, in the name of religious freedom, seek to roll back the progress made to protect 'human rights'.

At stake is the location of power and authority over secular or religious rights, amidst what many conservative religious people feel is the encroaching influence of secularization. The term says it all: 'human rights'. Where, religious leaders and adherents ask, is the preferred authority of 'divine rights'? It's important to note, when considering the discourse of human/divine rights, that perception may not accurately represent the cases on the ground. As Laura M. Krull describes in her research into liberal Protestantism and social justice in the United States (https://onlinelibrary.wiley.com/doi/pdf/10.1111/jssr.12641), scholars have observed that 'liberal Protestants have been quieter than conservative Protestants in articulating a distinctly religious viewpoint to bolster and motivate their involvement in advocacy (Wuthnow 2002)'. Krull argues that liberal Christians, while advocating and working for social justice, often refrain from overtly arguing against conservative Christians for fear of being branded conservatives by a wider public, mainly because it is the conservative voice that is more commonly heard and associated with aggressive political action. Krull (2020, 3) writes that:

This separation of social justice from politics likely reflects the liberal protestant understanding of the separation of church and state (Demerath and Williams 1992; Djupe and Gilbert 2002; Wald and Leege 2014). As such, even among the third of churches reporting they are 'politically active' (Chaves and Eagle 2015:22), they primarily support social services that address direct and immediate needs such as providing food or shelter, rather than advocating for political reform.

While many questions remain, the subject of human rights will increasingly arise in a more complex, globalized world. The question is perhaps more pertinent in contemporary society now as certain trends have helped position that issue more in the public eye.

Sample questions for private study

1   Discuss what constitutes a religious or secular organization for the UN?
2   What recent cases relating to human rights resonate with the themes of this chapter?

Sample class exercise

Discuss media reports involving current controversies.

Note

1   The first variation of the pledge to mark God was proposed in 1906 by the Daughters of the American Revolution: 'I pledge allegiance to my flag, and the republic for which it stands. I pledge my head and my heart to God and my country. One country, one language and one flag.' *The American Monthly Magazine* 29 (1906): 797.

Indicative reading

Ammerman, Nancy T. 2007. *Everyday Religion: Observing Modern Religious Lives.* Oxford: Oxford University Press.

Asad, Talal. 2003. *Formations of the Secular: Christianity, Islam, Modernity.* Stanford, CA: Stanford University Press.

Barak, Gregg. 1990. 'Crime, Criminology and Human Rights: Towards an Understanding of State Criminality.' *Journal of Human Justice* 2, no. 1: 11–28.

Barker, Eileen. 2020. 'Freedom of Religion' In: *The SAGE Encyclopaedia of the Sociology of Religion,* edited by Adam Possamai and Anthony J. Blasi. Thousand Oaks, CA: SAGE.

Berger, Peter (ed.). 1999. *The Desecularization of the World: Resurgent Religion and World Politics.* Grand Rapids, MI: William Eerdmans.

Cannell, Fenella. 2010. 'Anthropology of Secularism.' *Annual Review of Anthropology* 39: 85–100. https://doi.org/10.1146/annurev.anthro.012809.105039.

Carrette, Jeremy, and Sophie-Hélène Trigeaud. 2013. 'The Religion-Secular in International Politics: The Case of 'Religious' NGOs at the United Nations.' In *Social Identities between the Sacred and the Secular,* edited by Abby Day, Giselle Vincett and Christopher Cotter, 7–22. Farnham: Ashgate.

Day, Abby. 2016. 'Vicarious Belonging and the Persistence of Institutionalised Christianity.' In *The Brill Handbook of Contemporary Christianity: Movements, Institutions and Allegiance,* edited by Stephen J. Hunt, 223–42. Leiden: Brill:

Day, Abby, and Simon Coleman. 2013. 'Secularization.' In *Oxford Bibliographies Online: Anthropology.* New York: Oxford University Press.

Dinham, Adam. 2017. 'Religious Literacy in Public and Professional Settings.' In *The Routledge Handbook of Religion, Spirituality and Social Work*, edited by B. R. Crisp, 257–64. New York: Routledge.

Evans, Malcolm D. 1997. *Religious Liberty and International Law in Europe.* Cambridge: Cambridge University Press.

Falcetta, Sylvia, and Paul James Johnson. 2018. 'Migration, Sexual Orientation, and the European Convention on Human Rights.' *Journal of Immigration, Asylum and Nationality Law* 32: 210–31.

Fitzgerald, Timothy. 2000. *The Ideology of Religious Studies* . New York, Oxford: Oxford University Press.

Fitzgerald, Timothy. 2007. *Discourse on Civility and Barbarity: A Critical History of Religion and Related Categories.* New York, Oxford: Oxford University Press.

Fokas, Effie. 2015. 'The Secular Court? Trends in the United States Supreme Court and the European Court of Human Rights Compared.' In *Modernities, Memory and Mutations: Grace Davie and the Study of Religion,* edited by Abby Day and Mia Lövheim, 163–78. Farnham: Ashgate.

Forsyth, Miranda. 2016. 'The Regulation of Witchcraft and Sorcery Practices and Beliefs.' *Annual Review of Law and Social Science* 12. https://doi.org/10.1146/annurev-lawsocsci-110615-084600.

Freeman, Michael. 2011 *Human Rights: An Interdisciplinary Approach.* Cambridge: Polity.

Ganiel, Gladys, and Peter Jones. 2012. 'Religion, Politics and Law.' In *Religion and Change in Modern Britain*, edited by Linda Woodhead and Rebecca Catto, 299–321. Abingdon, Oxon: Routledge.

Gilliat-Ray, Sophie, Mansur Ali and Stephen Pattison. 2013. *Understanding Muslim Chaplaincy.* Abingdon, Oxon: Routledge.

Goodale, Mark (ed.). 2012. *Human Rights at the Crossroads.* Oxford: Oxford University Press.

Goodhart, Michael. 2013. *Human Rights: Politics and Practice.* Oxford: Oxford University Press.

Grewal, Kiran. 2016. *The Socio-Political Practice of Human Rights: Between the Universal and the Particular.* London: Routledge.

Harvey, Graham. 1996. *Contemporary Paganism: Listening People, Speaking Earth.* New York: New York University Press.

Johnson, Paul James, and Sylvia Falcetta. 2018. 'Sexual Orientation Discrimination and Article 3 of the European Convention on Human Rights: Developing the Protection of Sexual Minorities.' *European Law Review* 43 no. 2: 167–85.

Johnson, Paul James, and Sylvia Falcetta. 2019. 'Sexual Orientation Equality in Central and Eastern Europe: The Role of the European Convention on Human Rights.' *European Human Rights Law Review.*

Johnson, Paul James, and Robert M. Vanderbeck. 2017. 'Sexual Orientation Equality and Religious Exceptionalism in the Law of the United Kingdom: The Role of The Church of England.' *Oxford Journal of Law and Religion* 6, no. 3: 433–50.

Khalaf-Elledge, Nora. 2020. ' "It's a Tricky One": Development Practitioners' Attitudes towards Religion,' *Development Practice.* DOI: 10.1080/09614524.2020.1760210.

Mancini, Susanna. 2010. 'The Crucifix Rage: Supranational Constitutionalism Bumps Against the Counter-Majoritarian Difficulty.' *European Constitutional Law Review* 6, no. : 6–27.

McIvor, Méadhbh. 2019. 'Rights and Relationships: Rhetorics of Religious Freedom among English Evangelicals.' *Journal of the American Academy of Religion* 87, no. 3: 860–88. https://doi.org/10.1093/jaarel/lfz02.

Nash, Kate. 2015. *The Political Sociology of Human Rights.* Cambridge: Cambridge University Press

Potter, Pitman. 2003. 'Belief in Control: Regulation of Religion in China.' In *Religion in China Today,* edited by Daniel Overmeyer, 11–31. Cambridge: Cambridge University Press.

Sandberg, Russell. 2008. 'Religion and the Individual: A Socio-Legal Perspective.' In *Religion and the Individual: Belief, Practice, Identity,* edited by Abby Day, 157–68. Farnham: Ashgate.

Sullivan, Winnifred Fallers. 2005. *The Impossibility of Religious Freedom*. Princeton, NJ, Oxford: Princeton University Press.

Taylor, Paul M. 2005. *Freedom of Religion: UN and European Human Rights Law and Practice*. Cambridge: Cambridge University Press.

Tomalin, Emma. 2015. *Handbook of Religions and Global Development*. London, New York: Routledge.

Williams, Rhys, and Peter Berger. 2001. *The Desecularization of the World: Resurgent Religion and World Politics*. Washington, DC, Grand Rapids, MI: Ethics and Public Policy Centre and W. B. Eerdmans.

Part III

Contested borders

Chapter 7

Gender and sexuality

Introduction

This chapter looks at how religions monitor and regulate gender, sexuality and the body and builds on the discussions about human rights in Chapter 6. The body is an important sociological term as, scholars suggest, it is a site of both inscription and contestation, where bodies embody, reflect and often wear religion. How gender and sexuality are defined reflects broader influences and they are thought by contemporary scholars to be fluid and contested, in contrast to the way many religious people think about those categories. The difficulties facing women and men in patriarchal, fundamentalist religions are explored, together with some of their creative responses to adapt and resist. A variety of religious traditions, regions and historical periods are discussed, considering different approaches to gender and sexual difference. The approach here locates the discussion in intersectional discourse, searching for connections and comparisons, ensuring that social structures such as age and ethnicity are incorporated and analysed, rather than locating gender or sexuality in isolation.

The body in the sociology of religion

Social scientific and philosophical turns to studying the body have profoundly shaped contemporary sociology of religion and will help explain some of religion's beliefs and practices relating to gender and sexuality.

In her Presidential address to the Society for the Social Scientific Study of Religion, Meredith McGuire (1990) delivered a pioneering speech which helped shape the discipline's orientation to the body. She urged social scientists of religion to take theories of the body, and embodiment, seriously because the body 'matters'. She outlined (1990, 284) two ways in which it mattered. First, she pointed out, bodies matter to people. 'Part of the reason our bodies matter to us is that we strongly identify our very selves with our bodies. We experience things done to our bodies as done to ourselves.' Second, she continued, bodies are matter. The human body is material, and society inscribes itself on the body. She pointed out that a child starving of malnutrition in a famine is not an idea. And yet, she lamented (McGuire 1990, 285), sociologists of religion may ignore the body in favour of the mind or spirit.

> Rather, let us assume that the human body is both a biological and a cultural product, simultaneously physical and symbolic, existing always in a specific social

and environmental context in which the body is both active agent and yet shaped by each social moment and its history.

McGuire proposed that conceptions of the body could usefully engage scholars of the sociology of religion in several ways. She urged scholars to consider the body in terms of one's self-experience and experience of others, its role producing and reflecting social meaning and its relationship with power. She described how, although each one of us is unique, our embodiment and the way we relate to other bodies outside ourselves are 'profoundly' social. She elaborated by emphasizing that those social meanings do not need to be conscious. As Pierre Bourdieu (1977, 124) argued, the 'socially informed body' is acquired through processes of socialization that determine the tastes, likes and dislikes people tend to think, erroneously, are highly individualized. Whether a sense of smell registers an object as appealing or revolting, or a sense of style or morality guides people's daily behaviour, the way those senses have been cultivated is both social and, particularly in 'western' societies, to some extent malleable. That means the individual and her or his body become a site of competition and struggle: 'The specifically symbolic power to impose [such] principles of the construction of reality ... is a major dimension of political power' (Bourdieu 1977, 165). McGuire also emphasizes the work of Michel Foucault (1980, 1977), particularly the way in which he analysed society's technologies or regimes of power that order, discipline and punish individuals, trying to determine that what is being assumed is the correct, or at least most expedient, mode of thinking and behaviour.

Bryan S. Turner (1991, 1—4) discussed how 'the body' has long been of central interest to anthropologists, primarily because anthropologists were concerned with what generalized concepts or 'universals' could be found to explain the processes and conditions for human beings' survival and flourishing. Further, central issues in anthropology revolved around the relationship between nature and culture, and what, if anything, would determine or justify a human's special place amongst living creatures and distinction from other animals and how such a human might evolve. Sociology as a discipline (and see Chris Shilling 1993) inherited three of those concerns, he argued, primarily because:

1   The human body has, sometimes conflicting, embodied and socio-cultural potentialities and constraints.
2   There sometimes arise contradictions between sexuality and society.
3   Those first two facts vary according to gender, itself an ambiguous concept that covers the nature/culture divide.

Drawing mainly on the work of anthropologist Mary Douglas, Turner describes the body as the central metaphor for political and social order. For sociologists, he argued, that recognition was of interest but did not command the attention of sociological thinkers in ways that economy and rational action did, as a legacy of Marx and Weber. Turner turns to the work of Adorno and Horkheimer (1979) who discussed how Christianity and capitalism conspired to create a dominant view that work was virtuous, and the body was evil. Western social thought can therefore, Turner explained, be seen as focused on the apparent dualities of body-soul and nature-culture. He also explains that social theory cannot be separated from society, and reminds us that it is important to see how social changes, such as consumerism, a post-modern turn in the arts, feminism and what Foucault called 'bio-politics' all influence the development of social theory.[1] A significant factor in society's relationship with the body was what Turner described as the collapse of puritanical Christian authority. Indeed, this point has been further explored by scholars since, who have argued that the rise of feminism in the 1960s precipitated a catastrophic decline in Christianity (Day 2017; Brown 2012; Woodhead 2007; Brown 2001).

Turner proposes that another important development was how the relationship between the sexes changed with the rise of feminism and subsequent attention to sexuality, gender and biology. Another factor he identities as influencing the sociological attention to the body is the phenomenon of an ageing population and the consequent interest and challenges of health, attitudes towards dying and related technologies.

While Max Weber may have had considerable focus on, as Turner wrote, theories of rational action and capitalism, he also theorized about religion and sexuality, particularly arguing that the tension between sex and religion is irreconcilable. One of the reasons, he argued, was that the chaotic nature of sexual desire may interrupt the need to rationally pursue life and economy; another reason may be that the achievement of theodicy, whereby people rationalize the place of evil in a God-created world, would be threatened by something as unpredictable and unmanageable as sexual desire.

Defying definition

As increasingly contested terms, 'gender' and 'sexuality' are understood sociologically as fluid, rather than biological, concepts without stable definitions. They are social constructs, reproducing the attitudes and behaviours society applies to what are usually, but erroneously, seen as binary differences between males and females. These norms are internalized by individuals to the extent that they may feel inherent and 'natural', when, in fact, they are ascribed and continually reinscribed through action. As Simone de Beauvoir (1949) famously put it: 'One is not born, but rather becomes, a woman.'

Judith Butler (1990) described this process of becoming gendered as 'performative' acts, bringing into being and reinforcing those norms according to pre-assigned scripts. She argued that there is no essential essence to gender; it is not a natural fact but occurs in specific historical situations as a performative accomplishment. Gender, she wrote, is not 'a role which either expresses or disguises an interior self' (Butler 1990, 412) but represents 'cultural fictions' of what it is to be a real woman or a real man. Butler's illustration of the 'Heteronormative Matrix' (Butler 1990, 85–193) refers to the processes that regulate gender, linking bodies to norms to create the seemingly natural distinctions of heterosexual males and females. These norms can be reflected in and subverted through, for example, emotions, desires and mourning.

She echoes here the work of Erving Goffman (1959), who argued that there was no such thing as a stable 'self' or 'identity', but that these shift according to time, place, circumstances and audience, just as 'culture' is not a fixed, static entity. He suggested that one's 'scripts' reflect the roles and expectations others have of us, the interpretive 'frames' people use, the type of parts one plays and the routines one creates. What may be described as internalization was the process Goffman employed, drawing on Max

Weber, as bureaucratization, where a 'certain bureaucratization of the spirit is expected so that we can be relied upon to give a perfectly homogenous performance at every appointed time' (Goffman 1959, 64).

Nancy Fraser (1996, 17) argued that gender contains both a cultural and an economic dimension, noting that 'gender contains both an economic face that brings it within the ambit of redistribution and a cultural face that brings it simultaneously within the ambit of recognition'.

As social structures, gender and sexuality are bound up with other social structures such as age, class and ethnicity. Exploring the experience of women in Islamic societies, Valentine M. Moghadam (2013) foregrounds those structures within the framework of economy, particularly capitalism, where she examines three transnational social movements: Islamism, feminism and global justice.

In non-Muslim majority countries, controversies have arisen over whether Muslim women should be allowed to wear coverings such as headscarves (*hijab*), body coverings such as *jilbab* and *burqa*, and face coverings such as the *niqab*. Some European countries have banned these coverings in public spaces, others have regulated them and a few have resisted. Sociologists may ask what the fuss is about: in a 'free' society, is it not permitted to wear what one wants? The situation, however, is more complicated and relates to assertions about who 'belongs', who is 'other' and the extent to which religious freedoms should be protected (see e.g. Woodhead 2009; Scott 2007). A tension between a theological and sociological approach resides, once again, in struggles for power, legitimacy and authority. Monotheistic religions in particular have traditionally located gender and secularity in beliefs about the supremacy of god and his creation. And yet, as will be discussed here, these beliefs have changed significantly in recent years and may represent only a minority of religious opinion – despite what religious leaders will say and do to retain that traditional stand. It is to that theme we now turn, in particular the creation and imposition of power on embodied, gendered, sexualized human beings.

On power

Of the many ways sociologists may conceive of 'power', Stephen Lukes's (2005) approach is one that may be most helpful for this kind of analysis. Power is not, he points, out, most effectively wielded through force, but through being able to determine the agenda, the shape of debate and its parameters and boundaries. One of the most obvious ways that religion exerts power on gendered and sexualized bodies is through prescriptions and laws. Questions of sexuality, gender and the body appear to be central to most religions, and the degree to which they matter to any religion seems to be shared along a similar spectrum, from those who are most conservative at one end to those most liberal at the other. What is interesting to a sociologist is not the religion's sacred scriptures or doctrines, but how those matter to the religious adherents themselves, and how they are policed and protected. There are certain issues that appear to be touchstones, sharply dividing religious people within their own faiths, and often demonstrating a significant difference from the general population.

Linda Woodhead, as part of her 'Westminster Faith Debates' programme in London, conducted several social surveys with the polling agency YouGov and discovered that religious people are not always out of step with public opinion (http://faithdebates.org.uk/research/page/2/ LAST ACCESSED FEB. 2020).

The opinions of people with religious affiliations on abortion are not markedly different from the general view, she found. The survey showed that 43 per cent of people who identify with a religion are in favour of keeping or raising the current 24-week limit on abortion. This was similar to the views of the general population, at 46 per cent. The proportion of those who would like to see it lowered, 30 per cent, were again similar to the general population at 28 per cent. Only 9 per cent of religious people supported an outright ban, in line with the views of the general population at 9 per cent. Significantly, Woodhead points out, although the Roman Catholic Church teaches that abortion is always wrong and should be illegal, only 14 per cent of Catholics share that view.

While those statistics provided a general view, Woodhead pressed the question further and wondered if characteristics such as gender, age or voting preferences would explain hostility to abortion. She found that they did not, but certain other characteristics did, with hostility towards abortion highest amongst those who believe in God with absolute certainty and rely on scriptures or other kinds of religious sources and teachings for guidance. While, as she observed, only 8 per cent of the UK general population fits that profile, of those who do, a third support banning abortion. That group included Catholics, Muslims and Baptists. In other words, a literalist Muslim has more in common with a literalist Baptist than a liberal Muslim.

Religious people from the three main monotheistic religions share certain biblical books and take prohibitions about sexuality from, largely, the books of Genesis and Leviticus:

You shall not lie with a male as with a woman. It is an abomination.

(Leviticus 18:22 KJV)

If a man lies with a male as he lies with a woman, both of them have committed an abomination. They shall surely be put to death. Their blood shall be upon them.

(Leviticus 20:13 KJV)

People who argue against adhering to a literalist reading of the texts are keen to point out other biblical prohibitions which are not observed today, such as wearing clothing made of more than one cloth, or killing someone who does not observe the Sabbath. They may also point out that prohibitions change, even those thought to be 'modern'. Homosexuality was illegal in most countries only a few decades ago and is still punishable by death in some countries. A case study by Paul James Johnson and Sylvia Falcetta (2019) describes, for example, how polticans in Uganda, encouraged by church members, have been debating amendments to reintroduce a withdrawn 2014 law that made homosexuality illegal and punishable by life imprisonment.

Psychiatrists practised 'aversion therapy' to 'cure' someone of their homosexuality in recent times, and many religions still encourage that. But, when we consider the issue sociologically instead of theologically, we are left to explain why it is that abortion, homosexuality and divorce appear to be such major issues for certain groups of religious people. As Meredith McGuire (1990, 293) argued, the 'engendered body is also both the instrument of power and the site of struggles over power. The most obvious power struggle is in the arena of reproductive control, in which religious legitimations and organizations are prominent.'

As discussed in Chapter 4, Roger Friedland (2001, 2002) argued that one of the reasons religions police so earnestly boundaries of gender and sexuality is that they recognize the political and nationalistic, performative and transformative power of the family. Friedland (2002) tied that anxiety to the 'traditional' family's power for reproducing certain norms and structures, a point he elucidated in a slightly earlier work (Friedland 2001, 134) as he drew on Foucault (1990), presenting the family not just as a source of order and government, but of creation:

> Religion nationalisms are animated by a family drama; they all center their fierce energies on the family, its erotic energies, its gendered order. This is because the institutional logic of religion centers on the order of creation, locating humanness in the cosmos, replicating cosmology through ritual, a practical metaphysics that necessarily points before life and after death.

The American conservative Christians' concern with the family intensified with the rise of divorce, he argued, to the point where all matters of gender and sexuality that threatened the family became pivotal. In a similar example, he noted the first major statement of Sayyid Ruhollah Musavi Khomeini in 1961 in Iran was to attack the Shah for relaxing regulations about women, permitting them entry into the armed forces, the civil service, the judiciary and allowing them to vote. Those initiatives were all reversed by the Islamic revolution he led in 1979, founding the Islamic Republic of Iran. In her study of Moroccan gender dynamics, Fatima Mernissi (1987) argued that a wave of more conservative Islam occurred primarily because men saw women's sexuality as dangerous, and with growing female empowerment and participation they wanted to suppress what they saw as competitive and threatening.

Many sociological and political commentators concur that the rise of religious conservatism can be understood as a response to the liberalism of the 1960s counter-culture, the rise of feminism, a perception of 'secular humanism', the economic recession caused by the 1973 oil crisis and perception of a threat to the world standing of the United States (Beyer 1994; Bruce 1988; Liebman and Wuthnow 1983; Fackre 1983). These issues are responded to by the 'New Right's social traditionalism which is concerned with 'the breakdown of family, community, religion, and traditional morality in American life' (Himmelstein 1983, 16). These concerns then formed a political agenda as a political response to 'pursue legislation against the Equal Rights Amendment, the Gay Rights Bill, abortion, gun control, and sex education in public schools' (Hunter 1983, 152). The rise of 'populist' and far-right groups more widely spread from the mid-2000s onwards containing the same features of anti-abortion and anti-LGBTQ+ rights, often housed in religious rhetoric.

Adapting and resisting

Human beings, however socialized and habituated they may be, have powers of analysis and agency. Sociologists are interested in how people adapt and resist, contest and condemn, the uses of power they find to be anathema.

Following decades of campaigning, the governing body of the Church of England, the Synod, agreed in 1994 that women could become priests. The battle for inclusion in the higher echelons of the church would continue for decades and it was not until 2014 that Synod voted to allow women to be bishops. Women priests are still not universally accepted amongst Anglicans.

Even those women who have managed to overcome hierarchal obstacles and attained the status of Christian priesthood are still aware that they are somehow different, and not entirely accepted on their own terms. Reflecting on her experience as one of the Church of England's first woman priests, Diane E. Rees (2015, 132) wrote:

> Since my ordination in 1996, I have come to understand that although there is generally an acceptance of my priestly ministry, it is, even now, not entirely 'normal'. I am still a 'woman' priest rather than simply a priest.

Not everyone welcomed the ordination of women in the worldwide 'Anglican Communion'. The Synod, allowed women to become deacons in 1985. Deacons play an important role in the leadership team but are not regarded as important as priests. This can indicate more than different views of church hierarchical practice, but reveal what kind of religious life is deemed to be properly 'religious'. A woman deacon once explained in conversation (Day 2017, 161) that she felt her job was to help the congregation cohere as a group, while the (male) priest busied himself 'with the magic'. And yet, women's leadership of and participation in such social and 'cohering' activities indicates a specific kind of religiosity which tends to be undervalued in many societies, as Marilyn Strathern (1984) discussed, showing how ethnocentric views of women sometimes ignore or denigrate how women value their own positions and labour.

Related themes of connection and community come through in Caroline Starkey's (2020 study of 25 ordained British Buddhist women in the UK. Some had met with resistance within their Buddhist networks, and all had to navigate the often difficult terrain of both curiosity and prejudices in wider British society.

Eileen Campbell-Reed's (2016) research about Baptist clergywomen makes a similar point, privileging relationality over theology. In the struggle for Baptist identity between conservative and moderate members of the American Southern Baptist Convention (SBC) between 1979 and 2000, the role of women has been generally ignored. Campbell-Reed suggests that historians and theologians fail to appreciate more nuanced forms of the 'struggle': the psychological, the spatial and the gendered theological. Her book narrates the period through stories of five clergywomen, offering important insights into how religion and gender relate to relationality.

Michael Keenan's work explores how the institution of the Church of England has tried to repress homosexuality and gay experience by constructing a narrow view of what it can find acceptable, and yet gay clergy have found it possible to adapt to and even flourish in that environment. It is a complicated story, as Keenan describes, where in trying to meet increasing internal and external pressure, the church is (Keenan 2015, 95):

> in effect constructing a picture of 'acceptable homosexuality' which fails to fully engage with experiences of lesbian and gay Christians (particularly those in the clergy). Instead Church engagement continues to focus on lesbian and gay Christians as a problem, requiring silence, constraint and assimilation which further marginalizes and excludes.

The problem with that position is that it can further silence and marginalize people, he writes, because being assimilated into existing structures without overtly changing or challenging them only continues to allow the dominant discourse to prevail. The church's early attempts to reconcile their preferred theology with the reality of gay lived experience was in itself a barrier to understanding, Keenan argues, citing the wording of a 1954 Church of England document: 'The Problem of Homosexuality, an Interim Report'. After more discussion and studying, the church reached a new conclusion that allowed gay people to become clergy, providing that they remained celibate. That resulted not only in the difficult and at times contradictory expectation that a gay couple should remain celibate, but also closed the possibility of discussing one's sexuality in an open, accepting environment.

Keenan draws on his research, consisting of interviews and questionnaires with gay clergy, to illustrate the complexity of their lives and feelings. He chooses two quotes to give a sense of the anguish these men often feel (Keenan 2015, 104):

> With gay people it's like, we've bought you a brand new car but you can't have the keys, you can admire it, but you can't take it out.
> So, I'm probably perceived at the moment as relatively 'safe', because I will be assumed to be going around like a castrated cat.

In his analysis of his data, Keenan (2015, 104) points out the role of power: 'acceptable homosexuality is also a homosexuality which understands its place in the hierarchy'. It is not simply that the church envisages homosexuality as dangerous and morally wrong, but it is of a lower status than heterosexual relationships. In discussing the comparable case of the church refusing to allow women priests, Keenan quotes one respondent drawing attention to the sense of power relations within the institution.

> What they actually cared about was whether you were for it or against it, and if you were for it you belonged to one club and if you were against it you belonged to another club.

In that way, Keenan (2015, 106) continues:

> the debates of the Church are seen to be more political than theological – for this respondent the debate became more about the winning than it did about the result and the consequences of that result for the Church. The Church therefore was seen to be presenting as an institution of judgement and infighting. It was not seen to be an open and welcoming arena for reflection and sharing. Again, here 'safe' homosexuality is silent homosexuality.

Keenan has usefully demonstrated that the position of gay people within the church is linked to wider issues of power and structure, and of whether someone is going to be a member of a certain club. Do they fit in? Are they like 'us'?

Momin Rahman (2010, 945) pursues a similar point when he discusses Muslim sexuality in the American context. He begins by arguing that to be 'Muslim in North America is, in these examples, antithetical to an American or Canadian identity, reflecting in large part the wider cultural positioning of Muslim culture and values as antithetical to those of the West'. He charts the effect the 1993 book written by Samuel Huntingdon had on public discourse and imagination. Huntingdon's argument followed his book's title: 'Clash of Civilizations: Remaking of World Order', in which he argued that there are irreconcilable differences between 'western' countries he described as secular, progressive and democratic and Islamic countries he characterized as undemocratic, theocratic and ultra-conservative. Rahman reviews critiques of Huntingdon and says that the touchstones of gender and sexuality have come to be used as part of the arsenal in 'clash' discourses, creating the glossed but dominant 'clash' idea that gender and sexual equality have been created in the 'west' but not in Islamic cultures due, primarily, to the inherent nature of each. Gay is therefore positioned uniformly as 'western', which 'feeds assumptions about Muslims as "other" to western culture and its values of democracy, secularism and tolerance of sexual minorities' (Rahman 2010, 948). He provides an alternative view in placing gay Muslims in a intersectional space, by which he means, following Patricia Collins (2000) that their identities are constructed at the intersections of other social hierarchies, that they are plural, that cultures and identities overlap and that attention must be drawn to the standpoint of the oppressed, recognizing that the knowledge claims of those in authority often exclude those, perhaps challenging, claims of marginalized people. Using feminist analytical theory, Rahman discusses how 'difference' should always be nuanced and analysed, to provide more complex categories that account for different forms of difference, including gender, sexuality, class and race. He urges (Rahman 2010, 949) readers to take intersectionality even further, to consider sociologically the realms in which it occurs and thereby to understand how 'the existence of gay Muslims, either within the West or Muslim majority cultures, presents a fundamental challenge to the cultural opposition thesis because their identities refute the mutual exclusivity of culture inherent within this discourse'. Further, he continues, intersectional analysis may disrupt the monolithic cultural presentation of 'gay' in 'western' societies and consider other forms of gay identity.

Along with intersectional analyses, Rahman (2010, 954) argues that queer theory offers a useful analytical framework as it stresses uncertainty, resistance and subversion in response to essentializing, universalizing dominant discourses. He points out that the dominant discourse on gay rights is itself tied to assumptions about modernity, where people are apparently free of the influence of institutions and religions and can therefore lead 'true', authentic lives:

> Queer intersectional Muslim subjects remind us that there are only *possible* selves, never true selves. That reminder, being so close in time to the very recent arrival of LGBT rights, is an uncomfortable and perhaps unwelcome fact, precisely because it reminds us – those of us living the western identity – that our own existence is ontologically and politically tenuous rather than somehow inevitable.

As Andrew Kam-Tuck Yip and Peter Nynäs elaborate in the introduction to their edited collection (Nynäs and Yip 2012), which covers topics ranging from emotion, activism and relationality to abortion and homophobia, the intersection between religion, gender and sexuality is multi-faceted. It is personal *and* political, sociological *and* psychological, because those complex identities are performed and influenced at personal, institutional and cultural levels within national, regional and international contexts.

Saving and surrendering 'self'

A question that perplexes many people, including sociologists of religion, is why some people would willingly belong to an organization that may appear to be inimical to their needs and desires. One answer is that the people being discussed do not have clear or attractive alternatives, that they are emotionally, intellectually and habitually locked into a community or religion that they cannot leave, either through fear of being harmed or because it is the only life and source of support they know and, subsequently, they believe, probably correctly, that strangers will not look after them.

Case example: Amish youth running around

For example, a frequent source of media attention is the Amish practice of 'rumspringa', or 'running around', a period of relative relaxation of rules in the otherwise strict and separatist sect. The Amish, originally European Anabaptists, emigrated to what is now Pennsylvania in the United States in the mid-18th century. They believe it is necessary to live away from 'the world', living in self-sufficient communities (but trading and doing business with outsiders), eschewing modern technology, including engines for cars or tractors and wearing simple clothes evocative of their German roots. Family, community and work life follows strict gender lines, with the men in charge and women subservient, carrying out domestic tasks and focusing on home life and their (typically large) families. The main practice of Amish spiritual, community and family life is best summed up, according to Donald Kraybill (2003) as 'Gelassenheit', a multi-layered, nuanced word generally meaning surrendering and denying the self in obedience to God and other forms of religious authority. Members practise 'giving up', whether that is in material, emotional, spiritual or physical senses. While much of that is antithetical to modern, 'western', values, it describes, argues Kraybill, the essence of what makes and sustains an Amish community. And yet, during the period of adolescence, most communities encourage a period of 'rumspringa', varying from allowing minor transgressions of authority within the physical boundaries of the community, to permitting short or even more extended visits to the outside world. What surprises people, when these events are covered in media or popular culture, is that most teenagers return to their former lives, marry and settle back into the Amish way of life. This is perhaps not surprising when the options are considered: being separated forever from family, friends and all that has been learned and familiar.

There is often a similar reaction to accounts of women who stay in religions that are patriarchal and often overtly disallow women from taking an equal part in worship or management of the institution. One of the most important early studies was Elizabeth

Weiss Ozorak's (1996) study of 61 white, middle-class women aged between 18 and 71. Most were Christian, Jewish and Unitarian women who belonged to religious institutions that varied in their patriarchal structures, from highly patriarchal to minimally so. Two were of no faith. Her research question was simple: 'Why do women disproportionately invest in an institution that systematically devalues them?' (Ozorak 1996, 17). During her interviews she asked about people's religious backgrounds, their beliefs and values, the groups they belonged to and whether and why anything may have changed. Sometimes, the issue of gender relations arose during the interview but if not, the question was asked directly: 'Do you think your church (synagogue, etc.) treats men and women about equally, or not?' 'If the woman thought not, she was encouraged to explain.' (Ozorak 1996, 20). Although there was considerable diversity amongst responses and different examples of how women perceived the gender gap, a significant hypothesis in the study was proven: 'that women conceptualize religion in terms of relationship rather than individuation ((Ozorak 1996, 22). The individuation theme included such characteristics as autonomy and the perception of God as controlling and distant, whereas the relationship theme focused on matters such as connection, emotional support and a caring, personal God. One of Ozorak's most significant conclusions was that the women usually reconceptualized the idea of power itself, not accepting unproblematically the vision of a top-down, male-led hierarchal patriarchy but instead nesting themselves and their experiences in a web-like entity. She writes (Ozorak 1996, 25):

> Many women referred to their congregation, or a subset of it, as their 'family.' The religious community resembles the web of mutual care, at least in theory, and in practice the community provides opportunities for women to work together and to form close friendships with other women. Christian women of all ages tended to describe a personal and often intensely emotional relationship with God, even when they were not entirely certain what God was like.

That web-like perspective allows the possibility of a community without losers, in which power emanates from the support of the community and so is increased by being shared (Ozorak 1996, 27). She reported that while most of her research participants accepted that, if measured by hierarchical social standards, they are not treated as well as they could be by their religion and much of the hard work they perform for their churches is not valorized, 'in absolute terms, they do not see themselves as disenfranchised. The power of connection and relationship, most essential to their own views of the faith experience, is available to them in abundance' (Ozorak 1996, 27).

The strength of belonging may be overlooked when assessing the apparent contradictions of patriarchy and women's religiosity. It is 'Strange to consider our common mother as a black woman of Africa', reflected Brigalia Bam (1998, 347), who went on to say that she believes black women have been 'doubly cursed' by being oppressed both as black and as women. Her reflections did not, however, cause her to reject religion, particularly the Anglican form established by colonizers and missionaries: She writes (Bam 1998, 349):

> We are grateful to the people of the Church [...] I am a member of the Anglican Communion. I am glad to be able to say that. My great grandfather was baptized

and confirmed in this Church and with experiences of joy and pain in that member-ship over the years my family has been pleased to call itself Anglican since that time. I am Anglican. But I am not English and I am not male.

Another reason women value religion is their sense of making a contribution to the wider institution and society. Ozorak found that the women emphasized their service to others as an integral part of their religious practice, as the following example may illustrate.

Case example: the Mothers' Union

The Mothers' Union was created in 1876 by Mary Sumner, a Church of England clergyman's wife, to promote marriage (between heterosexual couples only) and raise Christian children. In the UK, it was both a social club and a fund-raiser for Christian missions abroad. Its main purpose was to promote values of an idealized Christian woman as wife and mother. Its key principles were (www.salis-bury.anglican.org/mission/mothers-union/mothers-union-news/the-mary-sumner-story, last accessed Apr. 2020):

> That the prosperity of a nation springs from the family life in its homes
>   That family life is the greatest institution in the world for the formation of the character of children
>   That faith is the foundation of family life
>   That the tone of family life depends upon the married life of the parents – and ultimately, that example is stronger than precept

Part of the organization's early work including campaigning, such as raising the age of marriage for girls from 12 to 16. While its popularity has declined in the UK, it still exists in Britain and Ireland, mainly as a fund-raiser for projects in the global south in the region of £4 million per year. Projects range from lit-eracy and financial skills training, campaigns and resources to combat gender based-violence and community-driven social action to alleviate poverty. Critics point out that its focus on marriage and family stigmatizes single women. Esther Mombo (1998, 219–24) has argued that domestic abuse is rooted in 'a tradition reinforced by Judeo-Christian religion' and that the Mothers' Union's emphasis on family serves to allow people to ignore domestic abuse. Oswald Swartz (1998, 188) writes that the organization's family focus marginalizes single women and allows hierarchal patriarchy to flourish: 'Despite the vital role women play in the Church they are often disempowered – as in the community, the workplace and the home in this patriarchal society'.

This raises the important question not simply about whether women may or not be more religious than men, but about whether they understand what religion is differently. As always, the question may be studied in a variety of ways and contexts (Trzebiatowska and Bruce 2012; Walters and Davie 1998). Research I conducted into the religious lives of religiously active women (Day 2005, 2017) concluded that women's spiritual labour is often overlooked or dismissed as not being equal to men's. That may be, however, an indication of what sociologists of religion tend to view as what counts as religion.

My study of a small Baptist women's prayer group revealed that the substance of their prayers was the everyday problems and challenges being experienced by their families or friends. The research by sociologist of religion Robert Wuthnow (1994) into the nature and purpose of small women-dominated groups, including church groups, in the United States found that the content of their discussions and prayers often included such everyday issues, with members talking about how to remedy or rise to the associated challenges. He lamented, however, (Wuthnow 1994, 358) that a certain kind of wisdom was absent, because the women were not using theological concepts or arguments:

> In simplest terms, the sacred comes to be associated with small insights that seem intuitively correct to the small group rather than wisdom accrued over the centuries in hermitages, seminaries, universities, congregations and church councils.

The wisdom to which he is referring was male wisdom, as only men have historically been the main and certainly most powerful members of such institutions, and he was also privileging a certain kind of male-generated spiritual wisdom and labour. Fiona Bowie (2006) has discussed at length the problem of male-led research projects, particularly of the colonial era, that ignored the religious practices and experiences of women, and therefore universalized and marginalized them. Linda Woodhead (2000, 67–84) called attention to the roots of 'gender-blindness' in the sociological study of religion, citing both Max Weber's idea of the 'iron cage' created by rationalization and bureaucracy and Émile Durkheim's concept of 'anomie' as male-focused issues. Both are intrinsically located in a public realm from which women have long been excluded. Indeed, when considering Weber's (Weber 1993, 95–117) theories of religion, it is apparent that the occupational groups he selected to explain differing affinities towards religion are male-occupied: the warrior, the peasant, the artisan, the missionary, the tent-maker. He leaves unmarked and unexplained the religiosities of female domestic labourers, queens, nurses, teachers or wives.

Marianne Weber drew on (as cited in Lengermann and Niebrugge-Brantley, 1998, 204) and extended the sociology of her husband Max Weber's by adding several other human needs to the primacy he gave to meaning. Openly and emphatically adopting a woman's standpoint, she argued that there were other human needs that became subsumed within patriarchy as men were granted entitlement to have those needs satisfied at the expense of women, who had to sublimate them and provide them to men:

> the embodied practical need for material existence; the embodied sensual need for erotic and sexual gratification; the psychic need for agency, or self-directed action; the emotional need for intimacy; and the ethical needs for moral autonomy and harmony with others.

Bryan Wilson, in his well-known study on the nature of secularization, also missed the substance of women's religious involvement. He describes, for example, a problem with churches where (Wilson in Bruce 2016, 130) laypeople 'often persist in commitment for community and family rather than for well-articulated ideological and intellectual reasons'. His tone suggests that this is a problem and not, as Ozorak (1996) found, the key strength of why churches matter to some many laypeople, the majority of whom are women. Steve Bruce, revisiting Wilson's work 50 years after its first publication, suggests that (Bruce 2016, 235) churches in the United States and northern Europe may remain popular 'for secular reasons (such as providing social services and legitimating national integrity)'. Students of the sociology of religion will question why such activities are considered non-religious, when most religious women will say (Ozorak 1996; Day 2017) that service to others and maintaining the strength of their beloved institutions, principally home and nation, is at the heart of their religious impulse and activity.

One such means of reconceptualizing women's religious labour is through problematizing the concepts of 'self' and 'duty'. Saba Mahmood (2005), a Pakistani-born American woman strongly influenced by critical Marxism, explored a growing trend for Muslim women to re-engage with Islam. She introduced her work by summarizing the feminist relationship to religion and Islam where, she suggests, it is largely believed that 'women Islamist supporters are pawns in a grand patriarchal plan' (Mahmood 2005, 1). Her research began by asking (in a similar vein to Ozorak (1996) discussed above) why so many women across the Muslim world joined what is sometimes described as the 'mosque movement' or 'piety movement'? Since the 1970s, Muslim women have been engaged in an Islamic revival, attending mosques for instruction, forming women's study groups, training to be preachers and increasingly wearing the *hijab*. Why, asked Mahmood (2005, 2), would such a large number of women across the Muslim world actively support a movement that seems inimical to their 'own interests and agendas', especially at a historical moment when the same women appear to have more emancipatory possibilities available to them? In most Muslim institutional contexts, as in many Christian, women are not allowed to be in a position of leadership or teaching over men. One of the goals of the mosque movement that interested Mahmood was duty: 'da'wa'. Often used to denote a call or summons, da'wa has been central to the piety movement as an invocation for women to adopt their 'religious duty that requires all adult members of the Islamic community to urge fellow Muslims to greater piety, and to teach one another correct Islamic conduct' (Mahmood 2005, 57).

Mahmood's analysis of the piety movement moves beyond simply the role of women and contested versions of feminism, to central anthropological concerns about the nature of freedom and construction of self. By immersing herself for two years with female teachers, their followers and other religiously engaged women of different social classes and ages, she created a nuanced, complex ethnography. She found that the idea of an autonomous, western, secular self was a popular illusion of which the women were aware, but it was not what they desired. More important were ways to actively live out their religious beliefs in community and wider society. Far from being subordinated, submissive women, she found they had powerful forms of agency that allowed them to choose to engage in rituals in which they found their sense of self, a connected, embodied self.

Women's negotiations with conservative religion are nuanced and often not visible to external observers. Line Nyhagen (2019) shows through interviews with Muslim women in Norway and the UK that the socially constructed space of a mosque is complicated for western European Muslim women who simultaneously accept and resist the gendered practices and sometimes engage male Muslims as allies. She concludes (Nyhagen 2019, 15) that her findings:

> indicate that a binary reading of Muslim women's religious discourses and practices as representing either subordination or resistance does not capture the complexity of Muslim women's reflexive engagement with sources of religious knowledge and with male power and authority. The interviewed Muslim women engage in a complex discursive positioning of 'authentic Islam' as supportive of gender equality and women's rights and of women's inclusion in the mosque, whilst also invoking natural-biological and religious justifications for the ubiquitous unequal allocation of mosque space, power, and authority in men's favor.

Research conducted by Sarah-Jane Page and Andrew Kam-Tuck Yip in the UK, 'Religion, Youth and Sexuality: A Multi-Faith Exploration Focusing on Young Male and Female Adults Aged between 18 and 25', aimed to examine how young people manage and negotiate their gender identities in everyday contexts. Mostly students, the participants' religious self-identifications included Christian, Muslim, Jewish, Buddhist, Sikh and mixed-faith. A majority were white (64.9 per cent) and heterosexual (74.3 per cent). A significant finding was that, sometimes in conflict with their religion's teachings, most participants of different religious traditions and genders were committed to gender equality.

The researchers also found that participants often felt stigmatized by discursively produced tropes and stereotypes about gender equality and, often, gender-based violence (Page and Yip 2017, 9):

> women's bodies were frequently are marked as carriers of gender inequality and even gender violence (i.e. female genital mutilation), regardless of whether this is actually reflected within lived experience. These sweeping assumptions and framings are so powerful that they disrupt young women's ability to articulate the gender inequalities they *actually* experience.

While some participants affirmed gender equality within their religious traditions, others were explicitly critical, as two of the participants said (Page and Yip 2017, 9):

> What my religion teaches me is equality. That is one of the biggest fundamentals of Sikhism… [But] at the temple, in the committees, it's mainly men.
>
> (Ajeet, Sikh man; interview)

> Islam has been distorted by men to oppress women. The Qur'an gives women rights … But the Islam practised by the majority refers to other scripture to promote gender inequality.
>
> (Amreen, Muslim woman; questionnaire)

Note

1   Turner may not be giving enough weight to Foucault's arguments about conceptions of the body being acculturated to the point that they are internalized as a (false) sense of individual choice – a point stressed by others including, as discussed below, Meredith McGuire (1990).

Indicative reading

Adorno, Theodor, and Max Horkheimer. 1979. *Dialectic of Enlightenment*. London: Verso.
Bam, Brigalia. 1998. 'All about Eve: Woman of Africa.' In *Anglicanism: A Global Communion*, edited by Andrew Wingate, Kevin Ward, Carrie Pemberton and Wilson Sitshebo, 347–53. London: Mowbray.
Beyer, Peter. 1994. *Religion and Globalization*. New York: SAGE.
Bourdieu, Pierre. 1977. *Outline of a Theory of Practice*. Cambridge: Cambridge University Press.
Bowie, Fiona. 2006. *The Anthropology of Religion*. Oxford: Blackwell.
Brown, Callum. 2001. *The Death of Christian Britain*. London: Routledge.
Brown, Callum. 2012. *Religion and the Demographic Revolution*. Woodbridge: Boydell Press.
Bruce, Steve. 1988. *The Rise and Fall of the New Christian Right: Conservative Protestant Politics in America, 1978–1988*. Oxford: Clarendon Press.
Bruce, Steve. 2016. *Religion in Secular Society Fifty Years on*. Oxford: Oxford University Press.
Butler, Judith. 1990. *Gender Trouble: Feminism and the Subversion of Identity*. New York: Routledge.
Campbell-Reed, Eileen. 2016. *Anatomy of a Schism: How Clergywomen's Narratives Reinterpret the Fracturing of the Southern Baptist Convention*. Knoxville, TN: University of Tennessee Press.
Collins, Patricia Hill. 2000. *Black Feminist Thought: Knowledge, Consciousness and Empowerment*, 2nd edition. Boston, MA: Unwin Hyman.
Day, Abby. 2005. 'Doing Theodicy: An Empirical Study of a Women's Prayer Group.' *Journal of Contemporary Religion* 20, no. 3: 343–56.
Day, Abby. 2017. *The Religious Lives of Older Laywomen: The Last Active Anglican Generation*. Oxford: Oxford University Press.
De Beauvoir, Simone. 1949. *The Second Sex*. Harmondsworth, Middlesex: Penguin Books.
Fackre, Gabriel. 1983. *The Religious Right and Christian Faith*. Grand Rapids, MI: William B. Eerdmans.
Featherstone, Mike, Mike Hepworth and Bryan S. Turner. 1991. *The Body: Social Process and Cultural Theory*. London: SAGE.

Fraser, Nancy. 1996. 'Social Justice in the Age of Identity Politics: Redistribution, Recognition and Participation.' In The Tanner Lectures on Human Values. Delivered at Stanford University, 20 Apr.–2 May 1996.

Foucault, Michel. 1977. *Discipline and Punish*. New York: Pantheon.

Foucault, Michel. 1990. *The History of Sexuality*, vol. 1, translated by Robert Hurley. New York: Pandom House. First published in 1978.

Friedland, Roger. 2001. 'Religious Nationalism and the Problem of Collective Representation.' *Annual Review of Sociology* 27: 125–52.

Friedland, Roger. 2002 'Money, Sex and God: The Erotic Logic of Religious Nationalism.' *Sociological Theory* 20, no. 3: 381–425.

Goffman, Erving. 1959. *The Presentation of Self in Everyday Life*. London: Penguin.

Himmelstein, Jerome L. 1983. 'The New Right.' In *The New Christian Right,* edited by R. C. Liebman and R. Wuthnow, 15–30. New York: Aldine de Gruyter.

Hunter, James D. 1983. 'The Liberal Reaction.' In *The New Christian Right,* edited by R. C. Liebman and R. Wuthnow, 150–67. New York: Aldine de Gruyter.

Huntingdon, Samuel P. 1996. *The Clash of Civilizations: Remaking of World Order*. New York: Touchstone.

Johnson, Paul James, and Sylvia Falcetta. 2019. 'Beyond the Anti-Homosexuality Act: Homosexuality and the Parliament of Uganda.' *Parliamentary Affairs,* 3 August, 1–27.

Keenan, Michael. 2015. 'Conditional Love? Assimilation and the Construction of "Acceptable Homosexuality" in Anglicanism.' In *Contemporary Issues in the Worldwide Anglican Communion: Powers and Pieties,* edited by Abby Day, 95–112. Abingdon, Oxon: Routledge.

Konieczny, Mary Ellen, and Mark Chaves. 'Resources, Race and Female-Headed Congregations in the US.' *Journal for the Scientific Study of Religion* 39, no. 3: 261–72.

Kraybill, Donald B. 2003. *The Riddle of Amish Culture*. Baltimore, MD: Johns Hopkins University Press.

Liebman, Robert C., and Robert Wuthnow. 1983. *The New Christian Right*. New York: Aldine.

Lengermann, Patricia M., and Jill Niebrugge-Brantley. 1998. *The Women Founders: Sociology and Social Theory, 1830–1930*. Boston, MA: McGraw-Hill.

Lukes, Steven. 2005. *Power: A Radical View*. Basingstoke: Palgrave Macmillan.

Mahmood, Saba. 2005. *The Politics of Piety: The Islamic Revival and the Feminist Subject*. Princeton, NJ, Oxford: Princeton University Press.

McGuire, Meredith B. 1990. 'Religion and the Body: Rematerializing the Human Body in the Social Sciences of Religion.' *Journal for the Scientific Study of Religion* 29: 283–96.

Mernissi, Fatima. 1987. *Beyond the Veil: Male-Female Dynamics in Modern Muslim Society*. Bloomington, IN: Indiana University Press.

Moghadam, Valentine M. 2013. *Modernizing Women: Gender and Social Change in the Middle East*. London: Lynne Rienner.

Mombo, Esther. 1998. 'Resisting Vumilia Theology: The Church and Violence against Women in Kenya.' In *Anglicanism: A Global Communion*, edited by Andrew Wingate, Kevin Ward, Carrie Pemberton and Wilson Sitshebo, 219–24. London: Mowbray.

Nyhagen, Line. 2019. 'Mosques as Gendered Spaces: The Complexity of Women's Compliance with, and Resistance to, Dominant Gender Norms, and the Importance of Male Allies.' *Religions* 10, no. 5: 321. 10.3390/rel10050321.

Nynäs, Peter, and Andrew Kam-Tuck Yip (eds). 2012. *Religion, Gender and Sexuality in Everyday Life*. London: Routledge.

Ozorak, Elizabeth W. 1996. 'The Power, But Not the Glory: How Women Empower Themselves through Religion.' *Journal for the Scientific Study of Religion* 35: 17–29.

Page, Sarah-Jane, and Andrew Kam-Tuck Yip. 2017. 'Gender Equality and Religion: A Multi-Faith Exploration of Young Adults' Narratives.' *European Journal of Women's Studies* 24, no. 3: 249–65. https://doi.org/10.1177/1350506815625906

Rahman, Momin. 2010. 'Queer as Intersectionality: Theorizing Gay Muslim Identities.' *Sociology* 44, no. 5: 1–18.

Rees, Diana A. 2015. 'To Boldly Go: How do Women in Senior Positions in the Church of England Construe their Leadership?' In *Contemporary Issues in the Worldwide Anglican Communion: Powers and Pieties,* edited by Abby Day, 129–48. Abingdon, Oxon: Routledge.

Scott, Joan. 2007. *The Politics of the Veil.* Princeton, NJ: Princeton University Press.

Shilling, Chris. 1993. *Body and Social Theory.* London: SAGE.

Skeggs, Bev. 1997. *Formations of Class and Gender: Becoming Respectable.* London: SAGE.

Starkey, Caroline. 2020. *Women in British Buddhism: Commitment, Connection, Community.* Abingdon, Oxon, New York:. Routledge.

Strathern, Marilyn. 1984. 'Domesticity and the Denigration of Women.' In *Rethinking Women's Roles: Perspectives from the Pacific,* edited by Denise O'Brien and Sharon W. Tiffany, 13–31. Berkeley, CA: University of California Press.

Swartz, Oswald. 1998. 'New Wine, Old Wineskins: Possibilities for a Rural Diocese in a Changing Society.' In *Anglicanism: A Global Communion,* edited by Andrew Wingate, Kevin Ward, Carrie Pemberton and Wilson Sitshebo, 182–8. London: Mowbray.

Trzebiatowska, Marta, and Steve Bruce. 2012. *Why are Women More Religious than Men?* Oxford: Oxford University Press.

Turner, Bryan S. 1991. *The Body: Social Process and Cultural Theory.* London: SAGE.

Walter, Tony, and Grace Davie. 1998. 'The Religiosity of Women in the Modern West.' *British Journal of Sociology* 49, no. 4: 640–60. www.jstor.org/stable/i225043.

Weber, Max. 1993 [1922]. *The Sociology of Religion.* Boston, MA: Beacon Press.

Wilkins, Amy. 2008. *Wannabes, Goths, and Christians: The Boundaries of Sex, Style, and Status.* Chicago, IL: Chicago University Press.

Woodhead, Linda. 2000. 'Feminism and the Sociology of Religion: From Gender Blindness to Gendered Difference.' In *The Blackwell Companion to Sociology of Religion,* edited by Richard Fenn, 67–84. Oxford: Blackwell.

Woodhead, Linda. 2007. 'Gender Differences in Religious Practice and Significance.' In *The SAGE Handbook of the Sociology of Religion,* edited by James Beckford and N. J. Demerath III, 550–70. Los Angeles: SAGE.

Woodhead, Linda. 2009. 'The Muslim Veil Controversy and European Values.' *Swedish Missiological Themes* 97, no. 1: 89–105.

Wuthnow, Robert. 1994. Sharing the Journey: Support Groups and America's New Quest for Community. New York: Free Press.

Yip, Andrew Kim-Tuck, and Sarah-Jane Page. 2013. *Religious and Sexual Identities: A Multi-Faith Exploration of Young Adults.* Farnham: Ashgate.

Chapter 8

Generations

The reason generation is important is because it allows us to think with, through and against the concept. Sociologists cannot be deterministic and claim that 'all' young people or 'all' old people are or are not religious, as the context will be too different and is itself unstable. What does one mean by 'young'? How does religiosity vary by culture, social class or location? And, perhaps most importantly, how do we know? Arguably, young people and children are so under-researched that any broad statements and generalizations need to be treated cautiously (https://discoversociety.org/2016/02/02/the-missing-third-that-skews-sociology/). For a number of good studies exploring the formation of children and religious transmission see, for example, Rachael Shillitoe and Anna Strhan. 2020; Anna Strhan and Rachael Shillitoe 2019; Anna Strhan 2015a, 2015b; Jonathan Scourfield, Sophie Gilliat-Ray, Asma Khan and Sameh Otri 2013; Susan B. Ridgely 2011.

The broad sociological literature on ageing and generation tends to neglect religion, lacks diversity and often conflates separate but similar terms such as cohort and life course.

Thinking with words

Life course theory is a way of analysing a person's life relative to a number of other factors. Elizabeth Hutchison (2011) suggests the principle components include: relationships to others sharing the same time period (cohorts), transitions, trajectories, life events and turning points. Those who advocate the theory stress that each individual element, such as a 'transition', can only be properly understood within the context of the whole life story. Critics argue that the theory can be essentialized, applying it equally to all people and conflating it with biology.

Cohort is a word originally applied to a group in the military, but is now commonly used to refer to people grouped by the researcher according to a single variable, such as 'all students in year two' or, commonly in statistical analysis, age. Norman B. Ryder's (1965, 845) long-standing definition is 'the aggregate of individuals (within some population definition) who experience the same event within the same time interval'.

Generation is a term adopted by sociologists who imagine a 'cohort' as something more than a group, or strata of people identified by being born around the same time and experiencing similar events, but who, as Karl Mannheim (1952 [1923]) suggested, were formed by self-recognition of each other as formed by those events.

Broad, large-scale research indicates that the prevailing trend is for young people to be religious to the same or lesser extent than the previous generations. The Pew Research Center (www.pewforum.org/2018/06/13/young-adults-around-the-world-are-less-religious-by-several-measures/) regularly conducts global surveys asking respondents in 106 countries to state their current religion, if any, with country-specific options, including having no religion. They report that there was no difference in age groups' responses in the majority (63) of countries, but in 41 countries younger people are more likely than older to claim no religious affiliation, with only two countries (Chad and Ghana) having young adults who are more likely than older to identify with a religion. When analysed with a question about how important religion is in their lives, Georgia showed a similar age differential of younger adults compared with older. The age gap between affiliated and non-affiliated respondents was larger in those countries with a predominantly Christian population. By way of explanation, the report suggests that economic development may explain the pattern, as: 'worries about day-to-day survival become less pervasive and tragic events become less frequent'. The report added that, 'According to this line of thinking, each generation in a steadily developing society would be less religious than the last, which would explain why young adults are less religious than their elders at any given time.'

When sociologists consider how religion may change over time, generation is one of several analytical tools that is used to allow scrutiny of one variable, but it is just one variable. For example, looking at broad trends by age in many northern European countries, it might be said that young people, considered in terms of what they 'believe', how they practise church-based religion or how they consume popular culture, may be less religious than previous generations, and this would be generally uncontested. It would also mean, however, that in applying theories to this trend the sociologist must avoid attributing too much causality to that single variable. If, for example, that trend was explained by engaging with theories of modernity and secularization, the researcher might conclude that a more scientific, rational way of thinking of the world is more prevalent as societies become more 'modern', and that would explain the trend. Additionally, some might argue that a development of the roles of government, including the growth of welfare states, replaced religion and contributed to less religious generations (see e.g. Bäckström 2015; Davie 2005). What, however, would we make of large numbers of people in their twenties who have become more religious? Is this, too, to be seen within modernity theory as, perhaps, a reaction against a trend to modernize? What of teenagers who strongly believe in a life after death, yet would not self-identify as religious or spiritual? Are teenagers who participate in witchcraft irrational or unscientific? Or perhaps some other theory is required, such as post-modernity, or post-secularity.

The challenge, therefore, is to look at 'generations' while avoiding generalizations (Day 2014). Young people may be seen variously as more religious and less religious than their parents, depending on place and social context. Simultaneously, there is rapid growth amongst previously secular youth adopting the dress and religious habits of their parents' religions. This chapter explores here how religion can be a strong social marker for young people who seek both to differentiate themselves from others and to experience new forms of 'community' and social identity. The arguments to be explore here will draw from much prevailing theory about authenticity, individualism and relationality, but also take a critical, circumspect stand to avoid a crass correlation that would imply older, more religious generations are not authentic or relational.

'Generation': a contested concept

Although the term 'generation' is often used unproblematically, the critical scholar will dig into the assumptions that are embedded: is generation an age group? Can generations be compared cross-culturally? Is there a set time between generations that mark the younger from the older? Who is a young person? An old person?

One of the first steps in untangling this problem is to realize that 'young' and 'old' are relational terms. One can only be 'young' by being compared to another group that is considered 'old'. Sociologists are usually therefore careful to define more precisely what they mean by the term. Perceptions of age are socially determined and change by context. Some have legal implications, such as the age when a person can marry, vote, have sex or drink alcohol, but all are perceptions that reflect a certain society at a certain the time, rather than a biological age.

Age and alcohol

Consuming or buying alcohol is often illegal for all people, regardless of age, because of religious prohibitions. Many countries ban alcohol for everyone, even visitors. Some, but not all, countries set legal age limits for drinking alcohol and different limits for buying it. And yet, these are difficult to compare easily as often the conditions for legal consumption also vary. This may mean, for example, drinking is legal at home but not in restaurants, or with parents but not alone. In the United States, it is generally illegal for anyone under the age of 21 to consume alcohol in a public location, but many states allow drinking for religious purposes or at home with parents. In Wales, one can legally drink at home from the age of 5 whereas in the Central African Republic it is 15. At the time of writing, there were nearly 100 countries in the world, from Belgium to Uganda, without age limits relating to consuming alcohol.

Age and voting

The average age in the world at which voting begins is 18, although for some countries, such as Ecuador and Scotland, it is 16, and in others much higher: the oldest is the United Arab Emirates at 25.

Age and marriage

The worldwide average age for legal marriage is 16, with considerable variation. In China, men must wait until they are 22, and women until 20. In parts of the United States, children as young as 12 can be married with parental consent. Early-age American marriage is generally related to religion, writes Jeremy Uecker (2014), with the most conservative Christian sects tending towards younger marriages.

Age and military service

Most countries have either voluntary or compulsory military service, with an average age of 18. Some countries allow 'conscientious objection' for religious reasons, and many interpretations of Islam prohibit killing other Muslims, making military service in countries at war with Muslim countries problematic.

Anthropologists have distinguished between an 'age grade', such as infant or elderly, and an 'age set' which refers to a cohort of people, who are usually in a similar age grade, who engage together through initiation practices that mark their transition to a more mature stage, able to acquire responsibilities in kinship and community groups. Even so, such terms as 'kin' have become challenged and more nuanced over time, following David Schneider's (1980) study which showed that people did not necessarily view their 'kin' in strictly biological terms. Who and what is a family is often more than simply the people one is raised with, but those with whom one has developed strong bonds.

Early anthropological studies into initiation practices are often given as examples to explain socially symbolic rituals that mark a passage through time towards full person-hood and the recognition of acceptance by an older, established community. Arnold van Gannep's (1960) three-part schema is widely used in both sociology and anthro-pology: first a person leaves behind their old life, perhaps by leaving home to be married; then, there is a period of no-life, no-identity, an in-between or 'liminal state', perhaps in a car *en route* to the wedding venue; and three, where the person is admitted into another social group that confers a new identity, perhaps by a religious or judicial figure proclaiming them part of the new, married couple. This is a means of initiation not linked to age, van Gannep argued, but to becoming a member of a new group.

When Kati Niemelä (2008) decided to research the phenomenon of young people's engagement with the Evangelical Lutheran Church, the national church of Finland, the *rite de passage* of 'confirmation' was only part of the story. In many Christian sects, a Christian family will have their child baptized as an infant or young child, marking their welcome into the church. When a child is older, they usually embark on a process of 'confirmation'. Confirmation is an important stage in a Christian's spiritual journey when candidates study, usually for a year, details of their church's theology and then, at a special ceremony, make a lifetime pledge to Christ. In Finland, the preparation process lasts approximately one year, consisting of several meetings, church visits and an eight-day summer camp.

That so many young people engaged in confirmation was not surprising to Niemelä; that they left the church only a few years following their confirmation was the real puzzle, particularly when 'confirmation' symbolizes a person's transition from religiously passive to fully committed. The interesting question was not 'why did they choose to commit?' but, after only a short while, 'why did they choose to leave?', and in such unprecedented numbers? In her study, Niemelä (2008, 48) asked respondents several questions about their beliefs in God, designed to probe their sense of both belief and belonging. Of those who had completed the confirmation training, 46 per cent agreed with the statement 'I believe in God but I am not a "believer"'. Only 9 per cent agreed that 'I am a believer' and only 7 per cent chose 'I do not believe that there is a God'. When I asked Kati Niemelä if that meant the respondents did not feel they belonged to a group of religious people, yet wanted to express their belief in God, she replied:

> When the youngsters in Finland talk about 'believers' they tend to refer to that small group of very religious and often also morally strict. So when one agrees to this item, she/he is most likely saying something like (and our open questions in the survey also reveal this): 'Yes, I do believe in God and have a faith in Him, but I do not I belong to that small group of active ones nor do I totally live according to my faith.'

This suggests that the idea of 'belief' is located for many people in specific social contexts and not others. Niemelä's answer to unlocking the puzzle posed at the beginning of her longitudinal study lay in participants' familial background. Although many participated in the confirmation training, and particularly enjoyed the summer camp, those who came from non-religious backgrounds did not continue with their church involvement, and said they had never found the experience particularly meaningful. And yet, as most children in Finland are not raised in religious family life, those who stayed would also have come from a non-religious background. The pattern of religious belonging in Nordic countries is itself unusual: traditionally, people are automatically members of their national churches unless they decide to opt out. The majority stay, even though the majority will also say they do not believe in God or find religion significant in their lives. Niemelä argued that the generation she studied, described as Generation Y born from the 1980s and to early 2000s, is different from the older generations and more likely to opt out. This is partly because, in Finland, the rules were changed to allow opt out by email rather than in person, and also, she concluded, because (Niemelä 2015, 184):

> For members of Generation Y, their attitude to religion and the Church follows a different pattern from that of earlier generations. They primarily make individual decisions based on their own beliefs and life-view and no longer belong to religious institutions because of tradition.

Age and religious change

One of the most keenly contested concepts in the sociology of religion relates to the definitions proposed at the outset of this chapter: do people change their religious beliefs or practices through life-course influences, and become less or more religious as they age, or do they change because of some wider 'cohort' or 'generational' effect? The argument is lost or won depending on how the data are interpreted. For example, simply comparing a current population in their twenties with people in their eighties may show that the older group is more religious and thus could lead to an assumption that people become more religious as they age. This approach, however, would not take into consideration longitudinal data; what, for example, happens to those same people over time? When analysed longitudinally, research often shows that religious change is usually generational, not life-course-based. For example, research in the Netherlands (De Graaf and Grotenhuis 2008, 595–6) concluded that religious belief will continue to decline due to cohort replacement. They found that people did not become more religious as they age: 'in the Netherlands for the years to come, a continuing "silent secularisation revolution" in which both religious belief and religious affiliation decline is the most likely longitudinal trend and not a large-scale religious revival'. (For similar studies in the UK and Europe see Pollack 2008; Crockett and Voas 2006).

Exploring why those generations are different requires careful and complex analysis, considering what factors contribute to those 'cohorts' being different especially if, as Mannheim (1952 [1923], 191) argued, generations are not defined by biology or time spans:

> Whether a new generation style emerges every year, every thirty, every hundred years, or whether it emerges rhythmically at all, depends entirely on the trigger action of the social and cultural process.

It is the act of identifying with other members of one's cohort shaped by a social and cultural process that creates the 'generation'. Many who were young adults in the 1960s recognize each other as members of the 'flower-power' or 'counter-cultural' generation, just as many of their parents may recognize each other as members of the 'war-time' or 'air-raid' generations. Research on the oldest age strata in the Anglican churches of the UK and North America (Day 2017, Day 2015) concluded that salient identity differences between those two generations could help explain the churches' rapid generational decline, a phenomenon that is generally accepted. The Church of England's director of finance, John Spence, said in 2015 that the evidence for decline being due to demographic changes was 'indisputable' (www.theguardian.com/world/2015/nov/21/justin-welby-church-englandnew-synod,   last accessed Sept. 2016):

> Twenty years ago the demographics matched the population as a whole. Now we're 20 years older than the population. Unless we do something, the church will face a real crisis.

Archbishop of Canterbury Justin Welby told the *Guardian* newspaper that the church's renewal campaigns were trying to defuse the Church of England's 'demographic time bomb' (www.theguardian.com/world/2015/nov/21/justin-welby-church-englandnew-Synod, last accessed Sept. 2016).

It is not only older people in the mainstream churches that show the impact of being a final, active generation. Eileen Barker (2011) explored the changing demographic profile of new religious movements and found there was a variety of patterns. Nonetheless, if understood by her definition as a movement that only exists and grows because it attracts converts, a new religious movement (NRM) is likely to have an ageing profile if the group fails to reproduce or quickly attract new members. The nature of NRMs was discussed in more detail in Chapter 3, but here it is worthwhile noting that a strong characteristic of an NRM is its communal nature. Retaining worldly goods and money for individual use is often discouraged, and therefore the care of elderly people is often difficult because sufficient 'pension' money may not have been set aside.

In his study on religion, ageing and (in)equality, Peter Kevern (2019) examined how the main UK religions – Christianity, Judaism, Islam, Hinduism, Sikhism and Buddhism – created both equality and inequality for older people. He found that the results could be placed on a continuum, with at one end religions which created positive, equal environments for elderly people, and, at the other end of the spectrum, those that did not. In positive ways, some religions created healthy, connected environments and helped elderly people, particularly from ethnic minorities, access government services they might otherwise miss. The more negative experiences were created often because, for example, some religious beliefs and the institutions that promote them (Kevern (2019, 218) 'may impede access to resources by misdiagnosis (e.g. of mental illness as a spiritual condition) or as a result of concerns about how service provision may violate religious codes (e.g. by having a female non-relative bathe an older man)'. Whether positive or negative, Kevern (2019, 219) points to the difficulty of making generalizations, advising that 'the question of whether religions impede or promote equality for older people can only be answered by reference to particular individuals in particular social and historical contexts'.

A three-year, multi-country project, directed by Peter Nynäs at Åbo Akademi University, explored the religious and non-religious life views of young people (the often-called digital natives). The context the Young Adults and Religion in a Global Perspective project framed was one of global media influence, consumerism, social movements and increasing polarization between pluralism and radicalization.[1]

An important early paper developing the area of religious socialization was authored by Ghanaian scholar Ben-Willie Kwaku Golo with colleagues (Golo et al. 2019). They show that, while most theories, and emerging findings from the project thus far, identify family as a key area for religious socialization, the current millennial generation also ascribes secondary sources of socialization, such as friends, media and secular education.

Case example: young people and Anglicanism

What is defined as 'decline' varies according to what is measured. Leslie Francis and Gemma Penny (2015, 56) reviewed how claims about the decline of Anglicanism are measured, and urged scholars to ensure that analysis matches criteria: 'These three notions of belonging, practising and believing may provide three very different profiles of the Church of England, offering considerable scope for theoretical reflection and for empirical enquiry […] Each in its own way is a socially significant indicator of a different dimension of religiosity.' Francis and Penny analysed a large dataset of 33,982 teenagers, originally created by Francis in 2001, to explore self-assigned religious identity. They set out to respond to three questions: the worldview of young people who claim no religious affiliation (not belonging); a comparison between those teenagers with other teenagers who identify as Anglicans but do not attend church; and then an exploration of three categories of churchgoing Anglicans: those who attend occasionally, those who attend less than weekly and those who attend most weeks (weekly churchgoers). The researchers' new study updated the 2001 data by adding 12,252 schools. It was also decided only to focus on males aged between 13 and 15.

Their study generated some interesting findings, demonstrating considerable variety both within and in comparison to the selected categories. For example, while those in the unaffiliated group maintained a low knowledge and low interest in religion, roughly a third attended church for rites of passage and a high proportion expressed interest in other religions and ideas of immortality (and see Chapter 12 for a more detailed discussion of non-religious belief in immortality). They also maintained fairly strict moral codes. Those who did not attend church but affiliated as Anglican differed from the unaffiliated by holding stronger beliefs in God, the importance of the church and life after death. Their moral code was like the unaffiliated. The third group, whose attendance varied from rarely to frequently, expressed stronger beliefs in God but were much the same on moral issues, apart from pre-marital sex, which became less tolerated as church attendance increased.

Sylvia Collins-Mayo's (2015, 21) study of young people and Anglican identity found a similar range of activity amongst research participants. She also supported the idea that 'People's religious beliefs and practices tend to be settled by the time they reach their early 20s and if they are not religiously inclined in their youth, they are unlikely to become so in later years'. Her study analysed data collected for The Faith of Generation Y study, which had surveyed young people who attended Christian youth work projects in England. Nearly half those young people attending affiliated their religious identity to the Church of England, and yet many did not actively engage with the church. For example, one of the teenagers said (Collins-Mayo 2015, 27): 'hadn't thought about it really. … It don't really bother me'. Collins-Mayo found that while many of the young people maintained a Church of England or Christian identity, that kind of identity was based on their family's religious background or some kind of cultural identity: 'Ashley was a case in point: "Well, I haven't really got a religion. I'm mainly Christian because my family's a bit Christian".'

She also found (Collins-Mayo 2015, 28) that her research corroborated findings[2] from other researchers in the field:

> Various studies show young people rank family and friends as the most important aspect of their lives (Collins 1997; Savage et al. 2006; Day 2010). It is in these tangible relationships that they tend to put their trust and find their faith, rather than in God or Jesus. The same was found in this research.

Her study also discovered that, whether religious or not, young people maintained a strong belief in ethics and living a morally good life.

The 'baby-boomer' effect

In 2020, half of the UK population was aged over 50. The UK population became rapidly less Christian during the last 50 years, and many scholars argue that the catalyst was the baby-boomer generation – the post-World War II babies who were born between

1944 and 1960, raised in the 1950s consumerist boom and were the chief architects and agitators of the 1960s cultural revolution. Similar patterns exist in North America (principally Canada, whose national census mirrors closely the UK's religious demography) and northern Europe, at least amongst Protestants.

The boomers were less religious than their parents – 'Generation A' – and they then raised a generation of even less religious children, born in the 1980s and early 1990s, now known as the Millennials, and dominating the category of the non-religious 'Nones'. The most recent British Social Attitudes survey at the time of writing (2019, www. bsa.natcen.ac.uk/latest-report/british-social-attitudes-36/religion.aspx, last accessed May 2020) showed that the number of people with no religion and who were raised without religion, increased from 11 per cent in 1998 to 23 per cent in 2018. In these ways, boomers have been the catalyst of this century's intense religious change. Yet why so many gave up religion and transmitted non-religious values and practices to the next generation remains something of a mystery. A review of Gallup surveys covering religion from 1939 to 1999 (Field 2015) reveals that consistently most respondents affirm that their religious values were set as children. Despite their upbringing, many boomer Anglicans left the church, never to return apart from participation in occasional cultural and lifecycle events. The study is important because theories maintain that the key to religious sustainability is inter-generational transmission and yet most of those boomers rejected the religiosity of their childhoods in their late teens or early adulthood and have never reclaimed it, and nor have they raised religiously observant children, contributing to generational decline in Euro-American Christianity.

Many scholars cite the 1960s cultural revolution as the critical period when boomers apparently rejected church, religion, respect for institutions, care for community and obedience to a higher moral authority. Scholars tend to agree that the causal influences likely include feminism, consumerism, pluralism, the power of choice and a preference for an individualized, non-institutional authenticity (Brown 2000; Bellah et al. 1985; Roof 1993,1999; Snape and Brown 2016; Wilson 1966, Wuthnow 1998). Brown's claim for the death of Christian Britain: 'the demise of the nation's core religious and moral identity' (Brown 2000, 1) rests on what he perceives as a sudden shift in 1963 amongst the two generations who matured in the last 30 years of the 20th century. These would be the boomers and their progeny. The shift in the following decade was, he argued (Brown 2000, 176), sudden and violent, with a quick series of major changes as the 'institutional structures of cultural traditionalism started to crumble in Britain'. Some scholars (Brown 2012, 2015, 2017; Cook 2004; McLeod 2007) suggest the 1960s cultural milieu, particularly the feminist turn, may have had a longer tail. Brown (2017; Brown and Lynch 2012; Snape and Brown 2016) refer to the 'long sixties' of 1957–75, in which there arose a new 'moral cosmos' as people began to more and more doubt the supposed truths and authority of religion and turned to broader ideas of human and natural rights. It has also been observed that the porous boundaries between religion and spirituality may shift over time (Wink and Dillon 2003).

While most scholars focus on an apparent shift in cultural values during the 1960s, it is important to retain caution in adopting a single explanation for the idea of 'generation', particularly given the vast diversity of the women studied. While not a homogeneous group, the pattern was established for large swathes of women to attend church regularly in the 1950s and 1960s, with their families. In Euro-American countries, the challenges of wartime, nation rebuilding, austerity, domestication and consumerism all influenced the women of 'Generation A', who were teenagers and young adults during the World War II. Many had careers and families during the 1950s consumerist boom, and were often portrayed as ideal mothers and wives. Their lives and beliefs have been relatively unexplored but are frequently presented as the counterpoint to the counter-cultural and feminist revolutions of the 1960s. To some extent, those women and their characteristics may have been over-generalized and romanticized, with their progeny set up as clearly different and even liberated: where 'the individual is now free from the bonds typical of pre-individualist society – nature, church and the absolutist state – and could enjoy the advantages of independence and rationality' (Guibernau 2013, 16).

Perhaps the seeds of the cultural revolution were sown by the women who raised their children in the 1950s and early 1960s. The cultural changes that occurred in the 1960s were profound, affecting music, social and economic structures, and the rapid expansion of higher education. Global changes were occurring on an unprecedented scale, including increased migrations, modernizations, globalized economies, neoliberalism and mediatization (more of which will be explored in Chapter 10).

As one Generation A woman described it (Day 2017, 35), the cultural change began in the 1960s: 'the hippy era, what was this, the sixties? [...] Yeah. I think that's probably when it started. It was the sixties I think, yeah.' David Kynaston concludes that (2009, 596, 597): '1950s parents were, taken as a whole, significantly less old school than the previous generation of parents [...] The overall sense is of parenthood on the cusp of fundamental change by the early to mid-1950s.' Nevertheless, as he points out (Kynaston 2009, 558), the idea of motherhood and ideal family were clearly linked to ideas about the nation as a whole: 'Normative assumptions identifying the moral and social health of the nation with the moral and social health of the family.' These may be particularly strong in producing emotions and beliefs about nationalism, as discussed in Chapter 4.

The cultural, political and sexual revolution of the 1960s began to undermine androcentric assumptions for many teenagers and young women, who began to question institutions, patriarchy and authority in ways their mothers may have hinted at, but generally did not challenge directly. For religion, the impact was significant as the 1960s generation rejected much of what their mothers, the Generation A, had loved and held as sacred: God, the Queen, the family and nation, represented by and sedimented in the revered unchanging institutions of the Church of England and the wider Anglican Communion.

Young people retaining and reviving religion

As described at the outset of this chapter, there are theories of modernity which suppose that the more a society modernizes, the less religious it becomes. There are, however, counterarguments, particularly in light of the evidence of people maintaining or increasing their religiosity.

In his research into contemporary young British Sikhs, Jasjit Singh (2010) addressed such arguments as he conducted research into the processes of religious and cultural transmission in the lives of British South Asians, particularly young (aged 18–32) British Sikhs. He wondered how they were influenced by migration, ethnicity and minority status. He further explored, in the context of modernity theories that focus on subjectivization, how young British Sikhs negotiated their experiences of maintaining individual authority within membership of a religious community.

His research was based on 25 semi-structured interviews with young Sikh men and women holding varying degrees of visible observance of the five outward signs of adherence: uncut hair; comb, sword, cotton breeches, steel or iron bangle. Singh wanted to find out how young British Sikhs viewed keeping the hair and turban, what those symbols mean to them, what issues they faced in maintaining those outward signs, and how those symbols fit with their ideas of being both British and Sikh. He found that there were a number of reasons young British Sikhs continued to display those signs, ranging from: a desire post-9/11 to differentiate themselves from Muslims, even amongst non-religious British Sikhs; a feeling that they wanted to fit in with their religious families and communities; and a need to express their deeper forms of religious belief. Many also signalled that they wanted to exercise their right to wear religious clothing if they so desired. Singh (2010, 216) wrote:

> It is also clear that the majority of the respondents feel both British and Sikh; having been born in Britain, they feel that they have an automatic right to wear the turban. Indeed, it appears that young British Sikhs are confidently integrating the turban in their daily dress, with a new trend of different turbans for different social contexts emerging, possibly in response to the smart/casual dress culture.

This clearly showed that many young Sikhs held in place both their identities as a Sikh and as a citizen of a 'modern', western society.

Abamfo Ofori Atiemo (2013) explored why the Ghanaian population is strongly religious. He frames his discussion through a theoretical lens of 'spiritual capital' which he defined as (Atiemo 2013, 85) 'The widespread belief in Ghana that spiritual power resides in the invisible world and can be accessed for improving the quality of life'. He described a lengthy history of religious involvement in public as well as private life, including defiance against colonialism and other governmental breaches of human rights. Currently, he says, religion manifests strongly in people's daily lives. Most public events have a religious component, and even in the workplace it is common to break for prayers and to have religion-focused discussion groups. People in Ghana believe, he continues, that religion is not simply important to provide spiritual sustenance, but also assures material and career success.

Atiemo (2013, 99) confronts theories of religion and modernity by suggesting that ideas promulgated in social science theory about religious revitalization in Africa being linked to strategies to counter the anxieties of modernity are weak and should be challenged. Religion in Africa, he argued, has not been simply 'a reactive mechanism to crisis situations' and has a number of features, including causing significant social change. Religion also 'prompted changes in thought-patterns; provided new perspectives on fundamental issues of ultimate concern; generated alterations in existing worldviews; and provided new ideas and expressions that have challenged, or at least, shaken the older order'.

Another generally promoted idea in social science is about the comparatively recent tendency towards individualism, a quality Atiemo says was instituted by Christianity, with its focus on individual salvation and accountability. Further, he warns scholars against adopting a commonly held trope that western societies are individualistic and African societies are communal. This, he argues (Atiemo 2013, 102), is 'an overstatement; much of it is more an invention by scholars than a fact borne out of historical evidence'. Many traditional African and notably Ghanaian societies have been and are still individualistic, competitive and in many ways capitalistic.

The themes of individualism run through many scholars' works, to explain why they think young people have turned from religion to other sources of meaning and happiness, principally in human relationships, and why they think those sources may be insufficient for coping with life's problems and need for wider participation in society (Clydesdale 2007; Mason et al. 2007; Regnerus et al. 2004; Savage et al. 2006; Smith et al. 2011). In contrast, my longitudinal research (Day 2013) did not find that young people were drifting through an amoral universe or unable to cope with life's challenges, but were informed and sustained by their social relationships and sense of belonging.

Mathew Guest, Kristin Aune, Sonya Sharma and Rob Warner (2013a, 2013b), in the largest study of its kind to that date, surveyed 4,000 UK undergraduate university students from 13 universities and interviewed 75 (and 25 staff) between 2009 and 2012. They situated their research within a cultural milieu that generally associated university-based Christianity with evangelicalism, with a focus on 'belief' as synonymous with religious identity. They were interested in the extent to which Christian students associated with one or more Christian orientations, and whether the university educational and social experience influenced their religious identities.

As they discussed, a period at university is often thought to be a time of change for students from religious backgrounds, perhaps entering as devout adherents and leaving as atheist radicals. The reality is, they found, far more complex (and see also Sophie Gilliat-Ray 2000), with the supposed spiritual-religious boundary often crossed, and most students not identifying as evangelical. Of those who self-identified as 'Christian' 40.4 per cent regarded themselves as 'religious', while 31.2 per cent were 'not religious but spiritual'.

Another finding, pertinent to the understanding of religious change, was that few students claimed to be involved in alternative religious or spiritual movements, mirroring to some extent, the authors note, findings from other studies such as Savage et al. (2006), Heelas and Woodhead (2005) and Smith and Denton (2005). Further, they found that university chaplains were often central to the students' lives. In a later report, Kristin Aune, Mathew Guest and Jeremy Law (2019) discussed the increasingly multi-faith characteristics of universities and a corresponding, if slow, increase in multi-faith chaplaincies.

In conclusion, they saw that Christianity worked for the students as a portable cultural resource, helping them find new friendships and new meanings, while staying connected to their pre-university lives and values. In answer to one of their main research questions, they concluded that, for the majority, the university experience did not affect the students' religious identity that they arrived with: nearly three-quarters remained the same.

Religion, youth and politics

Religious youth were largely responsible for what has been variously described as the 'Arab Spring', a term that has become increasingly contested for being overly general and ignoring the considerable differences that existed within the countries involved. Most scholars and those directly involved prefer a more nuanced and accurate term such as 'transitions in the Arab world'.

The Egyptian revolution of 2011 relied significantly on the actions of the Society of Muslim Brothers, more widely known as the Muslim Brotherhood, which had been active for decades, particularly in rural regions where they delivered medical and educational materials and services. This kind of involvement led to them becoming 'the most successful grassroots movement across the entire region', writes Magdi Abdelhadi, former BBC Arab Affairs correspondent (www.theguardian.com/commentisfree/2012/jun/25/muslim-brotherhood-egypt, last accessed Feb. 2019):

> Their hospitals and other charity work have been a key component in their history to evolve as a movement from and to the people. This has often been criticised by their rivals as bribing the electorate. That may very well appear to be so at times of election. But their bond with their constituencies is not seasonal. Care for the poor and the weak is central to Islamic teaching, and they would not have enjoyed the support they do if they had not lived up to those ideals.

A young Egyptian involved in the revolution remarked that (Day 2019, 156) 'the cultural context I live in is the biggest influence in my life, and Islam more now than ever'. He said that the shift in Egypt towards increased religious involvement was mainly influenced by young people. Three decades earlier, he said, the political regime was opposed to conservative religious practices: 'you wouldn't see women in niqab but now people aren't against Islamists'. The sudden visibility in the political arena of conservative Islam was a surprise to many young people, one of whom mused that (Day 2019, 155): 'Our Salafi friends were never involved in the public sphere. We didn't know the difference between the Muslim Brotherhood or Salafis or that there were six different forms of Salafism.'

The nature of religious involvement in Egypt was affected significantly by politics. Ahdaf Soueif (2012) described the spectre of inter-religious violence as a feature of the Mubarak regime, and that it was something rejected by the young people, forcing his removal through revolution. She reported that, during the occupation of Tahrir Square during the first weeks of the revolution, both Muslim and Christian prayers were said on Fridays and Sundays, and 'Amens' rang out across the square after the prayers on both days. She also said that she had been reliably informed by young activists that the widely reported violence against Coptic Christians was carried out by state police, not the young revolutionaries. In one case, activists were able to convince the parents of young murdered Christians to demand autopsies. When these were carried out, they showed that the young people had been shot, with weaponry only available to the police or army.

A man from Tunisia, where the first revolution of the period took place, said (Day 2019, 154) that there had been significant in-fighting amongst religious and political groups. He described an incident when someone switched the Tunisian flag for the Salafi flag on a public building: 'this caught attention!'

Researching young people and the 2011 revolution in Tunisia, Ken Roberts, Siyka Kovacheva and Stanimir Kabaivanov (2017) found that most young people showed their strongest affiliation to Islamic groups, followed by Arab then Tunisian. And yet, when asked to agree or disagree with four statements about religion and politics, most said they wanted to see religion and politics kept separate, even though they would describe themselves personally as religious. The study also clearly showed that, while most political activists were more religious than other Tunisian youth, they also wanted politics and religion to be kept separate. This included being against religious leaders influencing government decisions or people with strong religious beliefs taking on representative posts.

In Chapter 4, the intersection of religion and politics is discussed more widely.

Sample questions for private study

1   What are some of the strengths and weaknesses of applying social transmission theories to a range of religions?
2   What do you think young people desire differently, compared to previous generations, that might explain their religious choices?

Sample class exercise

A visit to a space students would consider as 'sacred', considering how young people inhabit it and create it as a sacred space.

Notes

1   At the time of writing, most of the project's publications are still forthcoming and it is advised to check the project website for further information: www.abo.fi/en/yarg-young-adults-and-religion/ and, for an overview of findings, see www.pewresearch.org/wp-content/uploads/sites/7/2017/10/Nynäs-Pew-2017.pdf.
2   A vast literature on youth could be cited here: see Indicative reading section.

Indicative reading

Atiemo, Abamfo Ofori. 2013. *Religion and the Inculturation of Human Rights in Ghana* . London: Bloomsbury Academic.

Aune, Kristin, Mathew Guest and Jeremy Law. 2019. *Chaplains on Campus: Understanding Chaplaincy in UK Universities*. Coventry, Durham, Canterbury: Coventry University, Durham University, Canterbury Christ Church University.

Bäckström, Anders. 2015. 'Welfare, Society and Secularization.' In *Modernities, Memory and Mutations: Grace Davie and the Study of Religion,* edited by Abby Day and Mia Lövheim, 147–62. Aldershot: Ashgate.

Barker, Eileen. 2011. 'Ageing in New Religions: The Varieties of Later Experiences.' *Diskus* 12: 1–23.

Bellah, Robert N., Richard Madsen, William M. Sullivan, Ann Swidler and Steven M. Tipton. 1985. *Habits of the Heart: Individualism and Commitment in American Life*. Berkeley, CA: University of California Press.

Brown, Callum. 2000. *The Death of Christian Britain*. London: Routledge.

Brown, Callum. 2012. *Religion and the Demographic Revolution*. Woodbridge: Boydell Press.

Brown, Callum. 2015. 'How Anglicans Lose Religion: An Oral History of Becoming Secular.' In *Contemporary Issues in the Worldwide Anglican Communion: Powers and Pieties*, edited by Abby Day, 245–66. Aldershot: Ashgate.

Brown, Callum. 2017. *Becoming Atheist: Humanism and the Secular West*. London, New York: Bloomsbury.

Brown, Callum, and Gordon Lynch. 2012. 'Cultural Perspectives' In *Religion and Change in Modern Britain*, edited by Linda Woodhead and Rebecca Catto, 329–35. London: Routledge.

Clydesdale, Tim. 2007. *The First Year Out, Understanding American Teens*. Chicago, IL: University of Chicago Press.

Collins-Mayo, Sylvia. 2015. 'The Meaning and Inheritance of Anglican Identity amongst Young People.' In *Contemporary Issues in the Worldwide Anglican Communion, Powers and Pieties*, edited by Abby Day, 21–38. Aldershot: Ashgate.

Collins-Mayo, Sylvia. 2015. 'Young People and Residual Christian Culture.' In *Modernities, Memory and Mutations: Grace Davie and the Study of Religion*, edited by Abby Day and Mia Lövheim, 179–94. Aldershot: Ashgate.

Cook, Hera. 2004. *The Long Sexual Revolution: English Women, Sex and Contraception 1800–1975*. Oxford: Oxford University Press.

Crockett, Alasdair, and David Voas. 2006. 'Generations of Decline: Religious Change in Twentieth-Century Britain.' *Journal for the Scientific Study of Religion* 45: 567–84.

Davie, Grace. 2005. 'The Changing Nature of Religion in Northern Europe: Some Implications for the Study of Welfare,' In *Welfare and Religion: A Publication to Mark the Fifth Anniversary of the Uppsala Institute for Diaconal and Social Studies*, edited by Anders Bäckström, 133–44. Uppsala: Publications of the Uppsala Institute for Diaconal and Social Studies 10.

Day, Abby. 2013. 'Varieties of Belief over Time: Reflections from a Longitudinal Study of Youth and Belief.' In *Belief as Cultural Performance*, special issue of the *Journal of Contemporary Religion*, guest edited by Abby Day and Gordon Lynch, 28: 277–93. DOI: https://doi.org/10.1080/13537903.2013.783339.

Day, Abby. 2014. 'The Problem of Generalizing Generation.' *Religion and Society: Advances in Research* 4: 109–24. DOI:10.3167/arrs.2013.040107.

Day, Abby. 2015. 'Farewell to Generation A: The Final "Active Generation" in the Anglican Communion.' In *Contemporary Issues in the Worldwide Anglican Communion, Powers and Pieties*, edited by Abby Day, 3–20. Aldershot: Ashgate.

Day, Abby. 2017. *The Religious Lives of Older Laywomen: The Last Anglican Generation*. Oxford: Oxford University Press.

Day, Abby. 2019 'Lived Belief in Cross-Cultural Comparison.' In *Religious Imaginations and Global Transitions*, edited by James Walters, 143–8. London: Ginko.

De Graaf, Nan Dirk, and Manfred Te Grotenhuis. 2008. 'Traditional Christian Belief and Belief in the Supernatural: Diverging Trends in the Netherlands between 1979 and 2005?' *Journal for the Scientific Study of Religion* 47: 585–98. https://doi.org/10.1111/j.1468-5906.2008.00428.x.

Field, Clive. 2015. www.brin.ac.uk/wp-content/uploads/2011/12/Religion-in-Great-Britain-1939-99-A-Compendium-of-Gallup-Poll-Data.pdf.

Francis, Leslie J., and Gemma Penny. 2015. 'Belonging without Practising: Exploring the Religious, Social and Personal Significance of Anglican Identities among Adolescent Males.' In *Contemporary Issues in the Worldwide Anglican Communion, Powers and Pieties*, edited by Abby Day, 55–74. Aldershot: Ashgate.

Gilliat-Ray, Sophie. 2000. *Religion in Higher Education: The Politics of the Multi-Faith Campus*. Aldershot: Ashgate.

Golo, Ben-Willie Kwaku, Måns Broo, Sławomir Sztajer, Francis Benyah, Sohini Ray and Mallarika Sarkar. 2019. 'Primary Religious Socialization Agents and Young Adults' Understanding of Religion: Connections and Disconnections.' *Religion* 49 no. 2: 179–200. DOI: 10.1080/0048721X.2019.1584350.

Guest, Mathew, Sonya Sharma, Kristin Aune and Rob Warner. 2013a. *Christianity and the University Experience: Understanding Student Faith*. London: Bloomsbury.

Guest, Mathew, Sonya Sharma, Kristin Aune and Rob Warner 2013b. 'Challenging "Belief" and the Evangelical Bias: Student Christianity in English Universities.' In *Belief as Cultural Performance*, special issue of the *Journal of Contemporary Religion*, guest edited by Abby Day and Gordon Lynch, 28, no. 2: 207–23. DOI: 10.1080/13537903.2013.783326.

Guibernau, Montserrat. 2013. *Belonging: Solidarity and Division in Modern Societies*. Cambridge: Polity Press.

Heelas, Paul, Linda Woodhead, Benjamin Seel, Bronislaw Szerszynski, and Karin Tusting. 2005. *The Spiritual Revolution: Why Religion is Giving Way to Spirituality*. Oxford: Blackwell.

Hopkins, Peter. 2004. 'Young Muslim Men in Scotland: Inclusions and Exclusions.' *Children's Geographies* 2, no. 2: 257–72. DOI: 10.1080/14733280410001720548.

Hutchison, Elizabeth D. 2011. 'Life Course Theory'. In *Encyclopaedia of Adolescence*, edited by R. J. R. Levesque. New York: Springer.

Kevern, Peter. 2019. 'Ageing, Religion and (In)equality.' In *Ageing, Diversity and Equality: Social Justice Perspectives*, edited by Sue Westwood, 210–23. New York: Routledge.

Kynaston, David. 2009. *Family Britain 1951–57*. London: Bloomsbury.

Madge, Nicola, Peter J. Hemming and Kevin Stenson. 2014. *Youth on Religion: The Development, Negotiation and Impact of Faith and Non-Faith Identity*. London: Routledge,

Mannheim, Karl. 1923 (1952). 'The Problem of Generations.' In *Essays on the Sociology of Knowledge*, edited by Karl Mannheim, 163–95. New York: Routledge & Kegan Paul.

Mason, Michael, Andrew Singleton and Ruth Webber. 2007. *The Spirit of Generation Y*. Melbourne: John Garratt.

McLeod, Hugh. 2007. *The Religious Crisis of the 1960s*. Oxford: Oxford University Press.

Niemelä, Kati. 2008. *Does Confirmation Training Really Matter? A Longitudinal Study of the Quality and Effectiveness of Confirmation Training in Finland*. Tampere: Church Research Institute.

Niemelä, Kati. 2015. 'No Longer "Believing in Belonging": A Longitudinal Study of Finnish Generation Y from Confirmation Experience to Church-Leaving.' *Finland Social Compass* 62 no. 2: 172–86. https://doi.org/10.1177/0037768615571688.

Pollack, Detlef. 2008. 'Religious Change in Europe: Theoretical Considerations and Empirical Findings.' *Social Compass* 55, no. 2: 168–86.

Regnerus, Mark D., Christian Smith, and Brad Smith. 2004. 'Social Context in the Development of Adolescent Religiosity.' *Applied Development Science* 8, no. 1: 27–38.

Ridgely, Susan B. 2011. *A Methods Handbook: The Study of Children in Religions*. New York: New York University Press.

Roberts, Ken I., Siyka Kovacheva and Stanimir Kabaivanov. 2017. 'Still Troubled: Tunisia's Youth during and since the Revolution of 2011.' *Societies* 7, no. 29: 215–28. doi:10.3390/soc7040029.

Roof, Wade Clark. 1993. *A Generation of Seekers*. New York: Harper Collins.

Roof, Wade Clark. 1999. *Spiritual Marketplace*. Princeton, NJ: Princeton University Press.

Ryder, Norman B. 1965. 'The Cohort as a Concept in the Study of Social Change.' *American Sociological Review* 30, no. 6: 843–61. DOI: 10.2307/2090964.

Savage, Sara, Sylvia Collins-Mayo, Bob Mayo and Graham Cray. 2006. *Making Sense of Generation Y: The Worldview of 15–25-year-olds*. London: Church House.

Schneider, David. 1980. *American Kinship: A Cultural Account*. Chicago, IL: Chicago University Press.

Scourfield, Jonathan, Sophie Gilliat-Ray, Asma Khan and Sameh Otri. 2013. *Muslim Childhood: Religious Nurture in a European Context*. Oxford: Oxford University Press.

Sharma, Sonya, and Mathew Guest. 2013. 'Navigating Religion between University and Home.' *Social and Cultural Geography* 14, no. 1: 59–79.

Shillitoe, Rachael, and Anna Strhan. 2020. '"Just Leave it Blank": Non-Religious Children and their Negotiation of Prayer in School.' *Religion* 1–21. 10.1080/0048721X.2020.1758230.

Singh, Jasjit. 2010. 'Head First: Young British Sikhs, Hair, and the Turban.' *Journal of Contemporary Religion* 25, no. 2: 203–20. https://doi.org/10.1080/13537901003750894.

Smith, Christian, and Melinda Lundquist Denton. 2005. *Soul Searching: The Religious and Spiritual Lives of American Teenagers.* Oxford, New York: Oxford University Press.

Smith, Christian, Kari Christoffersen, Hilary Davidson and Patricia Snell Herzog. 2011. *Lost in Transition: The Dark Side of Emerging Adulthood.* Oxford, New York: Oxford University Press.

Snape, Michael, and Callum G. Brown (eds). 2016. *Secularisation in the Christian World.* London: Routledge.

Soueif, Ahdaf. 2012. *My City, our Revolution.* London: Bloomsbury.

Strhan, Anna. 2015a. *Aliens and Strangers? The Struggle for Coherence in the Everyday Lives of Evangelicals.* Oxford: Oxford University Press.

Strhan, Anna. 2015b. 'Evangelical Anglicans and the Formation of Children in Modern Britain.' In *Contemporary Issues in the Worldwide Anglican Communion, Powers and Pieties,* edited by Abby Day, 39–54. Aldershot: Ashgate.

Strhan, Anna, and Rachael Shillitoe. 2019. 'The Stickiness of Non-Religion? Intergenerational Transmission and the Formation of Non-Religious Identities in Childhood.' *Sociology* 53, no. 6: 1094–1110. 003803851985530. 10.1177/0038038519855307.

Uecker, Jeremy. 2014. 'Religion and Early Marriage in the United States: Evidence from the Add Health Study.' *Journal for the Scientific Study of Religion* 53, no. 2: 392–415.

Van Gannep, Arnold. 1960, *The Rites of Passage.* Chicago, IL: Chicago University Press.

Vincett, Giselle, Elizabeth Olson, Peter Hopkins and Rachel Pain. 2012. 'Young People and Performance Christianity in Scotland.' *Journal of Contemporary Religion* 27, no. 2: 275–90. DOI: 10.1080/13537903.2012.675741.

Voas, David, and Fenella Fleischmann. 2012. 'Islam Moves West: Religious Change in the First and Second Generations.' *Annual Review of Sociology* 38: 525–45.

Wilson, Bryan. 1966. *Religion in Secular Society.* London: C. A. Watts & Co.

Wink, Paul, and Michele Dillon. 2003. 'Religiousness, Spirituality, and Psychosocial Functioning in Late Adulthood: Findings from a Longitudinal Study.' *Psychology and Aging* 18, no. 4: 916–24.

Wuthnow, Robert. 1998. *The Restructuring of American Religion: Society and Faith since World War II.* Princeton, NJ: Princeton University Press.

Chapter 9

'Race', ethnicity, social class

Theories of 'race', ethnicity and social class help illuminate variations in religiosity and the way in which religious and non-religious people view each other. Power and identity are major themes here. Questions of classifications are also raised, to understand that being seen as an 'in' or 'out' group can take many forms and have both short- and long-term consequences. These can work to separate people on the grounds of birth, with social structures reflecting deeply embedded ideals, norms, stereotypes and prejudices.

The effect of post-colonial theory is explored, to investigate how sociologists understand the legacy of empire and its impact on religion, and how religion was employed and adapted to dominate and subject people. The chapter's emphasis on the social *construction* and *dynamic* of such social categories as 'race', ethnicity and social class aims to provide a demystifying look at a complex, dynamic topic.

Introduction

More than a century ago, sociologists Émile Durkheim and Marcel Mauss (1902 (1963) drawing on Aristotle, convincingly showed that all classifications are social classifications created by people and not inherent: 'The first logical categories were social categories; the first classes of things were classes of men into which these things were integrated.' The terms used in this chapter, such as 'race', ethnicity and social class, are socially constructed, contingent, fluid and contested. As all sociological terms and concepts are socially constructed, it is important to understand at the outset that the acts of creating such constructions have been unequally distributed over time and place and are therefore 'contingent', by which I mean unstable and resting on other equally unstable categories.

'Race'

The sociological contemporary critique on 'race' accepts that it is a comparatively modern and essentialized, fictional concept, which is why social scientists generally mark that acknowledgement by inserting quote marks around the word. And yet, while not an empirical fact, as an ideology it is real as are its effects on marginalized people. It also has, and continues to have, deep religious roots. Its first use in the English language has been traced to William Dunbar, a Roman Catholic priest and poet. He used the word in a poem in 1508, referring to a 'race of things', thus introducing it as an idealized, romantic notion. That formulation was revived in the late 18th century (Hogarth and Fletcher 2018, 3).

The ideology of distinctive 'races' and a hierarchy extends even further back into early religious formations, according to those who have used religious texts to justify their racist beliefs. Those religious people often cite the biblical story of the curse of Cain, who was expelled from the Garden of Eden, or Ham, whose son was cursed by Noah. Muslims, Christians and Jews share those texts as part of their own canons and have variously interpreted and employed them to justify their racialized beliefs that certain people, usually identified by skin colour, were destined to be enslaved. Early Christians were led to believe that their new religion superseded Judaism and should be seen to be superior, a position strengthened in the 4th century when Christianity was declared the official religion of Rome and all others deemed to be inferior and often illegal.[1] In his detailed discussion of how racism, Christianity and colonialization are mutually constitutive, Izak Spangenberg (2019, 8) wrote:

> Christian anti-Judaism, its anti-Semitism and its denigration of Muslims of medieval times gave birth to racism, which flourished during the period of colonisation. The 'hierarchising' of religions contributed to the 'hierarchising' of people. Christianity and Europeans rank at the top, while other religions and other people are of lower rank.

The concept was also embedded in the thinking and works of philosophers and scientists. Ivan Hannaford (1996) describes the development of racialized ideas through, for example, Kant, Locke, Hegel and Hobbes. An 18th-century essay by François Bernier clearly proposed the idea of separate 'species or races', swiftly followed by Georges Cuvier who introduced the notion that the first 'race' was white Caucasian, with all other colours being the result of some accident or catastrophe. The so-called white Caucasians created successful civilizations, he argued, whereas those of other colours did not. The era of 'scientific racism' ushered in by Cuvier thus created apparent evidence and argument linking different biological traits to intellect and morality. Other scientists went against that trend, notably Charles Darwin (1871; 1901, 307), who concluded in the 1870s that 'the great variability of all the external differences between the races of man [...] indicates that they cannot be of much importance; for if important, they would long ago have been either fixed and preserved or eliminated'.

Nevertheless, the idea of a human hierarchy built around colour remained strong in the 19th century and justified the colonizing activities of countries in the global north, who found non-white people in the lands they were exploring and deemed them inferior. Religion was, for the most part, complicit. As Kathy Hogarth and Wendy L Fletcher write (2018, 5), the ideal of 'Euro-descent normativity' was an ambitious programme for the early colonizers, where 'the enthusiasm of the religionists of the age was needed, and so churches and government partnered in the project of the suppression of and the then hope-for assimilation and renovation of the inferior other'.

The idea of 'race' was used to accelerate the persecution and genocide of Jews by the Nazis. Being able to operationalize the term, embedding it into the bureaucracy of a totalitarian regime, was one of the key factors that allowed the 'final solution' to occur (Bauman 1991; Mosse 2009), together with the Christian-rooted conviction that Christianity superseded Judaism.

Reflecting on his upbringing and theological training during South Africa's apartheid regime, Izak Spangenberg (2019, 2) describes how the church he attended, the Dutch Reformed, had 'four different churches for the different pigmented Christians. There was one for "whites", one for "blacks", one for "brown people" and one for people of Indian descent.' This conformed to segregationist policies imposed by the governing National Party, which often drew on biblical ideas to defend their policies, as did most of the theology faculty who taught him. Some of that thinking, Spangenberg writes (2019, 6), was based on the teachings of Martin Luther, whose anger at Jews for not converting to Christianity resulted in

> a vicious anti-Semitic tract with the title 'On the Jews and Their Lies' (1543). It was evident that the Reformation could no longer be seen 'as a movement of return to the Jewish foundations of Christianity, but as a casting off of the restraints that had safeguarded the Jews for centuries'.
>
> (Saperstein 1989:36).

While many South Africans may know that Christianity-mediated racism forms part of their history, Spangenberg (2019, 2) continues to say that:

> However, not many of them are aware that apartheid was practised throughout the Western world and that the Bible was equally used and abused by other Christians to support their governments' discriminatory legislation and practices. The United States may serve as an example. Prior to the civil rights movement of the sixties of the previous century, similar practices were the order of the day in the United States.

While legislated policies may not always be visible or overt, racialized ideas and practices still occur widely, particularly if the sometimes-false binary of religion and politics is analytically collapsed. By way of example, Bill Ashcroft, Gareth Griffiths and Helen Tiffin (2009, 222) point to recent practices of American fundamentalist Christians who 'while asserting their lack of political or racial bias ("It's not a black thing, or a white thing, it's a Jesus thing")' have continued to act in racially discriminative ways by opposing social 'welfare' or educational programmes designed to help minority groups.

The research finding that those who are most conservative, or 'fundamental', are more likely to act on racialized beliefs was corroborated in a European study by Stefanie Doebler (2015). Analysing survey data gathered from 47 countries along dimensions of believing, belonging and behaving, Doebler found that the habits of belonging to specific congregations or practising religion in certain ways were weak predictors of racial intolerance. She concluded that national contexts and varieties of belief were the most significant. Citizens of poorer, religious countries with a history of ethno-religious conflict were most likely to be racially intolerant, as were religious people who were most fundamentalist.

Stephen M. Merino (2010) showed that Christians who view the United States as a 'Christian nation' are less likely to include non-Christians in everyday life.

In the UK, one of the leaders of the Church of England, the Archbishop of Canterbury, said at a meeting of the Synod, the governing body, that the Church of England is institutionally racist: 'I'm ashamed of our history and I'm ashamed of our failure. There is no doubt when we look at our own Church that we are still deeply institutionally racist.' Synod members backed a motion to apologize for racism in the Church of England and to 'stamp out conscious or unconscious' racism. www.bbc.co.uk/news/uk-51469566.

Case example: racializing 'mercy'

Lizzie Seale and Alexa Neale from the University of Sussex, UK, conducted research they are calling: 'Racializing Mercy: Capital Punishments and Race in 20th Century England and Wales'. A short summary, pending publication, follows.

In the UK, the act of pardoning a convicted criminal their offence falls under what is known as the 'Royal Prerogative of Mercy'. In other countries, this is usually called a 'pardon'. In the UK, the Royal Prerogative's roots are unavoidably religious as the monarch is also the head of the Church of England. A recent well-known case in the UK was when in 2013 the deceased scientist and acclaimed World War II code-breaker Alan Turing was posthumously awarded by Queen Elizabeth mercy for his 1952 conviction of homosexuality, which had been a crime until 1967. While the title of 'royal prerogative' and Turing's case implies that this is an act personally performed by a monarch since its inception in the early 16th century, in practice it is carried out by government, in the UK, by the Home Secretary.

There are several roots of the word 'mercy': in Latin, it refers to *merces, merced,* meaning reward; in French it is related to *merci,* meaning thanks, or sometimes pity, while from the Middle English period it takes on biblical allusions to refer to, specifically, God's benevolence, favour and forgiveness to a wrong-doer. As the British monarch is seen as one appointed by and serving God, the sense of a 'Royal Prerogative of Mercy' inevitably links two sources of power, religious and secular. And yet, such acts are not evenly distributed amongst those who benefit.

In their recent socio-historical research, Lizzie Seal and Alexa Neale found that racialized discourse indicated that racist stereotypes were present in the judicial decisions overturning life or death sentences. Before capital punishment was abolished in the UK in 1965, appeals were sometimes made to higher judicial powers to overturn the sentence, using the authority of the 'Royal Prerogative of Mercy'. The decision-making process included reviewing police reports, witness statements and advice of civil servants, with the ultimate decision being the Home Secretary's (an elected official). During the period they studied, 1900–49, 36 white men were reprieved but only 17 men of colour were shown the same 'mercy'. Seal and Neale examined the reports written by the Home Secretary and proposed three main characteristics of what they termed racialized 'mercy narratives'. These drew on, they argued, colonial-derived racist paternalism that supported the writer's need to reinforce their background, as a form of cultural defence.

Seale and Neale identified three main mercy narratives, addressed chronologically:

1   'In hot blood', occurring mainly between 1900 and 1941, were paternalistic narratives about men of colour being passionate, overly emotional and lacking restraint. Only two such appeals were successful, for what appeared to be arbitrary reasons. For example, a man of colour who worked on ships fought with

and stabbed another crew member. The judge's court summary referred to the conduct of a man who had been wild and savage, and definitely not English. The jury found him guilty. His solicitor tried to obtain mercy but was unsuccessful and the man was hanged. In another case, another man of colour was also sentenced to death for killing someone in a fight, but the Home Office agreed that the fight was a result of the criminal being a 'hot-tempered' man and mercy was granted.

2   'Provocative prejudice', occurring mainly in the mid-1950s, referred to the convicted man's experience of 'racism' (although that term was not used) when, for example, he was taunted or otherwise aggressively targeted because of his colour. In one case, a man killed a woman after she called him 'n-r' (the full name not repeated here). The judgment stated that, while it was understandable that he reacted violently because he may not have been accustomed to hearing that word, the sentence would not be overruled. Seale and Neale argued that the case contested a prominent war-time narrative of Britain being welcoming, compared to Nazi Germany, and the man was executed.

3   'Dark Stranger', occurring mainly during the mid-1950s–1960s, was a narrative based on the idea that new migrants from the Commonwealth did not understand the cultural mores of their new home. A particular case Seale and Neale found had prominent religious overtones: a Christian Burmese man killed a Muslim man in a fight, and was reprieved on the somewhat flimsy and arbitrary argument that he did not understand the cultural norms of his new home and so should be shown mercy. As Loïc Wacquant (2005, 128) discussed, associations of blackness with danger are still active in the public imagination and amongst law-enforcers.

From 'race' to ethnicity

Given the troubled history of 'race', it became increasingly the norm for scholars to problematize and eventually lean away from the term. Ethnicity became, and remains at the time of writing, a frequently employed word to signify a difference between 'peoples' and is usually assumed to be more benign and less destructive than 'race'. There is a tendency for people to use the term 'ethnic' not to presume an inherent identity, but rather one constructed and reinforced in different social contexts and at different times. The sociologist of religion Max Weber (1978, 389) wrote that 'ethnic membership does not constitute a group, it only facilitates group formation of any kind'.

   In 1950, UNESCO issued a statement (Dunn 1975, 344) saying that the term 'race' was unscientific and should be dropped:

> All Homo sapiens were of common descent with no inherent biological or genetic group differences and that due to serious errors being habitually committed when the term 'race' is used in popular parlance, it would be better to drop the term 'race' altogether and speak of ethnic groups.

By the time the Human Genome Project in the 21st century showed that 99.9 per cent of humans' genetic make-up is the same, the argument for distinctions based on biology seemed entirely untenable. Steve Fenton wrote (2010, 22): 'the point of reference of difference is typically cultural difference, and cultural markers of social boundaries, rather than physical appearance'.

Such boundary creation may, itself, create new boundaries and hierarchies. The sociologist of religion therefore needs to maintain a critical eye to detect what is being imposed, what may be chosen and to what extent such choices may both empower and obscure. The significant contributions of fine-grained qualitative methods can be made here, with sociologists able to analyse social constructions and interactions that occur in daily life. As Fredrik Barth (1969) described it, identity is formed on the boundary.

It is important to interrogate the registers of power and dominance that may surround the term since, as Ashcroft et al. point out (2009, 76–7), it is a term given to immigrants and not those who see themselves as the dominant, extant group: 'Thus in **settler colonies** [*boldface theirs*] of the British Empire the dominant Anglo-Saxon group is usually not seen as an ethnic group because its ethnicity has constructed the mythology of national identity.' Those people who combine 'white', nationality and Christianity 'peddle these simplistic models of religion' and in so doing reinforce social divisions 'which collapse religion and race into new discriminatory signifiers of difference'.

The sociologist Stuart Hall introduced an idea of 'new ethnicities' as positional and conditioned by processes of diaspora-ization, predicated on difference, diversity and hybridity, not purity.

Case example: a census of Muslims

Following Ashcroft et al. (2009, 77), 'Inasmuch as group power is always a favoured solution to individual powerlessness, the ethnic group is a salient formation in the bid for political power within a society', the example here describes the effective use of group power to first identify with, and then reject, ethnicity as an identity marker.

One of the most significant cases to challenge the concept of 'ethnicity' was the Muslim Council of Great Britain's successful campaign to change the wording and available choices on the UK decennial census. The census figures are important in any country as they are used to inform and justify major government decisions, not only affecting how public money is spent, but how major policies affecting a wide range of issues are debated and decided (see Day and Lee 2014). The UK Census did not have a question about religion until 2001, but the Muslim Council of Great Britain argued that Muslims define themselves in terms of their religion, not ethnicity, and therefore a census religious question would give government necessary information about the Muslim community. As Sophie Gilliat-Ray (2010, 115–20) pointed out, the question about the size of the Muslim population had been unresolved for many years, and dependent on secondary data and extrapolation. Further, with government increasingly turning to 'faith communities' to bolster state welfare provision, it was in the interests of both the government and religious organizations to be more certain about the size of religious populations.

The importance of understanding Muslims through their identification as a religion rather than an ethnic group was emphasized in the American context by Aasim Padela, Amal Killawi, Jane Forman, Sonya DeMonner and Michele Heisler (2017, 846) who pointed out that:

> American Muslim health behaviors is challenging. Population-based representative samples of the American Muslim community do not exist because most national health care databases do not adequately capture religious affiliation, and naming algorithms used for proxies have not been fully validated. Although the qualitative literature does capture some Islamic influences on American Muslim health values and behaviors, most of these studies were focused only on one ethnic group within this diverse community.
>
> (Beine, Fullerton, Palinkas, & Anders, 1995)

Such information is important, they argue (Padela et al. 2017, 846), because members of some ethnic groups and religions might resist certain types of medical treatment based on different concepts surrounding illness (and see more discussion about religion and health in Chapter 11). Further, they argued, the influence of cultural conflicts, fears of discrimination and the way clinics may not accommodate their specific needs may add to their rejection of available secular treatments. For some communities, they note, religious beliefs, practices and values form important parts of their identities. All such complexity will mean an understanding of those aspects is important for health providers. The American Muslim community, they write (2017, 847) 'although diverse ethnically and racially, is bound together by a shared religious tradition that shapes its members' worldviews and informs their behaviors'.

It would also, as Serena Hussain and Jamil Sherif discussed (2014), help Muslims collaborate better if they were seen as a distinct, collective religious minority rather than as disparate ethnic groups based on country of origin, particularly in their ability to influence government to create protective legislation in the face of increasing Islamophobia. An Advisory Board was created to discuss the matter from a variety of secular and religious positions, and it was agreed to put a religion question on the 2001 census. Some people (Day 2011; Voas and Bruce 2004) have argued that a high Christian response to the census resulted from many people conflating ethnicity as 'white' with religion as 'Christian'.

Explaining racism

As the older, 'scientific racism' and colonial theories are disappearing, new forms of racism based on 'culture' or 'ethnicity' have taken their place. In some ways, it can be argued that 'religion' is the new 'race'. Martin Stringer (2014, 457) observed:

> A great deal has been said in recent years about the important shift in perception and language from identities built on ethnicity to those built around religion and

while I would not want to push this as far as some others (Stringer 2013, 71), it does have the consequence of making religion and religious identity a central feature of superdiverse society and an important plank in the study of superdiversity more widely.

There are several long-standing social theories to help explain racism and related forms of bigotry. Most centre on a theme of 'othering': people feel a stronger sense of identity when they can construct boundaries that mark them and 'others'. Therefore, the theory runs, in times of social anxiety exacerbated by, for example, economic problems and other forms of instability, the tendency to blame an 'other' increases. The process by which people claim a social identity is complex, but many social scientists will begin with the early 20th-century Canadian sociologist Erving Goffman (1959), whose key concepts about identity focused on dramaturgy, performance, front/back stage identities, boundaries, discordant events and the consequences of identities being stripped or merged into an institution.

Goffman understood identity, drawing on theories of Max Weber and George Herbert Mead, as a process of symbolic interactionism, by which people's actions reflect their interpretation of what is meaningful to them in the world. The self, he argued, is not pre-formed but is produced during social interactions in what people may describe as their 'culture'. But, he maintained, both the self and the culture are unstable, fluid identities. That point is instructive to help sociologists detect what is going on when people claim that they are acting in a certain way because of their 'culture', and then often create boundaries based on what they will argue is 'our' culture and 'theirs'.

Goffman's work strongly influenced the anthropologist Fredrik Barth, who described how Goffman's ideas about impression management and the self had influenced his and others' work on ethnicity. Reflecting on a meeting held to discuss research on identities, Barth (2007, 10) related:

> Our findings were fairly unambiguous. We documented situations where people change their ethnic identities under pressure, or as result of ecologic change, or where they clung to them in minority situations by careful impression management, or used impression management to deny patent cultural differences that might have been given ethnic significance. We argued that in view of such situations, the construction of ethnic identities was understood most readily by looking to the ethnic boundaries and modes of boundary marking.

The ideas of self, ethnicity, religion and culture therefore can become conflated, altered and weaponized in the arsenal of those who want to fight, for example, against immigration based on the idea that the 'Christian culture', as is often expressed, of their 'Christian country' will be threatened by non-Christian, typically Muslim, immigrants or, in the parlance of early 21st-century discourse, refugees and asylum-seekers. Responses by religious people vary, with some research showing that church-attending Christians are more tolerant than those who are more nominalist in their Christian identity (see e.g. research by the University of Bristol, www.bristol.ac.uk/sps/news/2018/faith-and-welcoming.html).

The now-banned far-right party, 'Britain First', justified its aggressive anti-immigration tactics by saying it was seeking the country's return to a former apparently homogeneous

Christian culture. As Ashcroft et al. (2009) consistently argued in their book, one of the tactics of colonial-inspired thinking is to invoke a mythological, pre- 'others', national identity.

Such a notion of a fluid, unstable culture is juxtaposed with earlier ideas about culture being a fixed, systematic whole. One such definition was proposed and largely adopted by the anthropologist of religion, E. B. Tylor who wrote: 'Culture ... is that complex whole which includes knowledge, beliefs, arts, morals, law, customs, and any other capabilities and habits acquired by [a human] as a member of society' (Tylor 1958, 1). Further, Tylor (1958, 23–4) proposed an idea of 'civilisation' that was not only ahistoric and universalized, but implicitly racist:

> Civilization actually existing among mankind in different grades, we are enabled to estimate and compare it by positive examples. The educated world of Europe and America practically settles a standard by simply placing its own nations at one end of the social series and savage tribes at the other, arranging the rest of mankind between these limits according as they correspond more closely to savage or to cultural life [...] ... ethnographers are able to set up at least a rough scale of civilization. Few would dispute that the following races are arranged rightly in order of culture: – Australian, Tahitian, Aztec, Chinese, Italian.

The critique which followed in the next century centred on Tylor's idea that culture could be reduced to a single, ahistorical, evolutionary entity rather than one that is historically and temporally contingent (see e.g. David Oswell's 2006 summary and discussion).

Religious leaders need not always look to a past 'golden age' to justify racialized intolerances. Chetan Bhatt (2000, 573–93) outlines how contemporary Hindu nationalists have constructed narratives of purity based on blaming a medieval period of Muslim dominance in India. In so doing, Bhatt (2000, 591) concludes that 'Virtually everything disagreeable within Hinduism is traced to this period and viewed either as a consequence of Islamic rule or an intrinsic attribute of Islam that has polluted Hinduism.' That list includes, *inter alia*, caste and tribe formations, women's oppression, educational limitations, harems, poverty and so on. Conversely, everything that is seen as agreeable within Hinduism is presented as an example of contemporary Hindu resistance against the 'invaders'.

Identity politics

The term 'identity politics' has been used both to mobilize groups of people who feel they share and should politicize a common identity, and those who will denigrate them for doing so. Vasiliki Neofotistos (www.oxfordbibliographies.com/view/document/obo-9780199766567/obo-9780199766567-0106.xml, last accessed Mar. 2020) defines 'identity politics' or, as sometimes described, the 'politics of identity' as:

> the deployment of the category of identity as a tool to frame political claims, promote political ideologies, or stimulate and orientate social and political action, usually in a larger context of inequality or injustice and with the aim of asserting group distinctiveness and belonging and gaining power and recognition.

Stuart Hall (1990, 223), writing about cinema, described the need for Black people originally from Jamaica to connect to a collective history shared by a 'one' people:

> This 'oneness', underlying all the other, more superficial differences, is the truth, the essence, of 'Caribbeanness', of the black experience. It is this identity which a Caribbean or black diaspora must discover, excavate, bring to light and express through cinematic representation.

And yet, he continued, while that conception is important for helping bring together some of the fragments of colonial and post-colonial experience, it is also deceptive, allowing a fiction of sameness that assumes a fixed, stable essence. In practice, he argues, those identities are always affected by history, culture and power and are being constantly transformed, rather than remaining somewhere hidden, waiting to be rediscovered and recovered. Hall describes (1990, 227), the forced removal of Africans to supply the needs of slave-owners, and argues that those Africans were from different regions and countries with different tribal identities and gods, all of which were significantly different from Christianity and its more limiting adherence to monotheism, thereby creating hybrids of Catholicism, Baptists and Pentecostalism. Hall's work was not primarily polemic but political, urging people to create new forms of identities in order to resist a Western desire to suppress and homogenize the 'other', arguing that 'every regime of representation is a regime of power' (Hall 1990, 226).

David Gellner and Sondra Hausner (2013, 75) point to this complex issue when exploring the experience of Nepalis in Great Britain, writing that identity politics can create tension 'between those who want to make particular identities the central and determining aspect of their social being and people who do not wish to do so or who refrain from doing so'. Further, they write, those who do not want make such identities the key aspect of their social being may do so strategically or tactically, recognizing that sometimes the state depends on formal identities for 'politically implicated process of regular counting, i.e. censuses, and (eventually) the distribution of resources'. They caution scholars, reminding them of a fallacy attached to the notion of categories: just because they can be counted does not mean they exist.

Their research revealed a multiplicity of belonging, where people of different religions would borrow and experience the resources of others, from gods to identities. Political environments affect such identities and the situation in Nepal, they write, has changed since the 1990s to one where categories and counting have become more important (Gellner and Hausner 2013, 78), with the rise of ethnic activism. This created a move from nation-building to ethnicity building: 'arguably it has now become one of religion building. In the new multiculturalist environment, it again became possible and required to count ethnic groups'. When carrying out their research in the UK, Gellner and Hausner (2013, 81–2) found that, when asked about their religious affiliation, Nepali respondents gave one, until they were told it was permissible to choose more than one, in which cases they often chose two or three (Hindu, Buddhist and/or Kirat).

Commenting on multiculturalism, Tariq Modood (2005) argued that British attitudes towards Muslims have changed over the years (see also Gilliat-Ray 2010). While racisms directed at colour may have been reduced, new forms of racisms are directed towards other differences such as family structure, language, religion and clothing. Defending multiculturalism (and see also Koopmans 2013), Modood argued that a more secular, less religious, approach was not the answer (www.theguardian.com/commentisfree/belief/2010/sep/24/multiculturism-hope-secularism-religion):

> Increasingly since the 1960s, European cultural, intellectual, and political life has become dominated by secularism, with secularist networks and organisations controlling most of the levers of power. Indeed, the accommodative character of secularism itself is being dismissed as archaic, especially on the centre left. Thus, respect for religion is made difficult and seems outlandish but may be necessary as one of the sources of counter-hegemony and a more genuine pluralism. So, respect for religion and moderate secularism are kindred spirits and are sources of hope for a multiculturalism that gives status to religious, as to other, communities.

Discussions of identity politics and the categories they create and reify were challenged by Kimberley Crenshaw (1995) in her work on intersectionality. While recognizing that identity politics can be effective by giving voice to many, and by revealing that violence and discrimination are systematic, rather than individualized, Crenshaw (1995, 357) showed that 'The embrace of identity politics, however, has been in tension with dominant conceptions of social justice'. Referring specifically to violence against women of colour, Crenshaw argued that only illuminating one aspect of a woman's identity, such as colour, failed to recognize other intersecting aspects, such as class. She argued that (1995, 358) women of colour who experience violence are sometimes further disadvantaged by economic structures which mean they do not have the same recourse to support as other women may have:

> Where systems of race, gender, and class domination converge, as they do in the experiences of battered women of color, intervention strategies based solely on the experiences of women who do not share the same class or race backgrounds will be of limited help to women who face different obstacles because of race and class.

Yet, color, class and gender all intersect in how male violence against women and children is committed, with nearly half of homeless women and children having fled violence in their homes; 'an estimated 63 percent of young men between the ages of eleven and twenty who are imprisoned for homicide have killed their mothers' batterers' (Crenshaw 1995, 361).

Above discussions of identity politics and intersectionality serve also to remind scholars of both the strengths and dangers of categorization, and the extent to which there is a shared understanding of 'politics' (see e.g. Glynn 2002 for discussion of young Bengali Muslims, discussed also in Chapters 4 and 5). Sociologists need to be aware and able to identify such claiming acts as the products of specific social interactions, which are often tightly secured to a specific time and place.

Social class

While some people may argue that class is an outdated concept and should be abandoned, most social theorists would say otherwise, arguing that it is a means of creating, maintaining and reproducing social structures, even (and perhaps through) someone's denial that it exists. It therefore can be important to consider social class in the context of one of several systems with which people engage in order to separate others into groups with whom they may or may not belong. The effect of categories such as social class, and resources, such as social capital, will be explored in this section to reveal how they not only confer advantage, but also create barriers: 'class concerns boundaries, those distinctions we make between ourselves and others' (McCloud 2007, 2).

The sociologist will not assume that 'class' is a pre-social category but will analyse it relevant to other systems of categorizations. Sociologists will also consider how people negotiate their sense of class position, realizing that such negotiations are not individualized creations, but, as Richard Jenkins (1997) described it, a process of dialectical identity formation and development that requires both an individual sense of belonging to a social group and an awareness that other people, 'outsiders', will also recognize that form of belonging and identity. Such negotiations required more creativity and agility than are available in economically or materially defined ideas about social class. In the UK, the National Statistics Socio-Economic Classification (NS-SEC) places people in one of seven main classes according to their occupation and employment status. It did not, however, allow more nuanced wider social and cultural views about the systemization of class. Many sociologists will therefore in their qualitative empirical work produce social classifications collaboratively, through asking research participants if and how they might describe themselves as members of a certain class.

In her study of white working-class women in northern England, Beverley Skeggs (1977, 74) found that: 'Class was central to the young women's subjectivities. It was not spoken of in the traditional sense of recognition – I am working class – but rather, was displayed in their multitudinous efforts not to be recognised as working class.' Through a process of dis-identification and dissimulation, the young women effected to ignore their structural positions in society and its limitations, while simultaneously, mostly through 'improving' narratives and practices designed to mimic and possibly attain middle-class status, reinforcing those positions. They were not, Skeggs argued, striving in a political sense for recognition, but denied such representations of their positioning. Skeggs's work contributed to theories about recognition and capital, as, she argued (Skeggs 1977, 75), class worked 'dialogically': 'In this process the designated "other" (based on representations and imaginings of the respectable and judgemental middle class) was constructed as the standard to/from which they measured themselves. The classifying of themselves depended upon the classifying systems of others.'

In distinguishing between 'class position' and 'class identity', Skeggs was able to show how the women she studied were aware of their 'place', mediated by how others represented and demonized working-class people, while also wanting to leave it. Skeggs also corroborated and then superseded Pierre Bourdieu's theories about social capital and habitus. While he effectively demonstrated how people adjusted to their class positions, Skeggs (1977, 2004) identified and theorized about the strategies they construct to adapt or resist those positions and related identities.

A new classification system arose in the UK following the largest survey of social class ever conducted: the BBC's 2011 Great British Class Survey. Analysis of the survey was carried out by sociologists (Savage et al. 2013) who identified how different forms of 'capital' will confer different advantages and affordances of power: economic capital, defined as wealth and income; cultural capital, defined as the extent to which people, largely through educational attainment, can appreciate and engage with cultural goods; and social capital, defined as the type and quantity of people's social networks. The researchers also disrupted conventional ideas of class that feminists had long challenged. Those ideas were based on typically male occupational data and did not pay attention to how class operates symbolically and culturally, stigmatizing and representing specific forms of personhood and value.

The seven new categories Savage et al. (2013) identified were: elite; established middle class; technical middle class; new affluent workers; traditional working class; emergent service workers; precariat. One of the ways the new classification became significant to researchers was to show how religious spaces might be most important to certain sorts of people who use them informally. In my study of Anglican churches that stayed open to offer tea and friendship to marginalized people (Day 2017), I suggested that those people might resemble the social class that Savage et al. (2013, 243) described as 'the precariat', a category composed of about 15 per cent of the population, having the lowest social and cultural capital of all classes, being either unemployed or in semi-skilled unskilled occupations. They would also have had the highest levels of capital insecurity, of all forms. Although their reasons for coming to the churches seemed, superficially, to be quite different, they had one thing in common: they had few other social places to go where they could be welcome, kept warm and offered free refreshments.

Sociologists and anthropologists have studied for decades how social institutions, from the family to the school, represent and reproduce certain social classes, as do religious organizations. Although class is a contested category, and researchers need to employ it carefully and indicate how they perceive it, most would agree it is a social category operationalized by people as part of a filtering process. Religious views on marriage are good examples. One of the most effective ways to preserve the homogeneous nature of a group is to protect against intermarriage. Robert E. Park (2000, 110) writes that every religious group keen on maintaining itself discourages people from marrying outside the group:

> The Catholic clergy are profoundly opposed to marriage outside of the church, and the Jews who are, perhaps, the most mixed of peoples have only been able to pre-serve their tribal religion for three thousand years and more because by endogamy they converted a religious society into a racial minority.

In her research into how evangelical Anglican leaders think about class, Joanne McKenzie (2015) found that many leaders discussed their strong theologically based commitment to operate as 'one humanity' and dissolve class distinctions, saying that they 'perceive congregations to be a rare space in society where sustained cross-class relationships can be forged and fostered'. And yet, they also said that their congregants were often mired in 'the significance of the middle class "habitus" of conservative evangelicalism in frus-trating the movement in its quest for more effective engagement with the working-class' (McKenzie 2015, 84). Many of her interviewees explicitly rejected a strategy popular with some Christian evangelical churches to focus on recruiting people who matched characteristics from their existing congregations on the assumption that homogeneity was more attractive than diversity.

Adrian Stringer (2015) noted that there had never been a systematic study of socio-economic classes and the Church of England, although he suggests that several studies provide proximate data and inference about the middle-class nature of Anglicanism. David Kynaston (2009, 53) wrote that in the 1950s: 'Women accounted for almost two-thirds of church attendances, with a bias towards the elderly, and a middle-class person was at least twice as likely to go to church each Sunday than a working-class person.' Stringer (2015) showed that studies in the United States demonstrated consistently that Episcopalians have been disproportionately drawn from the upper echelons of society, a finding that was supported in the work of, for example, Constance Buchanan (1992, 310–11) who wrote: 'the Episcopal tradition has always been small, exercising social and cultural influence vastly disproportionate to its size. More than any other Protestant denomination, it has been identified with the national power structure and destiny'. Sean McCloud (2007) drew attention to class-related religious cultures being transmitted through personal networks, thereby creating a stratification of religion mirroring the stratification of material resources in the wider society.

As discussed earlier, Max Weber (1922) proposed that different kinds of religion, from the salvationist to esoteric, attract people from different social classes, based on (men's) occupations.

Sample questions for private study

1   What theories of race help explain discriminatory practices in religions with which students are most familiar?
2   How may social class affect people's religious choices?

Sample class exercise

Discussion of media reports that are 'coded' examples of racialized or classist discourse.

Note

1   For further discussion see e.g. Goldenberg 2003; Haynes 2002.

Indicative reading

Ashcroft, Bill, Gareth Griffiths and Helen Tiffin. 2009. *Post-Colonial Studies: The Key Concepts.* London: Routledge.
Back, Les, and John Solomos. 2000. *Theories of Race and Racism: A Reader.* London: Routledge.
Barth, Fredrik. 1969. *Ethnic Groups and Boundaries.* Bergen: Universitetsforlaget.
Barth, Fredrik. 2007. 'Overview: Sixty Years in Anthropology.' *Annual Review of Anthropology* 36: 1–16. https://doi.org/10.1146/annurev.anthro.36.081406.094407.
Bauman, Zygmunt. 1991. *Modernity and the Holocaust.* Cambridge: Polity.

Bhatt, Chetan. 2000. 'The Lore of the Homeland: Hindu Nationalism and Indigenist Neoracism.' In *Theories of Race and Racism: A Reader*, edited by Les Back and John Solomos, 573–93. London: Routledge.

Buchanan, Constance H. 1992. 'The Anthropology of Vitality and Decline: The Episcopal Church in a Changing Society.' In *Episcopal Women: Gender, Spirituality, and Commitment in an American Mainline Denomination*, edited by Catherine M. Prelinger, 310–29. New York: Oxford University Press.

Crenshaw, Kimberlé W. 1995. 'Mapping the Margins: Intersectionality, Identity Politics, and Violence Against Women of Color.' In *Critical Race Theory: The Key Writings that Formed the Movement*, edited by Kimberlé Crenshaw, Neil Gotanda, Gary Peller and Kendall Thomas, 357–83. New York: New Press.

Darwin, Charles. *The Descent of Man*. 1871 (1901). London: John Murray.

Davison, Andrew, and Alison Milbank. 2010. *For the Parish: A Critique of Fresh Expressions*. London: SCM Press.

Day, Abby. 2011. *Believing in Belonging: Belief and Social Identity in the Modern World*. Oxford: Oxford University Press.

Day, Abby. 2017. *The Religious Lives of Older Laywomen: The Last Active Anglican Generation*. Oxford: Oxford University Press.

Day, Abby, and Lois Lee. 2014. 'Making Sense of Surveys and Censuses: Issues in Religious Self-Identification. Introduction.' Religion, 44, no.3: 345–56. http://dx.doi.org/10.1080/0048721X.2014.929833.

Doebler, Stefanie. 2015. 'Love thy Neighbor? Relationships between Religion and Racial Intolerance in Europe.' *Politics and Religion* 8, no. 4: 745–71. DOI: https://doi.org/10.1017/S1755048315000607.

Dunn, Leslie Clarence. 1975. *Race, Science and Society*. Paris, London: UNESCO, Allen & Unwin.

Durkheim, Émile, and Marcel Mauss. 1902 (1963). *Primitive Classification*, translated from the French and edited with an introduction by Rodney Needham. London: Cohen.

Fenton, Steve. 2010. *Ethnicity*. Cambridge: Polity.

Gellner, David N., and Sondra L. Hausner. 2013. 'How Nepalis in the UK Deal with "Religion".' In *Social Identities between the Sacred and the Secular*, edited by Abby Day, Giselle Vincent and Christopher R. Cotter, 75–88. Aldershot: Ashgate.

Gilliat-Ray, Sophie. 2010. *Muslims in Britain: An Introduction*. Cambridge: Cambridge University Press.

Glynn, Sarah. 2002. 'Bengali Muslims: The New East End Radicals?' *Ethnic and Racial Studies* 25, no. 6: 969–88. https://doi.org/10.1080/0141987022000009395.

Goffman, Erving. 1959. *The Presentation of Self in Everyday Life*. New York: Doubleday.

Goldenberg, David M. 2003. *The Curse of Ham: Race and Slavery in Early Judaism, Christianity, and Islam*. Princeton, NJ: Princeton University Press.

Hall, Stuart. 1990. 'Cultural Identity and Diaspora.' In *Identity: Community, Culture, Difference*, edited by Jonathan Rutherford, 222–37. London: Lawrence & Wishart. Tthe same article appears as 'Cultural Identity and Cinematic Representation.' *Framework* 36 (1989).

Hannaford, Ivan. 1996. *Race: The History of an Idea in the West*. Washington, DC: Woodrow Wilson Center Press.

Haynes, Stephen R. 2002. *Noah's Curse: The Biblical Justification of American Slavery*. Oxford, New York: Oxford University Press.

Hogarth, Kathy, and Wendy L. Fletcher. 2018. *A Space for Race: Decoding Issues of Racism, Multiculturalism and Post-Colonialism in the Quest for Belonging*. New York, Oxford: Oxford University Press.

Hussain, Serena, and Jamil Sherif. 2014. 'Minority Religions in the Census: The Case of British Muslims.' In *Making Sense of Surveys and Censuses: Issues in Religious Self-Identification*, special issue of *Religion*, guest edited by Abby Day and Lois Lee, 44, no. 3: 414–33, DOI: 10.1080/0048721X.2014.927049.

Jenkins, Richard. 1997. *Rethinking Ethnicity*. London: SAGE.

Koopmans, Ruud. 2013. 'Multiculturalism and Immigration: A Contested Field in Cross-National Comparison.' *Annual Review of Sociology* 39: 147–69. doi: 10.1146/annurev-soc-071312-145630.

Kynaston, David. 2009. *Family Britain 1951–57*. London: Bloomsbury.

McCloud, Sean. 2007. *Divine Hierarchies: Class in American Religion and Religious Studies*. Chapel Hill, NC: University of North Carolina Press.

McKenzie, Joanne. 2015. 'A Different Class? Anglican Evangelical Leaders' Perspectives on Social Class' In *Contemporary Issues in the Worldwide Anglican Communion: Powers and Pieties* ed. Abby Day, 191–212. Aldershot: Ashgate.

Merino, Stephen M. 2010. 'Religious Diversity in a "Christian Nation": The Effects of Theological Exclusivity and Interreligious Contact on the Acceptance of Religious Diversity.' *Journal for the Scientific Study of Religion* 49, no. 2: 231–46. https://doi.org/10.1111/j.1468-5906.2010.01506.x.

Modood, Tariq. 2005. *Multicultural Politics: Racism, Ethnicity and Muslims in Britain*. Edinburgh: Edinburgh University Press.

Mosse, George. 2000. 'The Jews: Myth and Counter-Myth.' In *Theories of Race and Racism: A Reader*, edited by Les Back and John Solomos, 195–205. London: Routledge.

Oswell, David. 2006. *Culture and Society: An Introduction to Cultural Studies*. London: SAGE.

Padela, Aasim I., Amal Killawi, Jane Forman, Sonya DeMonner and Michele Heisler. 2017. 'American Muslim Perceptions of Healing: Key Agents in Healing, and their Roles.' *Qualitative Health Research* 22, no. 6: 846–58. DOI: 10.1177/1049732312438969.

Park, Robert E. 2000. 'The Nature of Race Relations.' In *Theories of Race and Racism: A Reader*, edited by Les Back and John Solomos, 105–12, London: Routledge.

Savage, Mike, Fiona Devine, Niall Cunningham, Mark Taylor, Yaojun Li, Johs Hjellbrekke, Brigitte Le Roux, Sam Friedman, and Andrew Miles. 2013. 'A New Model of Social Class: Findings from the BBC's Great British Class Survey Experiment.' *Sociology* 47, no. 2: 21–5. https://doi.org/10.1177/0038038513481128.

Skeggs, Beverley. 1977. *Formations of Class and Gender: Becoming Respectable*. London: SAGE.

Skeggs, Beverley. 2004. 'Context and Background: Pierre Bourdieu's Analysis of Class, Gender and Sexuality.' *The Sociological Review* 52, no. 2: 19–33. https://doi.org/10.1111/j.1467-954X.2005.00522.x.

Spangenberg, Izak J. 2019. 'The Religious Roots of Racism in the Western World: A Brief Historical Overview', *HTS Teologiese Studies/Theological Studies* 75 no. 1: a5187. https://doi.org/10.4102/hts.v75i1.5187.

Stringer, Martin D. 2014. 'Evidencing Superdiversity in the Census and beyond'. In *Making Sense of Surveys and Censuses: Issues in Religious Self-Identification,* special issue of *Religion,* guest edited by Abby Day and Lois Lee, 44, no. 3: 453–65, DOI: 10.1080/0048721X.2014.903649.

Stringer, Adrian. 2015. 'Addressing the Problem of Socio-Economic-Classification.' In *Contemporary Issues in the Worldwide Anglican Communion: Powers and Pieties,* edited by Abby Day, 149–68. Aldershot: Ashgate.

Tylor, E. B. 1958 (1871). *Primitive Culture*. London: Murray.

Voas, David, and Steve Bruce. 2004. 'The 2001 Census and Christian Identification in Britain.' *Journal of Contemporary Religion* 10, no. 1: 23–8. https://doi.org/10.1080/1353790032000165087

Wacquant, Loïc. 2005. 'Race as Civic Felony.' *International Social Science Journal* 57, no. 183: 27–142. DOI: 10.1111/j.0020-8701.2005.00536.x

Weber, Max. 1922. *The Sociology of Religion*. Boston, MA: Beacon Press.

Weber, Max. 1978. *Economy and Society*, edited by G. Roth and C. Wittich. Berkeley, CA: University of California Press.

Part IV

Is nothing, or everything, sacred?

Chapter 10

Religion and media

Religion shapes and is shaped by media, both traditional and digital. This chapter reviews and explores in depth the three main approaches to studying religion and media, as Stig Hjarvard (2012) proposed: as 'religious' media, mainly controlled and performed by religious actors, and sometimes by the state; as religion through journalism, where news media bring religion to the public sphere, often as the main and sometimes only way people know about religion; and as 'banal religion' where religion is implicitly made visible through entertainment. His reference to 'banal' alluded to his earlier work (Hjarvard 2008) in which he drew on Michael Billig's idea of 'banal nationalism', as discussed here in Chapter 4. He described banal religion as a result of 'mediatization' created by media, whereby 'Through the process of mediatization, religion is increasingly being subsumed under the logic of the media. As conduits of communication, the media have become the primary source of religious ideas' (Hjarvard 2008, 9).

Religion, media and changing times

A study of media needs to be situated in the wider social context because that it is the essence of the relationship: media reflect and shape the context. Media scholars consider media in terms of their effects, and how they are managed through regulation, framing, structures and policies. Although media are related to and produced by powerful interests, they are also resisted and managed by individuals who may bypass certain sources and create their own content.

In his research about media as agents of change, Stig Hjarvard (2012) made the important observation that for most people in western societies, media have become the primary source of their religious ideas, and information about other religions. Further, he suggests that some of the roles religion had have been replaced by what can be offered by media, such as rituals and community. In turn, religious organizations now have internalized and behave according to the 'media logic', by framing their actions and activities in forms appropriate to the media, and to their audiences. His underlying theory of 'mediatization' argued that religion's main role as a 'sacred canopy' becomes weakened as people become more individualized and rely more on forms of media that can provide that function. In contrast, scholars such as Birgit Meyer (2013) take a different view of media influence. Religious forms and changes are always mediated and are an essential, not weakened, part of the process of how religion develops in different ways (see, for more discussion, Lövheim 2016; Lövheim andLynch 2011).

There may be a tendency to see the readers or consumers of media as passive, unthinking recipients and while it is necessary to explore the dynamics of 'mediatization', students also need to interrogate how the reader/consumer is participating in studies. For example, Dawn Llewelyn (2015) engaged in read-response analysis to contrast how different sets of women, religious and those becoming less religious, used literature as a spiritual resource. By positioning her participants as actual, rather than implied, readers she was able to identify the reading strategies they used, and also to contribute to critiques of secular/feminist divides and so-called second/third wave feminisms.

Webb Keane (2002, 47) argued that those who thought religion was on the wane or had left the 'public sphere' should pay more attention to media stories and other representations of religion as public discourse. The daily newspaper should make it obvious that religion has not retreated to the private sphere (see Casanova 1994): 'If news from the Middle East, Northern Ireland, or Sri Lanka, or, for that matter, Amsterdam and Copenhagen, does not demonstrate religion's persistence in public events, a glance at American presidential politics should confirm it.'

Keane also cites a report in the *New York Times* (26 May 2004, p. A12) to emphasize religion's role in the 'public sphere': the action of seven European foreign ministers who delayed the signing of the European Union constitution by demanding it acknowledge Europe's Christian heritage.

Thinking with words

Mediation: how something is **conveyed** or communicated through a medium.
Mediatization: how something is **changed** through being communicated by specific media.

Changes in values, structures, options and accessibility have occurred rapidly during the last few decades, and therefore so have how the media that engage their publics. Kim Knott and Jolyon Mitchell (2012) frame their discussion within that changing context, examining four key drivers and effects: fragmented audiences; transformed identities; reformed communities and distant suffering brought been closer. By 'fragmented audience' and 'transformed identities' they mean the disruption to a nuclear family where a stable unit of two parents and children would usually access media together, gathered around the one family television set or radio. It is more common today for households to be more individualized, with single parenthood more common than in earlier decades, and household members likely to consume media on their own devices and often in their own rooms. So, too, the more digitalized media offer customers more choice. Identities have changed considerably over the last few decades, affecting gender, religion, youth and sexualities, prompting more variety of media consumption and increased debates surrounding this. The phenomenon of being able to witness distant suffering from the comfort of one's own safe home creates further tensions. Through and in response to all these factors, communities reform in new ways to promote and sometimes resist such transformations.

What we understand as 'media', in both creation and dissemination, should therefore be situated in a larger framework of society, and particularly the production of 'discourse'. What scholars refer to as 'discourse' is mediated, and therefore related to symbolism and power. It is a way of communicating, some would say, an ideology, or normative worldview. Not value-neutral, discourse is the usually taken-for-granted conversation that shapes people's thinking in a manner authorized and to a large extent controlled by those in positions of power in institutions such as media, education, politics and law. Developing the idea of Critical Discourse Analysis, Norman Fairclough (1992) proposed that language, through speech and writing, should be seen as social-political acts and therefore needs to be understood through relationships amongst power, ideology and social practice.

Although its strength is its capacity to cloak itself in supposedly objective, acceptable presentations, such as 'news' or 'research' or 'truth', French philosopher Michel Foucault argued that 'truth' is a product of political struggles and therefore what becomes truth or false is political. He was intellectually interested in surveillance, discipline and regulation as the modes through which knowledge is bound up with the exercise of power and produced in discourse. He wrote (Foucault 1981, 52):

> In every society the production of discourse is at once controlled, selected, organised and redistributed by a certain number of procedures whose role is to ward off its powers and dangers, to gain mastery over its chance events, to evade its ponderous, formidable materiality.

Following Foucault's ideas of 'technologies of self', hegemony, knowledge and micro-processes can all aid an analysis of media within the context of 'discourse'. As an example, one might analyse the way media often produce what has been discussed in several disciplines, including the sociology of religion, as a 'moral panic'. Stanley Cohen (1972, 2002, 16), who credits the first use of the term to media scholar Marshall McLuhan and then to criminologist Jock Young, described a moral panic as a moral and political issue circulated by media in order to identify, constrain and to some extent control risk: 'there must be loss of cherished values and material objects resulting in death or injury or destruction to property'. Core to his thinking was the idea of risk, danger and pollution, first convincingly articulated by the anthropologist Mary Douglas. Cohen wrote: 1972, 2002, xxxii):

> More interesting than 'applying' risk theory to the study of moral panics is to remember that most claims about relative risk, safety or danger depend on political morality. As Douglas originally argued, substantial disagreements over 'what is risky, how risky it is and what to do about it' are irreconcilable in purely objective terms. Moreover, the perception and acceptance of risk is intimately tied to the question of who is perceived to be responsible for causing the hazard or damage to whom. This allocation of blame is intrinsic to moral panics.

Cohen defined seven stages of moral panic, subsequently collapsed to five to suit his chosen case of the 'Mods and Rockers' (2002, 16, 17):

1   Target: A person or group is identified as a a threat to values or interests.
2   Warning: the media circulates often coded ideas about something or someone who poses a threat to values or interests.

3　Impact: Public concern grows rapidly.
4　Inventory: Authorities or opinion makers respond and some kind of structure, or narrative, is created to explain the situation. 'This scurrying around for a causal theory – or, at least, a language for making sense – is found in all moral panic texts' (Cohen 2002, xiv).
5　Reaction: The panic recedes or results in social changes.

In his introduction to the book's third edition, Cohen (2002, vi–xliv) notes that sources of moral panics have shared similar characteristics over time, as have the identities of the 'folk devils': young working class, sometimes violent men, frequently referred to as 'yobs'; violence, shooting and bullying in schools; wrong drugs, used by the wrong people at wrong places; child abuse, satanic rituals and paedophile registers; sex, violence and blaming the media; welfare cheats and single mothers; refugees and asylum-seekers 'flooding our country, swamping our services'. In retrospect, Cohen reviews some of his work, updating examples, and critiques. The most salient point of his contribution may well be his reiteration of the 'moral' aspect of the panic. His reference to HIV/AIDS is an excellent example as it shows, he explains, how the nature of the illness was morally constructed, attributing responsibilities and accusations of moral failures to gay men. These moral beliefs are not individually constructed but usually shaped by media representations of some underlying myth or folk devil, such as those listed above (bad youth/mothers/sexually active people), which result in further stereotyping and myth making. Stuart Hall and colleagues (Hall et al. 1978, 220–2) argued that, although the media spread ideas and fuelled panics, they were not the originators of the panics. Such ideas, particularly about law and order, were generally produced by elite members of society, principally police and judiciary.

An example here can be shown by returning to the discussion in Chapter 6 of the four cases brought before the European Court of Human Rights where it was evident that Christian and national identities merged in some of the public discourse to convey a moral panic about threats to an apparently Christian heritage. As discussed in Chapter 4, Benedict Anderson (1991) coined the term 'imagined community' to convey a nationalistic sense of belonging, communicated mainly through media and novels. The 'community' was imagined because no one can actually meet most other members of the nation-community to discuss their shared sense of common values and English moral superiority that epitomize the 'nation'; these must be picked up through discourse.

The case of Nadia Eweida, the British Airways employee who wanted to wear her cross visibly above her uniform in defiance of BA policy, caught the imagination of religious leaders who spoke to media about their outrage. The then Archbishop of York (second most important Church of England clergyman) John Sentamu explicitly drew on moral nationality-based frameworks in comments made to the national broadcasting service, the BBC. He said that British Airways should reconsider its decision against cross-wearing, because such a ban would threaten 'the history of the country it represents, whose culture, laws, heritage and tradition owes so much to the very same symbol it would ban' (http://news.bbc.co.uk/1/hi/england/northyorkshire/6166746.stm, last accessed Feb. 2020). A former Archbishop of Canterbury, the most important Church of England clergyman George Carey, warned in the Church of England's weekly newspaper, the *Church Times*, that there would be a serious threat 'to the social order' and called for a different composition of judges to hear such cases who might be more sympathetic to Christianity: 'it is difficult to see how it is appropriate for other religions to be considered by the judiciary where the practices are further removed from our traditions' (www.churchtimes.co.uk/articles/2010/23-april/news/uk/carey-backs-counsellor-amid-animus-to-christian-beliefs, last accessed Feb. 2020).

A columnist writing for the conservative-oriented *Daily Telegraph*, Christopher Booker, emphasized what he thought was the court's wrong decision to uphold the charity Relate's decision to fire the counsellor, Gary McFarlane, who refused to counsel same-sex couples. Booker wrote that: 'Under a law designed to bar religious discrimination, it is now perfectly legal to discriminate against someone's beliefs so long as these are based on religion – e.g. Christianity (but not of course Islam)' (www.telegraph.co.uk/comment/columnists/christopherbooker/7664681/The-divisive-law-of-Lord-Justice-Laws.html, last accessed Feb. 2020).

One of the strongest myths circulating in most societies is that everything was better 'before'. British historian David Kynaston, in an online article for a UK newspaper, the *Daily Mail* (www.dailymail.co.uk/news/article-1224231/A-vanished-Britain-50-years-ago-country-doors-left-unlocked-children-played-street.html#ixzz43RuAN5ZB, last accessed June 2019), wrote that 'To many people who grew up in the Britain of half a century ago, the Fifties are a clearly and dearly remembered age.' People remembered their childhoods when, apparently, house doors and bicycles remained unlocked, people were trustworthy and easy-going, families were intact and values such as respectability, conformity, restraint and trust were paramount. Of course, as some of Kynaston's interlocutors recalled, the decade was also authoritarian, illiberal and puritanical, the food was basic and fatty, and children were routinely bullied and sometimes abused at military-style schools. The rock star Mick Jagger was quoted as saying he thought his school had too much homework and bureaucracy: 'And too much petty discipline. Petty rules about uniforms and stuff.'

And yet, social change was happening. Divorces increased rapidly through the following decades, with UK figures showing that, for example, in 1971 there were 5.9 divorces per thousand of married population, compared to a peak 20 years later of 14.2, before slightly decreasing and levelling off. While many may welcome this as liberating, particularly for women, other, more conservative people and institutions, would see it as problematic, as was discussed in earlier chapters. Indeed, the very notion of 'family' is contestable, and in certain contexts retains a vestige of colonial and other repressive regimes. See Haley McEwen's (2017) discussion of the normative, western-imposed family discourse that has shaped, to their detriment, many countries in Africa.

Such social changes have also had a dramatic effect on religion whereby, as Stewart Hoover (2006, 279) suggested, individuals may concentrate less on the external demands of a religious tradition and more on their own internal well-being or spiritual needs, with media providing 'a range of symbolic resources to contemporary "religious" and "spiritual" questing'.

Media and the role of the state

The state often has a role in media regulation, depending on the country and its type of government. According to the Pew Research Center, the number and intensity of government restrictions on religion increased significantly between 2007 and 2017, as has the level of social hostility involving religion. Pew Research has focused on two main ways that government regulates religion: regulatory frameworks including laws and policies that impact on religious freedom, and religious favouritism, whereby the state may give preference through policy or funding to a particular religion and not others through, for example, education, clergy and property (see www.pewforum.org/2019/07/15/a-closer-look-at-how-religious-restrictions-have-risen-around-the-world/, last accessed Feb. 2020).The role of the state in regulating media speaks directly to one of the fundamental human rights established by the UN in 1948, and incorporated into the constitutions or legal frameworks of contemporary democracies: 'Everyone has the right to freedom of opinion and expression; this right includes freedom to hold opinions without interference and to seek, receive and impart information and ideas through any media regardless of frontiers.' In undemocratic states, governments will often take an assertive stance, controlling media through, for example, ownership, editing or banning certain outlets. The line between 'democracy' and 'non-democracy' is not always so clear, as democratic states also often control media through both direct and non-direct means, often defending their actions as necessary to defend national security, or through regulations against 'obscenity' or 'indecency'. The former is defined by its likelihood to deprave or corrupt, and the latter by being a matter of 'anything which an ordinary decent man or woman would find to be disgusting or revolting'. The state may also regulate against hate speech, whether religious, misogynist or racist. It may also have a role in cases of 'defamation', a civil rather than criminal wrong, where someone may be sued for damages for committing libel (written) or slander (spoken).

When does freedom of expression cross the boundary into blasphemy or hate speech? That question continues to vex religious leaders, politicians, members of the judiciary and the general public. The act of defaming, or speaking sacrilegiously, against a deity or sacred thing, is known as blasphemy. Blasphemy is a crime in many countries, with Christians tracing the interdiction to a text in the Bible: 'But whoever blasphemes against the Holy Spirit never has forgiveness but is guilty of an eternal sin' (Mark 3:29, KJV).

Writing in the UK newspaper the *Independent,* Andrew Copson, chief executive of Humanists UK, points to a variety of blasphemy cases and calls for their repeal. In many countries blasphemy is illegal and, in 13 Islamic countries, punishable by death. He cites a number of cases (www.independent.co.uk/voices/stephen-fry-blasphemy-ireland-getting-worse-around-the-world-a7723631.html, last accessed Feb. 2020):

> Mohamed Cheikh Ould M'kheitir in Mauritania, charged with 'insulting the prophet' for an article challenging slavery; humanist Ahmadreza Djalali, who worked as a Professor in Brussels but is now sentenced to death in his native Iran; and Saudi Arabia, which just last week sentenced Ahmad Al Shamri to death for 'atheism', while others such as Raif Badawi also sit on death row.

He also gives examples of the blasphemy laws used in predominantly Christian countries such as Greece, where in 2014 Philippos Loizos was given a ten-month suspended prison sentence for mocking and criticizing Orthodox Christianity (the main religion in Greece) and a well-known, revered Greek Orthodox patriarch. In Russia, where Orthodox Christianity is also dominant and often extolled by leader Vladimir Putin, three members of the all-female feminist punk band Pussy Riot were accused and imprisoned on the basis of spreading religious hatred, after performing songs critical of Putin and the Orthodox Church in a Moscow cathedral.

In the UK, blasphemy was illegal throughout the country until 2008 when it was taken off the books in England and Wales. During the political debate (www.telegraph.co.uk/news/1942668/Blasphemy-laws-are-lifted.html, last accessed Mar. 2020) Maria Eagle, the junior justice minister, said 'These offences have now largely fallen into disuse and therefore run the risk of bringing the law into disrepute. Given that these laws protect only the tenets of the Christian Churches, they would appear to be plainly discriminatory.' She was contradicted by Edward Leigh, a Conservative MP, who claimed their abolition would encourage more people to make fun of Christianity. The law remained in place in Northern Ireland and Scotland. The well-known humourist and television presenter Stephen Fry was accused of blasphemy in 2015 after appearing on Irish television where he said, in answer to the question of what he might say to God if they met: 'How dare you create a world in which there is such misery? It's not our fault! It's not right. It's utterly, utterly evil. Why should I respect a capricious, mean-minded, stupid god who creates a world which is so full of injustice and pain?' He went on to say that Greek gods 'didn't present themselves as being all seeing, all wise, all beneficent', adding 'the god who created this universe, if it was created by god, is quite clearly a maniac, an utter maniac, totally selfish' (www.bbc.co.uk/news/world-europe-39830447, last accessed Feb. 20).

Police were called by one man to investigate on the grounds that Fry had committed a crime by blaspheming. The case was later dropped as there was no evidence that Fry's comments had caused widespread offence. Following a referendum in 2018 when the population voted overwhelmingly to repeal blasphemy laws, the law was officially repealed by the Irish government in January 2020.

In 1977 Mary Whitehouse launched a successful private prosecution against the publisher of *Gay News* for printing a poem depicting, in graphic detail, homosexual acts between a Roman centurion and Jesus Christ. It was the first conviction for blasphemy since 1922, and generated debate and a Law Commission review recommending, in 1985, that the laws of blasphemy be repealed. As Ganiel and Jones (2012, 305) describe, 'for the rest of the twentieth century, this was an issue that governments studiously avoided', even though, as they comment, it was clearly inequitable in an multi-faith country that it applied only to Christianity. The debate mostly centred on whether the law should be repealed or extended so that it applied to other religions as well.

There have been other cases of blasphemy or religious protests that have captured media attention, and several that have been produced through the performances of popular culture, such as the film *Life of Brianl,* released in 1979. Although not directly satirizing Jesus or Christianity, many people drew inferences that it had and the film was banned in Ireland, Norway and some regions in the UK, as well as inspiring protests from Christians and Jews in the United States. In 1988 Christians set fire to a Paris cinema during its screening of Martin Scorsese's *Last Temptation of Christ*, injuring ten people. In 2004, UK Sikhs protested violently against Gurpreet Kaur Bhatti's play

Behzti in Birmingham Repertory Theatre Birmingham for depicting violence and sex in a temple. The play closed early on safety grounds. In 2007, a UK Christian lost their judicial case that the film *Jerry Springer the Opera* was blasphemous.

The event that most dramatically polarized public opinion was the declaration of a fatwa, or religious death sentence, against the author Salman Rushdie for allegedly blaspheming in his novel, *The Satanic Verses*. The novel sparked outrage amongst Muslims for disrespecting their faith, leading to scenes of book-burning and mass protests in England's predominantly Muslim neighbourhoods, and an equally vociferous condemnation by non-Muslims of that behaviour.

Sometimes, the consequences can be deadly. A bloody, lethal decade followed the 2005 publication by Danish newspaper *Jyllands-Posten* of a series of cartoons of the Prophet Mohammed in a variety of violent and anti-Islamic depictions. As newspapers in Norway, Italy, and Spain reprinted the cartoons, protests broke out in the Middle East and embassies were attacked. The publication and republication of the original and similar cartoons spread, and offices were attacked, lives threatened and lawsuits launched. As part of the protest, Muslim leaders and organizations in Denmark wrote letters of protest and filed suits against the editors, citing legislation governing defamation, hate speech and blasphemy. None was successful, prompting many people to argue that there is an unfair balance against Muslims compared to Christians, as Jytte Klausen (2009, 87) observed:

> Muslims complained about double standards in how the press treats Muslims compared to Christians and Jews and decried the cartoons as another instance of spreading Islamophobia, an irrational fear of Muslims and Islam. The charge of double standards has merit. Blasphemy laws are common in Europe, and in countries where no such laws exist, the media often refrain from printing things that are perceived as objectionable to religious people. Advocates of the double-standard view argued that Christian sensitivities are readily recognized whereas Muslims' feelings are ignored and derided.

After publishing a feature on a novel describing France as an Islamic state, the newspaper *Charlie Hebdo*'s offices were attacked on 7 January 2015 and 12 people were killed. Thousands, including heads of state, marched in Paris and other cities to promote the ideal of 'freedom of expression'.

The UK government effectively replaced the blasphemy laws in 2006 with the Racial and Religious Hatred Bill and repealed blasphemy laws in 2008 in England and Wales. Ganiel and Jones (2012, 305) note that:

> How far free expression should be curtailed for the sake of religious belief is not an issue that will be settled by these or any other legal measures. In part this is because, in a global age, it is an issue that transcends national boundaries. But it is also because it is an issue for which a society's public culture on what constitutes acceptable treatment of religious subjects is likely to matter more than the letter of its law.

Case example: correcting the media

Government regulation of media sometimes happens indirectly. In the UK, this occurs through the Independent Press Standards Organisation (IPSO), a regulator for the newspaper and magazine industry, funded by the publications, not central government. Some of their rulings have been controversial.

1. *The Sun's* front-page headline on 23 November 2015 was '1 in 5 Brit Muslims' sympathy for jihadis'. This was false (as *The Times* admitted immediately). The reality was that the survey question on which the story was based did not specify whether Muslims supported or opposed 'jihadis' – only whether they had sympathy with fighters in Syria on either side of the fighting. Asking the question of non-Muslims gave similar results. A complaint was lodged, and three months later IPSO reached an adjudication which upheld the complaint of inaccuracy. IPSO had no power to require a correction, but *The Sun* published a correction on an inside page, rather than giving it equal prominence to its original story on the front page.
2. On 26 July 2015, the *Mail on Sunday* published an article headlined 'Welcome to Shadwell: Muslim gang sabotages immigration raid vans'. Following a complaint, three months later the *Mail on Sunday* printed a correction which conceded that (a) the religion of the assailants was in fact unknown, and (b) even if they had been Muslim this would have been irrelevant to the story. They published a correction in a far smaller size than the original.
3. On 17 April 2015, Katie Hopkins's column in *The Sun* described migrants as 'like cockroaches' and as 'feral'. IPSO could not rule on a complaint that was made because the discrimination clause in the Editors' Code does not cover groups. Hopkins could have swapped 'migrants' for 'Jewish people', 'Muslim people', 'black people' or similar and IPSO would have been equally powerless.

Perhaps it is not a coincidence that the complaints above all concerned non-white religious people. Robert Beckford has shown (http://news.bbc.co.uk/1/hi/uk/4704925.stm, last accessed May 2020) that black-led churches are treated more negatively in the media than white-led churches: 'It's rare that you find an unbiased analysis of black life in general and black church life in particular. Scandals within the Catholic church or within Anglicanism never get the same kind of negative reaction that a black case will, even if it's an isolated one.'

Stuart and Ahmed (2012) conducted a detailed media analysis of three bestselling British daily newspapers: the left-leaning *Guardian*, right-leaning *Daily Telegraph* and right-leaning tabloid, *Daily Mail*. Their analysis covered reports of 'claims' against a public or private organization by individuals on religious grounds. They found that between 2000 and 2010, Christians comprised 67 per cent of reported claims covered by the media, Muslims 31 per cent, and the other main religious groups less than 10 per cent. Christians also participated in most (96 per cent) of discrimination claims.

Scholars have debated how to respond to a populist demand for 'free speech' in the media, given the apparently open states of living in democracies. Offering a critique of some of the most popular arguments about free speech, Talal Asad, Wendy Brown, Judith Butler and Saba Mahmood (2009) explore the conflicts between blasphemy and free speech, between religious taboos and freedoms of thought and expression, and between secular and religious worldviews.

To paraphrase this important collection of essays, I will begin with the authors' acknowledgement that at stake is the term 'secular', which may mean anything in general discourse from ideals of 'non religion' to varying degrees of tolerance. Much is at stake, as the authors argue, because a popular treatment of secular inevitably links to ideals of a western, historically Christian, liberal and democratic 'civilization', cast as opposite and superior to a non-western, more religious, Islamic 'other'. The debate is further complicated because such terms as secular or religious are themselves produced in different times, and in different ways, and are thus temporally and spatially fluid and contingent. Those entanglements are particularly examined through the example of the Danish cartoons, discussed above, when 'free speech' is seen as a discursive-intellectual binary that sets ideas like 'Christianity, secularism, reason, tolerance, free thought and speech on one side, and Islam, fundamentalism, submission, intolerance, restricted thought and speech on the other' (Asad et al. 2009). Asad (2009, 24–7) points out that so-called European civilization is replete with occasions when free speech was denied, not least during periods of colonization and oppression of indigenous peoples. Even in contemporary times, free speech is curtailed through a variety of means, such as copyright, commercial secrets, patents and intellectual property rights. Societies also regulate access to material deemed to be harmful, such as child pornography. Writing in the same publication, Saba Mahmood (2009, 68) makes the point that blasphemy laws protecting Christian symbols exist in Britain, Austria, Italy, Spain and Germany. She (2009, 75) also discusses the ways the Muslims she interviewed expressed personal feelings of hurt, rather than just anger, a response she traces to the intimate, mimetic nature of the adherent's relationship to the Prophet:

> Those who profess love for the Prophet do not simply follow his advice and admonitions to the *umma* (that exist in the form of the *hadith*), but also try to emulate how he dressed; what he ate; how he spoke to his friends and adversaries, how he slept, walked, and so on.
>
> These mimetic ways of realizing the Prophet's behavior are lived not as commandments but as virtues where one wants to ingest, as it were, the Prophet's persona into oneself.

This sense of closeness produced, she argued, a feeling of moral injury because the relationship with Muhammad was deeply affective. It was not so much, for many Muslims, that a regulation had been broken, but that a dependency and lived experience of Muhammad's being had been shaken. More widely, the hurt also related to the feeling of being targeted (Mahmood 2009, 79): 'the cartoons are a particularly vicious example of the racism they have come to experience from their compatriots in Europe'.

Case example: North Korea

Probably one of the most restrictive states in relation to media is North Korea, where the internet is banned, and citizens are only permitted to use government websites and approved email systems. Phone calls are monitored by a government department, says Amnesty International, reporting that people are incarcerated for communicating with the outside world: 'In apparent attempts to dissuade anyone in the country reaching out to connect with anyone beyond its borders, the government is actively cracking down on those who attempt to talk to those outside North Korea from within the famously isolated state' (www.amnesty.org. uk/north-korea-surveillance-state-prison-camp-internet-phone-technology,   last accessed Mar. 2020).

The ban might not be as effective as the regime would like to think. South Korea's largest religious radio broadcaster, the Far East Broadcasting Company, tries to access potential and existing Christians in North Korea by broadcasting religious programmes to North Korea every day, using powerful transmitters that can reach North Korea and beyond, to China, Japan and Russia. Their goal is both religious and political, hoping to nurture Christianity and work towards a reunified country of both North and South Korea.

Although, for obvious reasons, it is not possible to calculate the number of listeners, the station's American-based strategist Mary Kay Park, suggests it is in the thousands: 'We transmit changed values, and different ideas of the gospel and what freedom looks like. The transformational message of the gospel will help if there is reunification' (www.theatlantic.com/international/archive/2018/04/north-korea-christian-radio/558755/ accessed Mar. 2020).

Digital religious spaces

Media scholars suggest that new media present novel ways to read, disseminate and create new forms of representation. Many also caution against uncritical embraces of the idea of 'the new'. Are new media necessarily better than old media? Are they really new at all? As Martin Lister, Jon Dovey, Seth Giddings, Iain Grant and Kieran Kelly wrote (2009, 11), perhaps the idea of the new needs elaborating:

> There is a strong sense in which the 'new' in new media carries the ideological force of 'new equals better' and it also carries with it a cluster of glamorous and exciting meanings. The 'new' is 'the cutting edge', the 'avant-garde', the place for forward-thinking people to be (whether they be producers, consumers, or, indeed, media academics). These connotations of 'the new' are derived from a modernist belief in social progress as delivered by technology. Such long-standing beliefs (they existed throughout the twentieth century and have roots in the nineteenth century and even earlier) are clearly reinscribed in new media as we invest in them.

In his study of media and Pentecostal churches in Botswana and Zimbabwe, Lovemore Togarasei (2012, 260) notes that a gap identified by Rosalind Hackett (1998) in the 1990s has started to be addressed. She had argued that the areas of media and popular culture were not treated seriously enough by scholars. Those lacunae have been filling, Togarasei suggested, but not evenly. Citing in particular the work of Walter C. Ihejirika (2009), he argues that scholarship in and about Africa has been increasing, but southern Africa continued to be neglected. Focusing on Pentecostalism, Togarasei discusses how, since its inception in the early 20th century, Pentecostalism has made wide use of media, 'including radio, CDs, DVDs, video recorders and cassettes, radio cassettes, electronic music instruments, public address systems, newspapers, books, computers, the Internet, and mobile phones as modern media technologies'. (See also Charles Hirschkind (2006) for use of audio cassettes for broadcasting Islamic sermons in Egypt.) As the radio is the most common form of electronic media in Africa, it has also been used significantly to broadcast Christianity, although this has been reduced in Zimbabwe due to tight government regulations over media use. Togarasei explored the theological justifications for using media by Pentecostal churches and found that, although media may be important for spreading Christianity, it also produces a risk of trivializing and commodifying and 'raises questions about belonging, binding, community, and membership' (Togarasei 2012, 271).

The term 'digital religion' has been defined by Heidi Campbell (2013, 3, and see also 2020) as 'the technological and cultural space that is evoked when we talk about how online and offline religious spheres have become blended or integrated'. Campbell discusses how new media are contributing to the formation of new kinds of virtual communities and yet, she suggests, the distinction between on and offline has become blurred. For example, she asks, how should we interpret the number of hits a site generates? Is this a pattern related to a growing religion? Or could it mainly be attributable to browsing behaviour which may or may not even be initiated by the user? Douglas Cowan (2005, 156) looked into how pagans use a variety of online and offline resources, as do many people who simply want to know more about paganism. He observes that 'external participation does not necessarily indicate internal identification. In terms of identity and investment there is an important difference between personal participation in external behaviour and the external presentation of a self-identified persona.'

Heidi Campbell and Forrest Rule (2016) turned to ritual as a lens through which to study digital religion as this can help scholars identify particular ways in which people act religiously both on and offline. After reviewing the way scholars have defined and interpreted 'ritual', they choose for the purpose of their study an approach that stresses the concept of the 'sacred', and discuss a definition proposed by Christopher Helland (2013, 25): 'a purposeful engagement with the sacred' (and see also Helland 2000). This definition allows the activity to be individual or communal. The framework they found most useful to analyse the use of the digital ritual was Ronald Grimes's (2002) model considering media presentations of rites, how media are used to extend rituals beyond constraints of time and place, how media can be framed as virtual places where rituals can be performed and how media can be religious icons.

Media can also provoke ritual practice across domains other than the digital. In her study of contemporary, popular televised astrology in Bangalore, India, Sahana Udupa (2017) showed how the astrologers engaged with their audiences in ways that legitimized and privileged everyday concerns through bringing them to television, particularly through live question-and-answer sessions. The astrologers frequently recommended that their audiences seek remedies for their problems through ritual acts, to be performed most frequently in temples. The growth and content of such programming, most popular for young and middle-aged adults, confound several binaries: public/private, individual/collective, secular/religious. Udupa (2017, 115) argued that the case provided opportune material to 'critique the orthodox assumptions that secularization and urbanization are intrinsically interlinked, and revealed how the city provides the social material for popular religiosities in and through the workings of commercial mass media'.

Sometimes, as Lynn Schofield-Clark (2007, 79) found, media are the main source of religious language and moral values, even amongst otherwise non-religious young people. Her study shows that that American teens, 'twice-removed' from institutionalized religion, expressed disapproval of atheists, and discussed their moral beliefs within a language of Protestant Christianity: 'teens who claim no interest in organized religion itself, may use religious language and images as means of identifying themselves as good moral people'.

Philosopher Tim Rayner considered new media, and in particular the internet, from a perspective inspired by Michel Foucault. Rayner suggests that, when considered 'from a Foucauldian perspective, social media is more than a vehicle for exchanging information. Social media is a vehicle for identity-formation. Social media involves "subjectivation"' (https://philosophyforchange.wordpress.com/2012/06/21/foucault-and-social-media-life-in-a-virtual-panopticon/ last accessed Mar. 2012).

Rayner takes, in particular, the idea of the 'panopticon', crucial to Foucault's thinking. A concept first introduced by English philosopher Jeremy Bentham as an architectural design for a model prison, the round, windowed structure allowed the guards and the prisoners to continually watch each other. As Foucault wrote (1995, 198), in the central tower, 'one sees everything without ever being seen'. The structure produced a visibility of bodies under centralized observation, becoming an 'all-seeing' surveillance machine with its dominating overseeing gaze. Because its visibility only worked one way, being designed so that no prisoner could ever see the 'inspector', the prisoners never knew when they were being watched, and therefore had to always behave correctly, just in case. For Foucault, the wider theoretical implication was that power was produced through a specific technology, employing various tactics within an overall strategy to submit bodies through a particular architecture. What had been produced was, he wrote, a system where (Foucault 1995, 198): 'There is no need for arms, physical violence, material constraints. Just a gaze. An inspecting gaze, a gaze which each individual under its weight will end by interiorising to the point that he is his own overseer, each individual thus exercising his surveillance over, and against, himself.' Foucault argued that this brought about a condition where power was exercised continuously and at a minimal cost. The ultimate result was what he described as 'carceral society', with prisons just one part of a disciplined space, organized and arranged to facilitate observation of those within. The goal of such a society is for citizens to internalize the required norms and behaviours so that they self-monitor without needing external observation. Power is then not simply a function or arm of the 'state', but exists everywhere on macro and micro levels: 'We can see that this model is based on the notion of networks of power, rather than a single central source for it, and on a whole series of elements including "walls, space, institutions, rules, discourses"' (Foucault 1995, 308). Foucault extends this to schools and universities, particularly the human sciences (such as sociology) which create 'regimes of truth'. All academe's disciplines, such as child psychology and development, pedagogy, architecture and medicine, are thus implicated.

Rayner writes in his blog that internet edifices such as Facebook work like Foucault's panopticon, always monitoring and often harvesting for marketing purposes the behaviours of its users. It is a site where users willingly allow themselves to be watched, and where users await and receive the affirmations or condemnation of their online communities.

Such theories inevitably raise the question of authority. Reflecting on the opportunities for new identities and modes of authority afforded by new media, media scholars Mia Lövheim and Evelina Lundmark (2019, 25) raise the question of how these new forms of authority relate to more traditional religious institutions:

> These shifts follow a trend where individuals to a larger extent than before are able to assemble and perform their identities online in new ways through digital resources (Lövheim, 2012; Campbell, 2012; Hutchings, 2014). However, more work is needed on the particular characteristics of these 'new' forms of authority that develop outside of, or parallel to, religious organizations.

Using data from their earlier projects on female bloggers and vloggers, they traced how the bloggers' authority often developed through the interaction with their followers and took on specific forms. It was relational, performed with the confidence, trust and respect of specific audiences; connected to the individual's personal qualities and values; fragile and constantly connected; authentic, by being connected to oneself and aware of one's dependence on others; vulnerable, through emotional labour and respecting one's audiences. Lövheim and Lundmark (2019, 36) concluded that such examples reflect how 'religion is experienced, articulated and practiced in digital media – and society in general – as a shift from religious institutions to individuals, then personal religious identity is not just "personal" anymore. It is also, to different degrees, public.' Another example of the trust required in the audience/blogger relationship is Deborah Whitehead's (2015) analysis of Christian 'mummy-bloggers'.

Jane Cameron (2013) discussed research she conducted with Reina Lewis and Emma Tarlo into how female bloggers (Muslim, Christian and Jewish) interested in the growing trend towards 'modest fashion' (Lewis 2013) created a space between 'sacred' and 'secular' on their sites, using visual material to convey strong emotional messages. The messages would differ depending on religious tradition, with, for example, Christian and Jewish bloggers allying with a biblical interdiction against the practice of women wearing trousers, while Muslim bloggers would support it: 'Many Muslim fashion bloggers show how short dresses can be made modest by wearing pants underneath. It is clear how different meanings can be read from the image depending on the audience, or who it is that is doing the looking and interpreting' (Cameron 2013, 27; and see Tarlo 2010).

An area neglected in the study media and religion, according to Mia Lövheim (2013), is gender. In particular, she suggests scholars need to engage with post-colonial feminist, queer and post-feminist theories. The case studies in the collection raise issues connected to authenticity, identity, sexuality, online spaces, masculine identities.

Sample questions for private study

1 How do media representations help shape a public understanding of religion?
2 Give recent examples of the power of digital religion, in relation to this week's lectures/reading.

Sample class exercise

Set up a mock interview where a 'religious' person is interviewed on a controversial subject by a TV or radio host.

Indicative reading

Anderson, Benedict. 1991. *Imagined Communities.* London: Verso.

Asad, Talal, Wendy Brown, Judith Butler and Saba Mahmood. 2009. *Is Critique Secular? Blasphemy, Injury, and Free Speech.* Berkeley, CA: Townsend Center for the Humanities. https://escholarship.org/uc/item/84q9c6f.

Cameron, Jane. 2013. 'Sartorially Sacred or Fashion Faux Pas? Visual Interpretations of Modesty Online.' In *Social Identities between the Sacred and the Secular*, edited by Abby Day, Giselle Vincett and Christopher Cotter, 23–39. Aldershot: Ashgate.

Campbell, Heidi. 2013. *Digital Religion: Understanding Religious Practice in New Media Worlds.* London, New York: Routledge.

Campbell, Heidi. 2020. 'Contextualizing Current Digital Religion Research on Emerging Technologies.' *Human Behavior and Emerging Technologies* 2, no. 1: 5–17. https://doi.org/10.1002/hbe2.149.

Campbell, Heidi, and Michael W. DeLashmutt. 2014. 'Studying Technology and Ecclesiology in Online Multi-Site Worship.' *Journal of Contemporary Religion* 29, no. 2: 267–85. https://doi.org/10.1080/13537903.2014.903662.

Campbell, Heidi, and Forrest Rule. 2016. *The Practice of Digital Religion.* Hessen: Springer Fachmedien Wiesbaden.

Casanova, José. 1994. *Public Religions in the Modern World.* Chicago, IL. London: University of Chicago Press.

Chambers, Deborah. 2013. *Social Media and Personal Relationships: Online Intimacies and Networked Friendship.* London: Palgrave Macmillan.

Cohen, Stanley. 1972 (2002). *Folk Devils and Moral Panics: The Creation of the Mods and Rockers.* Abingdon, Oxon: Routledge.

Cowan, Douglas. 2005. *Cyberhenge: Modern Pagans on the Internet.* Abingdon, Oxon: Routledge.

Fairclough, Norman. 1992. *Discourse and Social Change.* Cambridge: Polity Press.

Foucault, Michel. 1981. *The Order of Discourse in Untying the Text: A Post-structuralist Reader.* London: Routledge & Kegan Page.

Foucault, Michel. 1995. *Discipline and Punish.* New York: Vintage Books.

Ganiel, Gladys, and Peter Jones. 2012. 'Religion, Politics and Law' In *Religion and Change in Modern Britain*, edited by Linda Woodhead and Rebecca Catto, 299–321. London: Routledge.

Grimes, Ronald. 2002. 'Ritual and the Media.' In *Explorations in Media, Religion and Culture*, edited by Stewart Hoover and Lynn Schofield Clark, 219–34. New York: Columbia University Press.

Hackett, Rosalind I. 1998. 'Charismatic/Pentecostal Appropriations of Media Technologies in Nigeria and Ghana.' *Journal of Religion in Africa* 28: 258–77.

Hadden, Jeffery K., and Douglas E. Cowan. 2000. *Religion on the Internet: Research Prospects and Promises.* London: JAI Press/Esevier Science.

Hall, Stuart, Charles Critcher, Tony Jefferson, John Clarke and Brian Roberts. 1978. *Policing the Crisis: Mugging, the State, and Law and Order.* London: Macmillan.

Helland, Christopher. 2000. 'Religion Online/Online Religion and Virtual Communitas.' In *Religion on the Internet: Research Prospects and Promises,* edited by Jeffery K. Hadden and Douglas E. Cowan, 205–24. London: JAI Press/Elsevier Science.

Helland, Christopher. 2013. 'Ritual.' In *Digital Religion,* edited by Heidi Campbell, 25–41. New York: Routledge.

Hirschkind, Charles. 2006. *The Ethical Soundscape: Cassette Sermons and Islamic Counterpublics.* New York: Columbia University Press.

Hjarvard, Stig. 2008. 'The Mediatization of Religion: A Theory of the Media as Agents of Religious Change.' *Northern Lights: Film and Media Studies Yearbook* 6: 9–26.

Hjarvard, Stig. 2012. 'Three Forms of Mediatized Religion: Changing the Public Face of Religion.' In *Mediatization and Religion: Nordic Perspectives,* edited by Stig Hjarvard and Mia Lövheim, 21–44. Göteborg: Nordicom.

Hoover, Stewart. 2006. *Religion in the Media Age.* New York: Routledge.

Hunt, Arnold. 1997. 'Moral Panic and Moral Language in the Media.' *British Journal of Sociology* 48, no. 4: 629–48.

Ihejirika, Walter C. 2009. 'Research on Media, Religion and Culture in Africa: Current Trends and Debates.' *African Communication Research* 2, no. 1: 1–60.

Keane, Webb. 2002. *Christian Moderns.* Berkeley-Los Angeles, CA: University of California Press.

Klausen, Jytte. 2009. 'The Danish Cartoons and Modern Iconoclasm in the Cosmopolitan Muslim Diaspora,' *Harvard Middle Eastern and Islamic Review* 8: 86–118.

Knott, Kim, and Jolyon Mitchell. 2012. 'The Changing Face of Media and Religion,' In *Religion and Change in Modern Britain*, edited by Linda Woodhead and Rebecca Catto, 243–64. London: Routledge.

Lewis, Reina (ed.). 2013. *Modest Fashion: Styling Bodies, Mediating Faith.* London: I. B. Tauris.

Lister, Martin, Jon Dovey, Seth Giddings, Iain Grant and Kieran Kelly. 2009. *New Media: A Critical Introduction,* 2nd edition. Abingdon, Oxon: Routledge.

Llewellyn, Dawn. 2015. *Reading, Feminism, and Spirituality: Troubling the Waves.* Basingstoke, New York: Palgrave Macmillan.

Lövheim Mia, ed. 2013. *Media, Religion and Gender.* Abingdon, Oxon: Routledge.

Lövheim, Mia. 2016. 'Analyzing Media Transformations of Religion from a Gender Perspective.' *Media, Culture & Society* 38, no. 1: 18–27. doi.org/10.1177/0163443715615411.

Lövheim, Mia, and Evelina Lundmark. 2019. 'Gender, Religion and Authority in Digital Media.' *Journal for Communication Studies* 12, no. 2(24): 23–38.

Lövheim, Mia, and Gordon Lynch. 2011. 'The Mediatisation of Religion Debate: An Introduction.' *Culture and Religion* 12: 111–17. doi.org/10.1080/14755610.2011.579715.

Lynch, Gordon, Jolyon P. Mitchell and Anna Strhan. 2012. *Religion, Media and Culture: A Reader.* Abingdon, Oxon: Routledge.

McEwen, Haley. 2017. 'Nuclear Power: The Family in Decolonial Perspective and "Pro-Family" Politics in Africa.' *Development Southern Africa* 34, no. 6: 738–51. DOI: 10.1080/0376835X.2017.1318700.

Meyer, Birgit. 2013. 'Material Mediations and Religious Practices of World-Making.' In *Religion across Media: From Early Antiquity to Late Modernity,* edited by Khunt Lundby, 1–19. New York: Peter Lang.

Schofield-Clark, Lynn. 2007. 'Religion, Twice Removed: Exploring the Role of Media in Religious Understandings among "Secular" Young People.' In *Everyday Religion, Observing*

Modern Religious Lives, edited by Nancy T. Ammerman, 69–82. Oxford, New York: Oxford University Press.

Stuart, Hannah, and Houriya Ahmed. 2012. *Faith in the Public Sphere: A Study of Media Reporting of Faith-Based Claims*. London: Henry Jackson Society. http://henryjacksonsociety. org/wp-content/uploads/2012/12/HJS-Faith-in-the-Public-Sphere-Report.pdf.

Tarlo, Emma. 2010. *Visibly Muslim: Fashion, Politics, Faith*. Oxford, New York: Berg.

Togarasei, Lovemore. 2012. 'Mediating the Gospel: Pentecostal Christianity and Media Technology in Botswana and Zimbabwe.' *Journal of Contemporary Religion* 27, no. 2: 257–74. doi.org/10.1080/13537903.2012.675740.

Whitehead, Deborah. 2015. 'The Evidence of Things Unseen: Authenticity and Fraud in the Christian Mommy Blogosphere.' *Journal of the American Academy of Religion* 83, no. 1: 120–50. https://doi.org/10.1093/jaarel/lfu083.

Chapter 11

Disease, disability and the religious response

Introduction

Both within and outside institutionalized, formal religious spaces, people look to religions for healing and helping. It is an area that has often perplexed social scientists and invited both scorn and scepticism. And yet, promises of healing, and other forms of what may be regarded as miraculous transformations, are central to many religions' beliefs and practices. These may be performed and transmitted through prayers during a regular service, through special healing services, or in events sponsored by the religious organization or individuals. In a survey conducted in 2003, the popular American weekly newsmagazine, *Newsweek*, found that an overwhelming majority believed prayer could heal people: '72 percent of Americans say they would welcome a conversation with their physician about faith; the same number say they believe that praying to God can cure someone–even if science says the person doesn't stand a chance' (www.newsweek.com/faith-healing-133365, last accessed May 2020).

There is certainly an urgent need worldwide to help people with chronic illnesses and disabilities. According to the World Health Organization, about 15 per cent of the world's population is disabled www.who.int/disabilities/world_report/2011/report/en/ last accessed Mar. 2020). The number is increasing due to the ageing population and prevalence of disabling illnesses such as cancer, cardio-vascular disease and diabetes. Measured against virtually every outcome, such as education, occupation and transport, disabled people are worse off than the general population, and worse off globally in less advantaged communities. Poverty is much higher for people in families with disabled members. In the UK, around half of disabled people are in work, and the pattern is similar, or worse, in other countries. Helen Barnard, the Executive Director of the Joseph Rowntree Foundation, a UK-based Quaker charity, called for more recognition of the deleterious impact of disability. She pointed out that there are material, practical steps that governments and other organizations can take to help people with disabilities (www.jrf.org.uk/blog/its-not-right-four-million-disabled-people-are-locked-poverty, last accessed May 2020). 'It's not right that four million disabled people are locked in poverty', she said:

> In our country we believe in taking care of one another and protecting each other from harm – so it's simply unacceptable that 3.8 million disabled adults and 300,000 disabled children are trapped in poverty; and that over 3 in 10 disabled people live in poverty compared to only 2 in 10 non-disabled people.

A future crisis facing disabled people is how they will be disproportionately affected by climate change. Aleksandra Kosanic et al. (www.campus.uni-konstanz.de/en/science/climate-change-is-a-disability-rights-issue, last accessed May 2020) drew on their recent research to argue that global environmental change should be considered a disability rights issue. They argued that damage to ecosystems and exposure to infectious diseases will increase inequalities and marginalization globally, affecting the world's disabled populations disproportionately. Disabled people are already disadvantaged by poor access to resources, services and knowledge, which will only worsen with climate-change events and disasters.

There is a mixed response to the crisis of disability from religious organizations, with most focusing on healing rather than significant material assistance. And yet, there is disagreement about the extent to which such interventions are helpful, as opposed to, for example, social welfare programmes. With such a worldwide and growing issue, a sociologist of religion will research and analyse the roles of religious organizations and the wider societal response. As discussed in Chapter 7, 'the body' is a significant metaphor and communicator of society's norms and rules. The ways religions understand, classify, monitor and regulate 'the body' may differ, yet most share a separatist perspective of mind/body/spirit reflecting a sacred/profane binary that comes into sharp relief when illness or disability presents.

Case example: Moses unhealed

Imagine that the most powerful all-knowing being in the universe has an important task in mind that will ensure his Chosen People will be freed from slavery in Egypt and allow them to return to their Promised Land. He must choose someone to convince Egypt's ruler, the Pharaoh, to 'let my people go'. It will be the speech of the century, if not the millennium. And so, God chose Moses to confront the Pharaoh with his demands, after which, God decided, Moses would have another important task. On the way to taking the Chosen People out of Egypt to the Promised Land, God would meet him on the peak of Mount Horeb (today's Mount Sinai) and give him some tablets of stone upon which he would write God's rules, take them back down the mountain and read them aloud to the Chosen People waiting below. These would be God's Ten Commandments which would govern his people and others to come forever. It was important to get them right.

These would be challenging tasks for any strong and articulate person, yet there was one perplexing fact: God had chosen a man with a speech impairment, what future generations may call a 'stutter' (see e.g. Barbara Goldberg's 1989 reference to the Talmudic explanation of the origins of Moses's stutter). Being all-knowing, and all-powerful, one would think that God would have known that, so Moses instantly questioned God's instructions and drew his attention to the problem. These were two speeches that cannot go wrong, and so Moses urges God (Exodus 4:10 KJV) to think again: 'And Moses said unto the Lord, O my Lord, I am not eloquent, neither heretofore, nor since thou hast spoken unto thy servant: but I am slow of speech, and of a slow tongue.'

God, being all powerful, could have changed all that and healed him on the spot, but he did not. Instead, he chastized Moses for not realizing that God had this figured out all along, God does not make mistakes (Exodus 4:10 KJV): 'And the Lord said unto him, Who hath made man's mouth? or who maketh the dumb, or deaf, or the seeing, or the blind? have not I, the Lord?' He then reassures Moses that he will personally tutor him (Exodus 4:10 KJV): 'Now therefore go, and I will be with thy mouth, and teach thee what thou shalt say.'

Moses, not losing his nerve despite being up against God, is still not happy. He definitely does not want to do this alone, even with divine inspiration and intervention, so he asks God to send him someone to help him. God agrees to send Aaron, Moses's brother who he knows can speak well (Exodus 4:15–17 KJV):

> And thou shalt speak unto him, and put words in his mouth: and I will be with thy mouth, and with his mouth, and will teach you what ye shall do. And he shall be thy spokesman unto the people: and he shall be, even he shall be to thee instead of a mouth, and thou shalt be to him instead of God. And thou shalt take this rod in thine hand, wherewith thou shalt do signs.

So, in the end, God does a lot for Moses: he promises to back him up, tell him what to say, send his brother to speak for him and even gives him some sort of stick to further empower him. The one thing, some might think the obvious thing, God does not do is heal him. Why not?

God, as they say, works in mysterious ways and while rabbis, imams and theologians have discussed this question for centuries, a sociologist should probably work it out immediately. The point God was making was likely not about individual stardom where Moses outperforms the Pharaoh with his brilliance and eloquence. Perhaps it was, rather, a point about collaboration, caring and community and a reminder from God, who we are told has made people in his own image, that he has also made people who have other impairments besides a speech impediment: deaf people, blind people. If God can accept Moses as he is, can support him to go about his business without being healed, why do religious people mainly do otherwise and strive for healing for themselves and others?

The religious 'problem'

What has long been observed as a 'problem of evil' or 'problem of meaning' in the world is bound up in the concept of a good God in a bad world. It is a straightforward problem, without a straightforward solution: God is good; God is all-powerful; God is all-knowing; bad things happen; how can bad things happen in a world controlled by an omnipotent, loving God?

The process of reconciling what may seem contradictory is known in religious language as 'theodicy', a term originally used by the 18th-century rationalist philosopher Gottfried Wilhelm Leibniz. Based on two Greek words, a divine being or god (*theos*) and justice (*dike*), a theodicy is how people interpret divine justice. While Leibniz wrestled with this problem philosophically, of more relevance here is how groups of people have wrestled with it in their own lives.

Max Weber positioned his work on theodicy within his sociology of religion and general theories of sociology. He argued that such a resolution was impossible for monotheistic religions, particularly those which believed in the Bible as the literal word of God. He used as a main example Baptists, a religion reflecting what he described as ascetic Protestantism. Weber described this as a form of worldly asceticism, which is 'the religious rationalization of the world in its most extreme form' (Weber 1930, 1992, 147). The degree of rationalization present in any religious group will determine the extent to which they can create an effective theodicy, Weber argued, with the religion's existence becoming vulnerable with the rise of science. He concluded that this kind of religion offers 'no rational solution' to the problem of meaning, holding God and the world in constant unresolved tension.

Weber argued (1992, 144–54) that Baptists believe that God speaks to them through revelations coming through the Holy Spirit, and are therefore guided by what they feel as the spirit, rather than the doctrines of the church. They believe that they personally receive the Holy Spirit's guidance through periods of quiet prayer, occasionally interrupted by what they sometimes describe as being 'slain by the spirit', or by what Weber called 'hysterical conditions' (1992, 149). Their faith in a providential God reassures them that his goodness will prevail. Weber argued that their rejection of rules, priestly teachers and the Bible as the sole authority was the main characteristic of the Baptist sect. They renounce earthly pleasures and try for a kind of salvation earned by the spirit, available to anyone choosing to be reborn.

Weber therefore places the problem of meaning as irreconcilable within the Baptist sect. In contrast, he argued that the karmic belief in non-monotheistic that one's daily actions will earn or deny the adherent a more or less advantageous next life in rebirth was 'the most complete formal solution of the problem of theodicy' (Weber 1992, 145).

Magic is the other problem threatening the worldly ascetics, Weber argued. He wrote that providence was a form of magic, even though the adherents' would argue otherwise, because providence is essentially the idea of 'dynamic activity manifested in god's personal, providential rule over the world' (Weber 1992, 144). That's why, he said, prayer and sacrifice originate in magic, with prayer having a 'business-like, rationalized form' (Weber 1992, 26) where the petitioners need to show God why they are deserving. He also argued that salvation religion, with its emphasis on a personal saviour, is analogous to magic with its emphasis on a wizard.

In a more contemporary example, sociologist Robert Wuthnow follows a Weberian argument by suggesting some of the prayers he witnessed in small groups have a pragmatic tone that threatens the religion. He cites an example (Wuthnow 1994, 266):

> One group leader, for example, pointed out how troublesome it was for group members to assert God's existence based on having miraculously found a parking space. 'I want to say, well, does that mean that God is not loving me when I don't get a parking space? Does it mean that God is punishing me and not loving me if I get cancer or if my husband is killed in a car accident? ... Come on now, let's think a little more deeply!'

Wuthnow suggests this is an example where people show that they believe in a pragmatic kind of God, who might be able to help them through difficult situations, but did not want to ask him for anything they thought might be too difficult. Such belief, Wuthnow argued, 'puts their faith on shaky ground' (Wuthnow 1994, 266).

Mary Douglas (1966, 174), writing about the purpose of ritual, argued along the same lines. She suggested that religions which stress the material benefits of their rites are vulnerable:

> If the faithful have come to think of rites as means to health and prosperity, like so many magic lamps to be worked by rubbing, there comes a day when the whole ritual apparatus must seem an empty mockery.[1]

Those three social scientists – Weber, Wuthnow and Douglas – link the nature of prayer and its power to magic: they argue that adherents believe that God is the magician who can perform miracles when asked and their faith is threatened when their prayers are unanswered. Questions can be raised against them, of course. Both in my own ethnographic work with a women's prayer group (Day 2005) and R. Marie Griffith's research on a Christian women's prayer group, prayer was seen as a spiritual practice that helped the women even when their prayers for healing were not answered as expected: 'failed healings, then, are reinterpreted by these women as opportunities for spiritual growth' (Griffith 1997, 89).

One of most significant studies of contemporary ritual healing was Meredith McGuire's (1988) exploration of such practices in urban, middle-class New Jersey. Her large, qualitative study involved 300 interviews and observations in a variety of groups focused on healing: Christian healing, Eastern inspired, metaphysical, occult/psychic and technical (such as chiropractors). The study's major finding was how the research participants found ways to make meaning and sense out of the illness, in ways that would comfort and empower. The main difference between those involved in the alternative healing practices and those engaged with standard biomedicine was the extent to which the 'person' was conceived in terms of mind/body/spirit, rather than simply a body to be healed.

McGuire (1988, 5–6)[2] urged sociologists of religion to engage with salient sociological questions when considering healing practices: 'what does this suggest about society and the social location of these beliefs and practices? Of what larger social phenomenon in this an example?' Her insight into the phenomenon created two main arguments that run throughout the book. First, she found that participants did not come to the groups suddenly, as a last resort, with an illness to be healed, but rather were already involved in and committed to a version of reality that was wider and deeper than simply healing. Second, McGuire positions medical practices beside, not above, those alternative practices. Sociologists need to see medical reality as not the one, true reality but one amongst several approaches, that is, like other parts of a social system, socially constructed. McGuire (1988, 40) also opened up ideas of what 'healing' might mean, well beyond thinking only of the physical body:

> Respondents described as 'healings' such diverse situations as a broken lawn mower suddenly working, a chronically disorganized chequebook becoming balanced, receipt of some unexpected money or a pet surviving a particularly difficult labor.

She examined 'ritual' as a key part of the healing processes in three ways: language; non-verbal, concrete symbolic objects; and symbolism through imagery and visualizations.

Multiple healing agents

As described in Chapter 9, Aasim Padela et al. (2017, 847) argue that, while American Muslims are diverse ethnically, they share a religious tradition that shapes their beliefs and practices. Their review of relevant literature informed their assumption that, despite their origins and current places of residence in the United States, American Muslims generally incorporate both spiritual and biomedical strategies in their response to healing but vary in their views about how accepting the biomedical system was of their religion-informed worldviews, leading in some cases to mistrust. Their literature review also showed that many Muslims accepted an explanation that diseases such as cancer reflected the will of God. The research team then conducted focus groups at mosques whose compositions reflected African American, Arab American and South Asian American Muslims, asking questions covering the roles of God and other agents in the healing process. The groups were composed of mostly Sunni adherents, equally representative of men and women, with an age range of 18 to 75.

They found that participants viewed health as having spiritual, physical and health components, with the most important agent being God, followed by human agents such as family, imams and health workers. They actively engaged with God in their rituals of healing, primarily through prayer and recitation of scripture, and also believed he worked through other agents. It was important to the participants that health professionals recognized that they, and the treatments they might prescribe, were only tools of healing, with God being the ultimate giver of both disease and healing. Many participants spoke of disjuncture experienced in a medical setting, with medical practitioners being unaware of the Islamic spiritual dimensions or the patient's expectation of a holistic approach. Participants also cited the important role of imams, in helping the healing process through prayers and spiritual instructions and also through counselling and other forms of pastoral care. They stressed the significant role of imams during hospitalization and wished for more Muslim chaplaincy in hospitals. The researchers (Padela et al. 2017, 855) found that the important role of imams also in non-American examples: sermons given in Bangladesh about tuberculosis resulted in increased detection and treatment; in Afghanistan, an imam's outreach programmes promoted reproductive planning to reduce maternal death rates; the British Heart Foundation works with imams to deliver health awareness-based sermons during Ramadan. Family members were also important both for emotional as well as material support, as were, to a lesser extent, friends and other members of the community. The research team concluded by recommending that more data are required about the population distribution of Muslims so that health care provision is able to adapt, and can work to incorporate more partnership with the human agents in health and healing.

In their study of Muslims in northern England, Nussrat O. Hussain and Simon Dein (2018) found that it was common practice for UK South Asian Muslims to seek help from *pirs*, traditional spiritual healers, either exclusively or sometimes combined with their experiences with National Health Service. Those from a Pakistani-Kashmiri background were most likely to rely wholly on spiritual healing. The review by the authors

(Hussain and Dein 2018, 168) of other academic studies showed similar patterns throughout the UK with, again, some culturally specific variations depending on people's backgrounds. The evidence, they say, is that although visiting *pirs* for healing is a common practice amongst British Muslims, most will also seek help through standard secular sources, such as the National Health Service. The authors make a distinction between 'High Islam' and folk practices, and they write that, although contentious amongst some scholars and religious leaders, a belief in 'unseen worlds' (*Al Ghayb*) is central to Islam. They write that throughout the Muslim world mental illness and some forms of physical illness, particularly epilepsy, are attributed to three supernatural causes: jinn, sorcery and evil eye. They explain that 'jinn' refers to unseen spirits, sorcery to forms of spell-casting and evil eye to a malevolent, loaded look from someone who may not be even aware they possess such power. The practices of people engaged in related healing activities vary from drinking certain liquids, praying, acquiring amulets, reading or hearing and reciting scripture.

The beliefs and practices discussed in this chapter illustrate that there may not be a binary distinction between religion/spiritual healing and biomedicine, Sipco Vellenga (2008) suggested that such a clear distinction may not hold up under further scrutiny, In research carried out in the Netherlands he compared practices of services of salvation and healing at a Pentecostal church and a hospital's cancer centre. In exploring potential similarities and differences four main points were considered: concepts and objects; means and methods; 'healers' and patients; and effects and expectations. The study found that there were at least five principal points in common: a tendency to objectify the underlying framework; an instrumental way of working; 'healers' having a high ascribed status; efficacy along the indirect line of symbolic healing; and a comparable way of dealing with unknown and uncontrolled forces. Through observations and interviews, Vellenga found commonality in two approaches. First, they were each part of a larger belief system. Religious practitioners believed in a larger system of supernatural power and engagements, and the medical practitioners believed in a natural order that can be studied and to some extent restored by bioscience. The context is important, he discussed (Vellenga 2008, 328) in order to understand what it is that practitioners hope to change:

> Both types of healing can be considered as attempts to contribute to the improvement of health. In 1948, the World Health Organisation (WHO) defined the concept of health as 'a state of complete physical, mental and social well-being and not merely the absence of disease or infirmity'. Nowadays this broad definition is also shared by a large part of the Dutch population. According to data of surveys of the Netherlands institute for Social Research (SCP), the Dutch have related the concept of good health even more to 'feeling fit' and 'psychological balance' than to the absence of a disease since the 1980s.
>
> (Van Campen 2007)

That means some people have different, more subjectivized ideas and aspirations about health and healing. It is useful, he discussed (Vellenga 2008, 328) to differentiate the terms, with 'disease' referring to a physical disorder, and 'illness' referring to how people may define and experience their health. Accordingly, this distinction can also be applied to the terms 'curing' and 'healing', where the former means recovering from a disease and the latter to an improved experience of how a person experiences their health or sickness. Vellenga's description of a healing service shows that the man conducting the service explicitly links healing to conversion, saying that people must first enter into a relationship with Jesus Christ. As people come forward for healing, he combines prayer, touch, scripture and command techniques and has them confirm by either speech or action that they have been healed. When Vellenga observed interactions at the cancer centre, he also saw that there were a number of diagnostic techniques employed, as well as different treatments proposed. The engagement was between the patient, together with their friends or family who accompanied them, and the medical team. A psychologist was rarely present and nor were pastoral workers, who are only involved with patients once they become hospitalized.

Vellenga (2008, 330) considered how the dualistic relationships inherent in both the religious healing and the medical approach can be struggles for meaning and coherence. For the religious person, this can be a battle between good and evil, or God and Satan. That battle shows itself as illness in people which is why, he says, illness is more a religious than a physical problem. While the medical team at the cancer centre disavow the efficacy of unproven, alternative treatments, they acknowledge that in many cases, patients may find them helpful. Vellenga (2008, 331) quotes from a Dutch Cancer Society brochure that is distributed by centre which acknowledges that an additional, unproved therapy may be helpful accompanied by a regular therapy: 'because someone feels better if he/she is actively involved in the process of healing, or because someone believes that the additional treatment supports his/her recovery'.

In discussing how the religious 'healer' gains legitimacy and authority Vellenga (2008, 332) writes that his authority in the church community seems to be primarily based on the belief that God called him to do this work of healing, which conforms to a Weberian (1978) theory about charismatic leaders. Weber argued that believers assume such charismatic leaders have special, sometimes supernatural, powers. Doctors also have a high status amongst patients, with authority to rule over life and death.

Vellenga notes (2008, 335) that, while miraculous healings rarely take place in the venue he studied, and one that may have appeared to be a miraculous healing may have been a spontaneous, natural event, those who attend feel better and often empowered by the experience. Significantly, the healer offers little to those with chronic illnesses, leading Vellenga to comment that responsibility for failure to heal is put 'on the shoulders of the sick' who are blamed for lack of faith or openness to God, or a blockage caused by sin.

In contrast, the efficacy of the cancer treatments depends on the nature of the tumour and treatments available. Vellenga concludes by saying both practices assume they are dealing with forces that are beyond their immediate control. While the religious healing event may provide comfort to some people, patients in a cancer centre may also benefit from more pastoral support.

Care versus cure

Religious institutions, in their focus on healing and cure, have generally been running against the dominant trend of the 'social model of "disability"', which has dominated medical, policy and activist conversations and policy initiatives for several decades yet seems marginal at best and often absent from religious discourse and practice. In turn, religion is also markedly absent from disability discourses. Sarah Imhoff's (2017, 2; see also Creamer 2009) comprehensive review of disability literature found that:

> In general, scholarly works on disability, religion rarely appears. In three of the most widely read disability studies readers, together comprising more than 1000 pages, there is no sustained discussion of religion. The entire run of the Journal of Literary and Cultural Disability Studies has only a single passing reference to religion, apart from the obligatory lists ('gender, race, religion,' etc.). And when religion appears in disability studies literature as something more than just part of a list, it tends to be cast in a negative light. 'Religion' often becomes a monolith creating or upholding the idea of the 'normal' that oppresses and excludes people with disabilities.

Although there is a recognized sub-field of theology known as 'disability theology', its main weakness is the lack of disabled theologians contributing to the discourse, as John Swinton (2011, 276) writes:

> Firstly, most influential theologians, historically and contemporarily have been able-bodied and have thus assumed an able-bodied hermeneutic God. A consequence of this is that the experience of disability has not been allowed to voice itself effectively within the development of Christian doctrine and tradition.[…] Our 'normal' constructions mean that disability can only be perceived as an abnormality which, it is assumed, cannot reflect the true image of God.

Most religions have not taken disability as a separate issue to consider or theologize about. Melinda Jones (2007, 138) writes that little has been written about Judaism:

> Because the need to understand a Jewish perspective on disability is relatively new, there has been little research pulling together the relevant texts and ideas on the subject of disability. However, at the very centre of Judaism there is an approach to the world from which we can derive a Jewish perspective of disability, a perspective which is extremely supportive of the modern ideas of the human rights approach to people with disabilities.

Religious people and organizations also often draw on models of disability that cast the disabled person as someone abnormal, with their impairments arising from sin, to be taught virtues of suffering (Swinton 2011; Eiesland 1994).

Originally proposed by a UK disability rights activist organization, the Union of the Physically Impaired Against Segregation (UPIAS), the 'social model' began with the distinction between impairment and disability: an 'impairment' in this context is a physical attribute, such as blindness, whereas a 'disability' is the consequence of society creating, or not removing, obstacles or not providing assistance, respect or information. 'Being deaf is only disabling if the people around you haven't bothered to learn sign language. Being blind is only disabling if the environment around you is built around the assumption that everyone can see' (Swinton 2011, 279). That idea was subsequently developed by Michael Oliver (1996) and became a popular identity signifier. Critics, including Oliver himself, later pointed out that the model should not be adopted uniformly, as people's experiences and social contexts are very different, as is the nature of impairments.

An important difference between the social model and the medical model is an emphasis on cure and 'fixing'. It is usually demeaning to be cast as somebody who is seen as abnormal and, consequently, unequal and in need of repair. While the social model locates disability in society, and seeks to change social conditions to allow people with impairments to participate equally, the religious model more often focuses on healing and cure, shifting the responsibility for equal participation onto the individual and the extent to which they are 'blessed' with being changed. As a result of an ageing population, religious institutions will have increasingly to respond to the growing numbers of impaired people in their congregations with diverse and sometimes invisible impairments.

There appears to be a wider shift within secular health care settings away from 'cure' to 'care'. With the erosion of welfare states and the crises of national health care services, as well as an increasing ageing population, more people have a disabling condition that interferes with major life activities. The 'cure' approach may also be disempowering as most religious organizations still focus almost exclusively on searching for miracles, perhaps with consequences relating to inclusion, diversity, sustainability and resource management. This may result from theological constructions around healing, social constructions around disability and perceptions of how the religious organizations obtain legitimacy through showcasing healing successes by providing services of, for example, deliverance, prayer vigils and exorcisms. This focus on cure may have wider disempowering and marginalizing implications for people with impairments, leading to further social exclusion. There are, of course, exceptions and contrary evidence, often found in studies of the community practices church members undertake. Courtney Bender's (2011) ethnographic study of religious people making and delivering food to people suffering with HIV/AIDs is an excellent example.

The religious response often draws on views of the person based on modernity's ideas of the individual and autonomy, writes Swinton (2011, 291), drawing on Thomas Reynolds's Foucauldian (2008) analysis of power:

> Tom Reynolds, another systematic theologian, applies a Foucauldian analysis to push us to re-think issues of power, individualism, competitiveness and other social goods that have come to be highly valued within modern liberal societies. Normality, he argues, is the product of an accepted understanding of the nature of 'the good.' Within liberal cultures 'the good' is defined in line with the social goods highlighted. (autonomy, freedom, self-representation etc)

Miraculous healing

While there are several diverse religious responses to healing disability, disease and other conditions, most assume at some level supernatural intervention, generally focusing on prayer and 'deliverance'. What they tend to have in common is being framed within the language of 'miracles', usually understood as practices that heal people otherwise failed by biomedical practices. The religious term 'deliverance' covers a number of practices; the most publicly familiar, through media coverage and popular culture, may be 'exorcisms'. The assumption is that a person's disability or affliction is due to an external, malevolent force, such as a devil or witch.

Jörg Stolz (2011, 436) says that a main driver of Pentecostalism's worldwide growth is its promise of miraculous healings and claims that 'very impressive miracles and healings are routinely produced: paralytics arise from wheelchairs, cancerous ulcers disappear, legs grow, cavities are mysteriously filled, and the deaf suddenly hear'. Stolz (2011, 437) sets out in his study to separate a sociological undertaking from an anthropological one. While the latter has produced many studies about healing, the scholars tend to offer a largely descriptive account without analysing the 'social techniques' used by the Pentecostals to effect the phenomenon. Conversely, his sociological study of a Swiss healing conference, using both observation and interview, asked two questions: 'by what social techniques are miracles and healings in Pentecostal healing workshops produced? Second: why do these workshops continue to persist, even though people might learn over time that these healings and miracles are often greatly exaggerated?' He argues that 'social techniques' such as suggestion, rhythm and music, combined with 'context factors' of audience size and beliefs, interact with 'causal mechanisms', such as probability, latency, selection and editing effects, to produce the healing phenomena. Like the above study by Vellenga, Stolz's study notes that Pentecostals link disease and suffering to sin and evil, requiring the afflicted to put their faith in Christ and God in order to be healed. He acknowledges that healings are valued highly amongst Pentecostals and those belonging to charismatic movements more widely, with evidence of privileged knowledge and 'gifts' of healing proof that God's work as told in the scriptures is active in the world today. Further, as Vellenga found, the person carrying out the 'healing' does not claim to be the healer, but a channel for the Holy Spirit. They also do not usually reject biomedicine outright, but value religious healing as more pure and powerful. Stolz (2011, 459) cites a number of critical approaches that argue there is no such thing as supernatural healing but notes that these works often create such a negative view of the Pentecostals that the writers fail to appreciate the positive benefits experienced by adherents. His research method identifies what are described as macro and micro techniques. The first, macro, stage is when the 'healer' introduced techniques to prepare the audience members for healing. These usually consisted of short statements claiming that Jesus is present in the hall and that 'all things are possible' (Stolz 2011, 466). He then adopts techniques like hypnosis by urging audience members to, variously, close their eyes, or sing, or remain quiet. The healer then moves on to issuing commands, such as 'We take authority over sickness and disease and pain in this meeting right now' or telling the Holy Spirit to go to certain people or places in the room. The healer may also have music playing and will often vary the rhythm and pace of both his performance and the background music. At the point when the leader wants audience members to show that healings have occurred, he will increase the pace and urge speed in coming forward in order 'to create the impression that a "fireworks of healings" is occurring all over the auditorium' (Stolz 2011, 467). Stolz analysed several more aspects of the event, and, together with interview analysis, arrived at several important conclusions:

1   Miracles are perceived mainly through the style of interaction (quick-fire requests for quick testimonies) and the probability that at least one person in a large gathering will attest publicly to something miraculous happening.

2   Verifiability is limited to what occurs in the event itself, with unsuccessful interactions tending to be forgotten.
3   Healings are only reported by those who can claim they have felt something occur, and the leader will 'edit' the accounts to produce a positive version.

His analysis concluded that Pentecostals are not intellectually weak but use what he described as '(bounded) rationality'. This meant that Pentecostals have a 'normal' belief structure, are often quite sceptical, use a practical, rational system to explain both healings and non-healings, and reach conclusions on what they believe is good evidence.

   In their study of healing practices in Malawi, Nicolette D. Manglos and Jenny Trinitapoli (2011) explain the importance of context: Malawi is a country where the HIV/AIDS epidemic affects large segments of the population every day. They argue that faith healing should be seen as a 'The Third Therapeutic System' as it is often used in conjunction with traditional and biomedical interventions. While the more widespread access to medical treatments and condoms has affected the course of the disease, their study shows how faith healing influences how people interpret and live with the disease. Another important part of the context is the growth of Pentecostalism and its focus on miracles, showing how religion emphasizes 'the marketing of faith healing as an invaluable product in this context' (see also Dilger 2008; Becker and Geissler 2007; Gifford 2004). The authors discuss how 'traditional healing' is different from faith healing in that the faith healers depend on a specific religious tradition, such as Christianity or Islam. Further, they argue that a problem in understanding faith healing arises because most studies are limited to ethnographies of Pentecostal-Charismatic churches and therefore not enough is known about other religious healing practices. Their study, which they say is the first to use quantitative methods to study faith healing in Africa, consisted of three surveys in three distinct religious/ethnic regions in Malawi. They wanted to find out (Manglos and Trinitapoli 2011, 108): how prevalent across the religious groups faith healing might be; the relationship between faith healing and congregation-level engagement with both biomedical and traditional practices; and, measured by the level of individual worry about the AIDS epidemic, the experiences of people living within the epidemic. Those research objectives were framed to help them explore 'the extent to which faith healing functions as a third therapeutic system relative to the biomedical and traditional models, with distinct consequences for how individuals experience the generalized AIDS epidemic'. In setting the theoretical context, the authors position the topic of healing within the wider scholarship of colonial and post-colonial studies (see also Meekosha 2011), discussing how the formation of the biomedical subject in sub-Saharan Africa 'is the result of a complex process of agency and exchange on the part of both the colonizers and the colonized and that traditional and biomedical therapeutic systems coexist in contemporary sub-Saharan Africa'. That focus has resulted in two contemporary schools of thought, with one seeing health-seeking behaviour as essentially pragmatic, arising from individual experiences, while the second suggests it is driven by deep-seated cultural forms 'expressed through collective rituals (Comaroff 1980)'(Manglos and Trinitapoli 2011, 108). The authors contend (p. 108) that these two schools of thought will produce dramatically different conclusions, with the first assuming that the individuals can simultaneously navigate both systems, while the second depicts a 'contestation between systems, emphasizing the fundamental incongruities in the assumptions underlying Western medicine and African traditional medicine(Westerlund 2006; Some 1998; Okwu 1979)'. There are practical, as well as theoretical considerations in considering those two systems, the authors write: 'The generalized AIDS epidemic in sub-Saharan Africa has thrown these larger theoretical and historical issues into stark relief.' While governments and aid agencies focus on individual behaviour, treatment and testing, the traditional methods also emphasize community contexts and influences.

In Malawi, there are broadly two types of non-biomedical healing: 'traditional', incorp-orating herbs or divination, and faith healing. Evidence the authors cite from studies of African independent churches show that faith healing may be a hybrid system, with adherents also accessing biomedical resources. The faith healing components are some-times church-based prayer or water-immersion events, and also private consultations. Studies of Pentecostal churches show an emphasis on sin and salvation, and a public res-toration of the 'individual's moral status in the community while solidifying the notion that the ultimate causes of AIDS are moral and communal and that the only lasting cures are spiritual ones' (Manglos and Trinitapoli 2011, 109). They also note that evi-dence from other studies and their own fieldwork suggest that religious faith healing predates the Pentecostal movement in Africa and has been found in a myriad of other denominations.

Through their survey and analysis at both the congregational and individual level, the authors found that faith healers and adherents generally combine both biomedical and faith healing strategies, although there was a notable resistance towards the use of condoms, and to some elements of traditional healing if supernatural powers are invoked. They found that faith healing is most common in Pentecostal churches, followed by Mission Protestant churches, African independent churches, Catholic churches, New Mission Protestants churches and mosques. They write that (Manglos and Trinitapoli 2011, 118):

> The significant number of mosques engaging in faith healing is surprising and may indicate a substantial cross-fertilization among religious groups as well as the poten-tial of all religious traditions to adapt to the needs and concerns of the local context. While faith healing may have its roots in Pentecostalism or African-independent churches, it is not exclusive to these traditions.

Further, they found that there was a high level of new membership in churches prac-tising faith healing, suggesting that was a reason for joining and, given the nature of the epidemic, evidence that growth is likely to continue. They also found that the pragmatic reasons for joining featured highly, as one theoretical model suggests, but also the ritual-istic, communal nature of the associations and events were important.

Religion, disability and stigma

Many religious people link illness and disability to moral, as well as physical, health and therefore can easily slip into creating stigma and shame. Erving Goffman (1963) famously introduced the concept of stigma as a socially created sense of shame for not conforming to some pre-existing stereotype (see also Jacoby 2008).

While his definition and discussion have influenced ideas about stigma both in sociology and a wider public imagination, critics (see e.g. the themed issue of *Sociological Review* edited by Imogen Tyler and Tom Slater 2018; Parker and Aggleton 2003) point to its ahistoricity and neglect of how such experiences are unevenly distributed in societies. It may also assume that ideas about homogeneous norms (or stereotypes) are shared equally.

Sherry et al. (2020) write in their introduction to their edited collection about disablist health speech that disability hate speech is an everyday experience for many people. And yet, religious leaders and followers are often amongst the worst offenders. Beata Borowska-Beszta (2020, 166–75) explores how Marxist ideology in Poland damaged disabled people through its belief in a perfect socialist worker, but there was also no evidence that churches acted to reduce disablist rhetoric. In Nigeria, leprosy is still prevalent (Ebenso et al. 2019), with 3,500 cases detected annually, and so is the stigma and discrimination attached to it by Christian and Muslim leaders and followers.

A similar point was made by George Goggin and Christopher Newell (2005), describing Australian attitudes towards disabled people as discriminatory, producing a form of social apartheid. Further, Goggin and Newell (2005, 210) say the situation for religious organizations is unlikely to change until people with 'a publicly recognised disability' are appointed into senior positions:

> This entails far more than making churches physically accessible. It requires genuine recognition of the oppression of people with disabilities, and the fact that the poor and oppressed are supposed to have a central place in the doing of theology. For the churches and NGOs there is a significant opportunity to provide leadership, especially in terms of reconciliation, and embracing justice-making as part of this.

Sample questions for private study

1   How can a 'turn' to care, not cure, be justified in religion today?
2   Suggest at least three sociological explanations for supernatural healing events.

Sample class exercise

A visit from a disability activist.

Notes

1   For a contrary view, and discussion of how many religious people respond positively to 'partial' healings, see Day (2005).
2   See also her other work on healing, principally McGuire 1986, 1993.

Indicative reading

Becker, Felicitas, and P. Wenzel Geissler. 2007. 'Searching for Pathways in a Landscape of Death: Religion and AIDS in East Africa.' *Journal of Religion in Africa* 37: 1–15. DOI: https://doi.org/10.1163/157006607X166564.

Bender, Courtney. 2011. *Heaven's Kitchen: Living Religion at God's Love We Deliver.* Chicago, IL: University of Chicago Press.

Borowska-Beszta, Beata. 2020. 'Amputation of Disability as Hate Speech Pattern in Poland.' In *Disability Hate Speech: Social, Cultural and Political Contexts,* edited by Mark Sherry, Terje Olsen, Janikke Solstad Vedeler and John Eriksen, 166–75. New York, Abingdon, Oxon: Routledge.

Comaroff, Jean. 1980. 'Healing and the Cultural Order: The Case of the Barolong Boo Ratshidi of Southern Africa.' *American Ethnologist* 7: 637–57.

Creamer, Deborah. 2009. *Disability and Christian Theology: Embodied Limits and Constructive Possibilities.* New York: Oxford University Press.

Day, Abby. 2005. 'Doing Theodicy: An Empirical Study of a Women's Prayer Group.' *Journal of Contemporary Religion* 20, no. 3: 343–56.

Dilger, Hansjörg. 2008. 'We are All Going to Die: Kinship, Belonging, and the Morality of HIV/Aids Related Illnesses and Deaths in Rural Tanzania.' *Anthropological Quarterly* 81, no. 1: 207–32.

Douglas, Mary. 1966. *Purity and Danger: An Analysis of Pollution and Taboo.* London: Routledge.

Ebenso, Bassey, James Newell, Nick Emmel, Gbenga Adeyemi and Bola Ola. 2019. 'Changing Stigmatisation of Leprosy: An Exploratory, Qualitative Life Course Study in Western Nigeria.' *BMJ Global Health* 4: e001250. doi:10.1136.

Eiesland, Nancy. 1994. *The Disabled God: Toward a Liberatory Theology of Disability.* Nashville, TN: Abingdon Press.

Fibiger, S. 1994. 'Did Moses and Demosthenes Stutter?' *Journal of Fluency Disorders Abstracts of the First World Congress on Fluency Disorders* 19: 173.

Gifford, Paul. 2004. *Ghana's New Christianity.* Bloomington, IN: Indiana University Press.

Goffman, Erving. 1963. *Stigma: Notes on the Management of Spoiled Identity.* London: Penguin.

Goggin, George, and Christopher Newell. 2005. *Disability in Australia: Exposing a Social Apartheid.* Sydney: UNSW Press.

Goldberg, Barbara. 1989. 'Historic Treatment of Stuttering: From Pebbles to Psychoanalysis.' *ASHA* 31, no. 6/7: 71.

Griffith, R. Marie. 1997. *God's Daughters: Evangelical Women and the Power of Submission.* Berkeley, CA: University of California Press.

Hussain, Nussrat O., and Simon Dein. 2018. 'An Exploration of Spiritual Healing Methods amongst the South-Asian Muslim Community in the North of England.' *Journal of Historical Archaeology and Anthropological Science* 3, no. 2: 158–69. DOI:10.15406/jhaas.2018.03.00079.

Imhoff, Sarah. 2017. 'Why Disability Studies Needs to Take Religion Seriously.' *Religions* 8, no. 9: 186; https://doi.org/10.3390/rel8090186.

Jacoby, Ann. 2008. 'Epilepsy and Stigma.' *Journal of Religion and Health* 47: 326–37. DOI 10.1007/s10943-008-9175-0.

Jones, Melinda. 2007. 'Judaism, Theology and the Human Rights of People with Disabilities,' *Journal of Religion, Disability and Health* 10, no. 3/4: 101–45. DOI: 10.1300.

Manglos, Nicolette D., and Jenny Trinitapoli. 2011. 'The Third Therapeutic System: Faith Healing Strategies in the Context of a Generalized AIDS Epidemic.' *Journal of Health and Social Behavior* 52, no. 1: 107–22. DOI: 10.1177/0022146510395025.

McGuire, Meredith B. 1986. 'Religion and Healing.' In *the Sacred in a Secular Age: Towards Revision in the Scientific Study of Religion,* edited by Phillip E. Hammond, 268–84. Berkeley, CA: University of California Press.

McGuire, Meredith B. 1988. *Ritual Healing in Suburban America*. New Brunswick, NJ: Rutgers University Press.

McGuire, Meredith B. 1993. 'Health and Spirituality as Contemporary Concerns'. *Annals of the American Academy of Political and Social Science* 527: 144–54.

Meekosha, Helen. 2011. 'Decolonising Disability: Thinking and Acting Globally.' *Disability and Society* 26, no. 6: 667–82.

Okwu, Austine S. O. 1979. 'Life, Death, Reincarnation, and Traditional Healing in Africa.' *Issue: A Journal of Opinion* 9: 19–24.

Oliver, Michael. 1996. *Understanding Disability: From Theory to Practice*. New York: St Martin's.

Padela, Aasim I., Amal Killawi, Jane Forman, Sonya DeMonner and Michele Heisler. 2017. 'American Muslim Perceptions of Healing: Key Agents in Healing, and their Roles.' *Qualitative Health Research* 22, no. 6: 846–58. DOI: 10.1177/1049732312438969.

Parker, Richard, and Peter Aggleton. 2003. 'HIV and AIDS-Related Stigma and Discrimination: A Conceptual Framework and Implications for Action.' *Social Science and Medicine* 57: 13–24.

Reynolds, Thomas E. 2008. *Vulnerable Communion: A Theology of Disability and Hospitality*. Grand Rapids, MI: Brazos Press.

Sherry, Mark, Terje Olsen, Janikke Solstad Vedeler and John Eriksen. 2020. *Disability Hate Speech: Social, Cultural and Political Contexts*. New York and Abingdon, Oxon: Routledge.

Some, Malidoma Patrice. 1998. *The Healing Wisdom of Africa*. New York: Jeremy P. Tarcher/ Putnam.

Stolz, Jörg. 2011. '"All Things are Possible": Towards a Sociological Explanation of Pentecostal Miracles and Healings.' *Sociology of Religion* 72, no. 4: 456–82.

Swinton, John. 2011. 'Who is the God we Worship? Theologies of Disability; Challenges and New Possibilities.' *International Journal of Practical Theology* 14: 273–307. DOI10.1515.

Tyler, Imogen, and Tom Slater. 2018. 'Rethinking the Sociology of Stigma.' *Sociological Review* 66, no. 4: 721–43. DOI: 10.1177/0038026118777425.

Vellenga, Sipco J. 2008. 'Longing for Health: A Practice of Religious Healing and Biomedicine Compared.' *Journal of Religion and Health* 47, no. 3: 326–37. doi: 10.1007/s10943-008-9175-0.

Weber, Max. 1930 (1992). *The Protestant Ethic and the Spirit of Capitalism*. London: Routledge.

Weber, Max. 1978 *Economy and Society,* edited by Guenther Roth and Claus Wittich. Berkeley, CA: University of California Press.

Westerlund, David. 2006. *African Indigenous Religions and Disease Causation: From Spiritual Beings to Living Humans*. Boston, MA: Brill.

Wuthnow, Robert. 1994. *Sharing the Journey: Support Groups and America's New Quest for Community*. New York: Free Press.

Chapter 12

Future religion

Nones and beyond

Introduction

The category of 'no religion' has displaced Christianity as the largest religious category in the UK and other countries are not far behind. In the United States, for example, one-quarter of the population now identifies as not religious. But what do people mean when they self-identify as such? While some may be ardent secularists and atheists, others demonstrate that 'no religion' is not a rejection of an other-worldly, numinous quality of life, or even of afterlife, just as 'religion' does not always mean beliefs or practices relating to a god (for further discussions of atheism and secularization see Chapter 3 and e.g. van der Veer, 2017; Bullivant and Lee 2016; Carroll and Norman 2016; Hutchings 2016; Zuckerman 2011, Sjöborg 2013; Contractor et al. 2013; Calhoun et al. 2011; Campbell 1971).

Many people, according to Steven Kettell (2014), adopt an atheist stance not simply to signal an absence of belief in God, but to indicate their commitment to political activism towards reducing the influence of religion (although internal divisions threaten the coherence and future of the movement). In the United States, he reports, those who self-identify as 'atheist' specifically (rather than a more diffuse category of 'non-belief') has increased from 1 to 5 per cent of the population. The rise of activist atheism has been noted elsewhere, and often its adherents are referred to as the 'new atheists'.

It is more socially acceptable in the UK than the United States to admit to an atheist identity, write Rebecca Catto and Janet Eccles (2013), and the category itself is internally varied and diffuse. Indeed, survey findings in 2018 showed that a fifth of people who say they are not religious pray (www.theguardian.com/world/2018/jan/14/half-of-non-believers-pray-says-poll). Non-religious people also participate in activities, such as meditation, which have religious roots. As Alp Arat (2017) explores, the contemporary interest in 'mindfulness' has Buddhist connotations due to its focus on the present, the now and the immediate. And yet, those who participate, increasingly because medical practitioners recommend it, would often not see themselves as 'religious'.

Besides praying, many people who describe themselves as not religious believe in the continuing presence of deceased relatives and carry lucky charms. Those secular, supernatural experiences of sensing deceased loved ones share four characteristics of being socially binding, embodied, comforting and reflecting the same relationship in earth as beyond. Understanding these complexities and nuances is important, as will be discussed below: the lived, everyday beliefs and practices of non-religious people problematizes the secular/sacred and religious/non-religious binary and boundaries (and see Kim Knott 2013 for her discussion of a 'secular sacred').

Noting the 'nones'

As the theme so far has been to carefully deconstruct and review key terms and the methods used in social science, the cautionary note to begin this chapter will come as no surprise. As always, the task is to clarify how knowledge about the question or theme is being framed and sometimes measured.

Lois Lee (2015) defined 'non- religion' as anything which is primarily defined by a relationship of difference to religion. This was an important definitional landmark, together with her insistence on questioning what had become a common-place assumption, that a secular condition was thought only to be the absence of religion, giving non-religion an insubstantial quality. Lee (2015, 3–4) set out to discover:

> whether people who are not religious are characterised and identifiable by their lack of engagement with religion, as secularisation theorists anticipate, or whether they are developed in contradistinction to religious cultures so that they are substantially and meaningfully irreligious or non-religious – rather than insubstantially a-religious, post-religious or secular.

Lee chose to situate her research in the multi-cultural/ethnic/religious cosmopolitan city of London, UK, and used semi-structured interviews that drew on Day's (2009) formulation of interviewing participants about religion without asking religious questions but focusing instead on questions about meaning, morality, purpose and non-religious existential questions.

Lee concluded (2015, 476) that the rich, relational and varied forms of beliefs and practices she found showed that self-identifying as non-religious was a poor indication of secularity: 'affiliation data do not reveal anything more extensive about secularisation because it is not possible to differentiate between positive nonreligious identities and minimal or negative ones'.

Case example: non-religious believers

When interviewing people (Day 2011) about what they believed in and how they may act out those beliefs, it was obvious to me that many people did not want to identify as religious. Some, indeed, made enormous effort to distance themselves from religion of any kind. One man (Day 2011, 67), 43-year-old Chris, spent much of the interview raging against the Catholic Church, which he described as 'illegal'. He said several times that he was an atheist without any 'beliefs'. He never prayed and said he even refused to sing hymns when attending church weddings or funerals. And so, it was surprising when, in answer to the question of how he had self-identified on the UK census, he appeared to panic, saying that was a difficult question. He finally said that 'I may be very close to being a Christian. I'd help anybody out, things like that.' The example here is instructive to press the point that being religious means different things to different people, and in his case, the idea of 'Christian' being synonymous with being a good person may reflect both his Catholic upbringing and incorporation of a phrase often heard that 'it's the Christian thing to do'.

A further complication of his case was the admission that he believed in ghosts and aliens. In some ways, his views seemed contradictory, unless one could take his self-identification as an atheist literally: he was without God, but that did not mean he was without other kinds of moral values or beliefs which, he said, may not have a rational explanation but were no less real to him for that. Other people in the same study presented similar contrasts. Most of the people who discussed believing in the continuing presence of their deceased ancestors also described themselves as not religious: belief in another spatial or temporal plane of existence was not, in their view, a 'religion' but was something to them important and intrinsic about being human. Indeed, like Chris, another man was defiant in his distaste for religion and for the belief that there was an all-powerful God controlling the universe and people's actions. Such an idea was ridiculous, Patrick told me, but that did not mean he did not believe in what he described as the continuity of the human spirit, a belief which came to him following an experience he had sensing the presence of his recently deceased mother. A 19-year-old student, Briony, said she was not religious and did not believe in God but, awakening in hospital after a suicide attempt, she had felt the sense that her grandmother was there and, she added, continues to look after her.

Studies in other countries have explored how people believe that ancestor spirits exist to protect the living, and many people will recount instances of escaping from an accident or recovering from an illness that might otherwise be described as 'miraculous': the intervention by the ancestor is a more accepted cultural explanation. The living's relationship with the ancestors is markedly material, whether by leaving gifts on a Buddhist altar or shrine in the family home, or tending graves. The ancestor continues to exist as an influential spirit as long as members of the family are still alive. When the last member dies out, their spirits merge into a general family/spirit class.

What explanation can be given for those examples? First, it is important to analytically decouple religion from belief. A theological legacy has lacked such distinction and even the more recent development of the sociology of religion retains that heritage, with authors persisting in using the word 'belief' unmarked, as if it is sufficient to simply describe someone as a 'believer' without clarifying the object of that belief: a god? a value, such as democracy? angels? Such a broader, more nuanced idea of belief becomes possible once it can be seen that 'belief' does not necessarily refer to a statement that can be held as true but not provable: a so-called 'propositional' statement such as 'I believe God exists'. Then the capacity opens for belief to be understood as a statement of faith, most likely cognitive, emotional and relational.

The propositional and universalizing way of looking at belief was critiqued strongly by anthropologist Rodney Needham (1972), who argued that ethnographic studies never interrogated how scholars were using the term belief. Further, he wrote that 'it does not constitute a natural resemblance among men, and it does not belong to the common behaviour of mankind' (Needham 1972, 188) because it had a Christian legacy and therefore could not be used universally in research. Anthropologist Malcolm Ruel (1982) was also concerned about how the term 'belief' is used, primarily because it meant different things to different people at different times. That anthropological scrutiny of the word was not evidenced amongst sociologists of religion.[1]

Such an analytical move is necessary, for example, to explain what 14-year-old Jordan (Day 2011, 79) meant when he said he was a Christian, but did not believe in anything. He discussed how he knew what Christians *did* believe in, such as God and the Bible, but that was what he did not believe in. While that would seem contradictory for some scholars, a sociologist of religion would likely pursue the line of thinking and realize, from other parts of the conversation about Jordan's religious grandparents and his sense of national identity, that his identity as a Christian was familial and nativist. He believed that being a Christian was part of his English identity and therefore, if ticking the box on the census, he would have selected 'Christian' rather than 'none'.

Analytically, Jordan's identity might be usefully interpreted as an anomaly, in the sense that Mary Douglas (1966) gave it: a case that does not belong to the wider set of which it may have initially be seen as a part.

Thinking with words

Durkheim (1897) first sociologically discussed the idea of **anomaly** as analogous to an 'other' that helped a group define its social boundaries and identified. Mary Douglas (1966, 6). picked up that idea and argued that it fit within the wider conception of what is dirty and what is pure within religious identities: 'ideas about contagion can certainly be traced to reaction to anomaly'. Perceiving who and what is an in-group or out-group is important in maintaining social boundaries, she argued.

The larger, looming question is: what if, indeed, people being studied not only have complex beliefs but also are explicitly rejecting religion and, in Euro-American countries at least, particularly Christianity? The evidence for that assertion is mounting. Between the 2001 and 2011 UK censuses, the number of people who said they had no religion nearly doubled. As discussed in more detail earlier, this also may have had something to do with generational changes (most people who ticked Christian in 2001 were over 50) and how the question was phrased and where it appeared on the census form (Day 2011).

Nonetheless, it was a dramatic decline corroborated by other surveys both in the UK and elsewhere. In Canada, for example, the decline in mainstream Christianity is occurring because members of the mainstream denominations are ageing and not being replaced by younger generations. The American Religious Identification Survey 2008 (Kosmin and Keysar 2009) revealed that 22 per cent of Americans aged 18–29 years self-identify as 'Nones'. In the Netherlands, De Graaf and Grotenhuis (2008, 595–6) concluded that religious belief will continue to decline, mainly due to generational factors: 'in the Netherlands for the years to come, a continuing "silent secularisation revolution" in which both religious belief and religious affiliation decline is the most likely longitudinal trend and not a largescale religious revival'.

Linda Woodhead (2016, 246) reports that her first large, nationally representative surveys of beliefs and values in Great Britain in 2013 found that the number of people reporting 'no religion' was just under half; by 2015, that number had increased and replaced 'Christian' as the majority choice. (For more about young 'nones' see Drescher 2016.) Her results were like the 2013 British Social Attitudes survey whose studies showed that 'no religion' had risen by two-thirds in the previous 30 years. Woodhead also points out that the rise of 'no religion' began long before it was measured by pollsters. The number of marriages solemnized by a religion has, for example, fallen steadily and now represents only 30 per cent of marriages. Significantly, she continues (Woodhead 2016, 248), it is the national religion of the UK that has shown the most reduction:

> This shows that it is decline in the number of Anglicans that is the most important cause of overall Christian decline. Anglican numbers have halved since the 1980s, as has attendance in the Church of England, and the decline continues. BSA data reveal that for every one convert, the C of E currently loses 12 people, mainly through death.

The reasons for the decline are not so much a result of a personal loss of faith amongst young people, but generational factors (and see also Callum Brown's 2015 detailed oral history of ex-Anglicans). As Woodhead (2016, 249) notes from her analysis of the British Social Attitudes survey: 'children brought up Christian have a 45 per cent chance of ending up as "nones", whereas those brought up "no religion" have a 95 per cent probability of retaining that identification'. As discussed above in qualitative research (Day 2013, 2011), having 'no religion' is not the same thing as being an atheist. By probing her respondents' attitudes, Woodhead (2016, 250) found in her surveys that only 41.5 per cent were atheists, and that most had a belief in God or a higher power – the 'largest bloc of nones is made up of maybes, doubters and don't knows'. While she found that less than a quarter believed in a personal 'God', the rest believed 'in a spirit, life-force, energy, or simply "something there"'. She also is careful to locate her findings, often distinguishing between the qualities of being a 'none' in the UK and the US, whether in politics (no clear UK profile, against a significant American Democrat-None cohort) or practice: little 'none' communal practice, compared to a strong communal tendency in the US.

When looking at global trends, Woodhead refers to the Pew Research Center (but points out that they rely on census data), which finds that the areas of the most 'nones' are: China, Hong Kong, North Korea, Japan, the Czech Republic and Estonia. She also adds a longer list where at least one in five people declared they had 'no religion': 'Australia, Belarus, Belgium, Botswana, Canada, Cuba, the Falkland Islands, France, Germany (especially in the east), Latvia, Luxembourg, Mongolia, the Netherlands, New Zealand, Sweden, the UK, Uruguay, and Vietnam'.

As for their future, she shows that, because of their lower fertility rates, against a rising global population, the 'nones' will make up less of the population as time goes on: in other words, the world will become more, rather than less religious: 'Although they are projected to increase by more than 100 million by 2050 (to 1.2 billion) that represents a falling share of the total world population, from 16 per cent in 2010 to 13 per cent in 2050' (Woodhead 2016, 252).

On contemporary issues, which may have a political tinge, she found that UK 'nones' held more cosmopolitan views, being more in favour of EU relations and diversity than those who identified as Anglican. As with her other studies, Woodhead found that the general UK population is liberal on matters such as abortion, divorce and assisted dying, compared with conservative religious adherents, but nones were even more so. Woodhead (2016, 252) concludes that:

> Overall, then, a typical none is younger, white, British-born, liberal about personal life and morals, varied in political commitment but cosmopolitan in outlook, suspicious of organised religion but not necessarily atheist, and unwilling to be labelled as religious or to identify with a religious group. Other than that, my surveys do not reveal any particularly significant correlations – not by class, education, gender, political inclination or region. Nones are distributed throughout the population, and exhibit considerable diversity. They are not a distinct minority, but a confident and rather unselfconscious majority. The choice of 'no religion' seems to be a negative more than a positive choice: a refusal of existing categories and a *dis*-affiliation from the organised religious groups.

What are the salient factors driving a 'none' affiliation? There are significant global variations, and therefore Woodhead advises against hasty generalizations, but notes that in some regions, particularly the UK and Scandinavia, there seems to be a general tip towards greater liberalism, supporting the argument that pluralism makes it increasingly difficult for any one religion to claim and sustain absolute truth, particularly when freedom of religion and belief is becoming increasingly enshrined in legislation. She argues that this, in the UK at least, reflects an increasing trend towards ethical liberalism, where individuals want the right to choose their beliefs and practices while embracing the rights and practices of others. While many religions can be and have been liberal, Woodhead argues that an increasingly, vehemently conservative kind of Anglicanism since the 1970s has placed the church in opposition to the population, especially seen in the 'touchstone' topics of gender and sexuality where it successfully lobbied for exemption from key aspects of human rights and equality legislation. Woodhead then advances a more subtle argument, presenting differences between sectarian and societal religions, with the former being a stricter, more exclusive kind of religion at odds with the views and moral beliefs of most of the population.

Although, she concludes, those who self-identify as having no religion may be in the majority, and their aversion to institutionalized religion 'the new norm', a mythic form of cultural Christianity and the old, establishment religious seats of power, such as the House of Lords and Christian worship in elite private schools, linger.

What is certain is that a turn from organized religion is not necessarily a turn from matters spiritual or supernatural. Indeed, such beliefs and experiences appear to be growing, particularly in countries which are seeing decline in institutionalized religion. This may be part of the phenomenon predicted by Heelas and Woodhead's (2005) 'spiritual revolution', as discussed in more detail below.

Everyday ghosts: a 'secular', social, sensuous supernatural

Case example: sensing the 'social sacred'

Two scholars of religion walk into a church. Not just any church, but the Church of the Holy Sepulchre in Jerusalem. They join the lines of pilgrims who are pausing, praying and sometimes weeping at designated holy stations. The scholars neither pray nor weep: one is an Israeli secular Jew; the other, a British ex-Christian agnostic. They wander around the church, watching the pilgrims. They exchange knowing glances and whispered, erudite comments about lived religion, embodied religiosity, shared spaces: they are specialists in their field; they know such things. They are also hungry. The Brit says they should go for lunch. The other, the Israeli, says they should visit Christ's tomb. 'After all,' he says, 'this is Christianity, your culture'. She replies, 'Not anymore, gave up church when I was a teenager', but reluctantly agrees to join the queue. It is a long wait, but they eventually enter the tomb. After a few moments she feels uncomfortable. A sense of shivers, tingling, pins and needles are fluttering all over her body. She is glad to leave and walks quickly with her companion towards the church's exit. By the door he stops her and says:

'What was *that* about?'

'*What?*' she asks, surprised.

'That, in there, oh, awful', he says, rubbing his arms.

'You felt it, too?'

'Yes. Shivers, tingles, pins and needles, all over', he replies.

But (she wants to protest) how can he feel an embodied response to a sacred Christian space when he is a secular Jew? And yet, how can she, an ex-Christian agnostic, also respond in a similar matter?

What *was* that about?

What happened to me and my friend in Christ's Tomb seemed to collapse the distinction between observer and participant and confounded assumptions about the secular and sacred, belief and unbelief. To make sense of those experiences I deconstructed them in more detail and drew on relevant theories.

Little research, however, is available to help us understand how non-religious actors experience religious sites and why, as indicated by the above puzzle, they may appear to have a spontaneous emotional, embodied response. The purpose of this case example is help fill that gap by beginning to plot the phenomena I describe as of 'non-religious sacred experience.'

Sacred framing

Demerath notes that 'No city in the world can match Jerusalem's status as the sacred ground of three major religions' (2001, 93). The site had, therefore, an *a priori* status; that sense of the pre-existing sacred was strong. The 'framing' also occurred on entering the church. There is only a single, narrow entrance shared by people coming and going, squeezing through the narrow passage. There could have

been more provisions for crowd movement and control, but the relative inaccess-
ibility to the church only emphaszsed its nature as separate from and different
from the 'outside' world. People present in visible forms of emotional responses
further framed the experience. The immediate impression was being amongst
people intent on their inward spiritual life.

Sensing

The closer we drew, the more I began to be aware of intense visual imagery from my
past: I could see in my mind's eye those colourful Sunday school Bibles and related
picture books we coloured in. My visual memories from my own religious background were joined, although fleetingly, by visual memories from photographs of
the Muslim pilgrims' circumambulation of the Ka'ba in Mecca: although on a
much smaller scale, the familiar religious form of centre and periphery was being
evoked here. Sigmund Freud argued that uncanny sensations were related to a universal, inherent, attraction towards death. There is a certain plausibility to that
explanation. We were, after all, in a grave.

But how did the sense of 'sacred' arise? The term 'sacred' has multiple, often
implicit, definitions and associations. Durkheim (1915) did not need to define
'sacred' because his point was that 'the sacred' did not exist as a pre-social category: it was whatever the group decided it was.

Demerath (2000) argued that, because a distinction between functional and substantive is difficult to sustain, it is more useful to recognize 'sacred' as the term
of most consequence for people. Religion is just one expression of the sacred,
with 'secular' sometimes being a partner with sacred rather than its opposite. He
suggested an analytical method that first distinguishes between a sacred experience that is either confirmatory, binding the individual to another or to a group,
or a sacred experience that is compensatory, where it comforts or relieves. Next,
he proposed distinctions between sacred experiences that are marginal, that is,
self-consciously outside of the mainstream, and those that are institutional. Those
intersecting distinctions result in four separate kinds of sacred: the integrative, the
quest, the collective and the counter-cultural.

Jon Mitchell (1997), during fieldwork in Malta, experienced an uncanny sensation of a 'presence' while he was cleaning a statue of Jesus in a church. The
experience provoked him to observe how he interpreted that experience in contrast to how many of his informants, members of the congregation, might interpret the event. The physical sense of something sacred was, indeed, present and
overwhelming, but most of the literature on the topic focuses on people who are
religious or, at least, spiritual and no doubt wanted to experience 'the sacred'.
Mitchell suggests (1997, 81) that expectation informs explanation:

> These experiences present the believer with ready-made memories that are
> already explained and are part and parcel of the process of religious indoc-
> trination. These structured experiences act as a blueprint or reference-point
> for people's subsequent experiences

Of the many possibilities available some people might choose a sceptical, nat-ural approach while others would choose a supernatural explanation, drawing on a 'corpus of religious knowledge' (Mitchell 1997, 81, 88). How they reach those conclusions is, he argued, based on their feelings supported by social memories. This is an *a priori* explanation: we come to a site that is already designated sacred; we come with our own memories of similar sites.

Of particular interest here is Mitchell's (1997, 91) conclusion that an uncanny experience leads to feelings explained as a supernatural experience because: 'the logic by which it is felt in the first place depends on anticipation of supernatural intervention. Even before it is felt it is explained as religious experience.'

Deconstructing the experience through its 'framing' revealed how the obvious, subtle, yet relentless framing of the site as sacred provoked socially and emo-tionally embedded memories, prompting me to unconsciously follow the 'script' (Goffman 1959) I had learned and performed decades earlier. This, in turn, helped provoke physical sensations attesting to the felt presence of a sacred being, again in a way that could have been predicted by the script. While the sensation transformed the experience from a distanced, dis-embodied, unemo-tional, performance of conducting the right moves in the right order to a per-formative, embodied experience, it was scripted all the same. It may have gone further from a mere public polite performance that was socialized and idealized, conforming to social expectations and local social values, but the 'shivers' could certainly be interpreted as having been the embodied response to 'the sacred' as the sense of something-as-sacred becomes materialized through human sensation.

Many non-religious people do not believe in gods but may believe in ghosts and other extraordinary phenomena. Grace Davie (1994, 83) noted the persistence of 'the para-normal, fortune telling, fate and destiny, life after death, ghosts, spiritual experiences, luck and superstition'.

Belief in ghosts and spirits is widespread, and usually not religious (excepting such religious formulations as 'the Holy Ghost' or 'Holy Spirit'). A 2009 survey by the Pew Research Center (www.pewresearch.org/fact-tank/2015/10/30/18-of-americans-say-theyve-seen-a-ghost/ last accessed Apr. 2019) revealed that 18 per cent of those surveyed said they have seen or been in the presence of a ghost. Further, nearly a third say they have felt in touch with someone who is deceased. When Erlander Haraldsson (2006) analysed the European Values Survey, he found that a majority of those surveyed from Nordic countries believe in life after death and 43 per cent in reincarnation.

A Pew Research Center survey (pewresearch.org/fact-tank/2015/11/23/millennials-are-less-religious-than-older-americans-but-just-as-spiritual/ last accessed Oct. 2017) showed that younger people, specifically millennials, are less religious than their parents, but two-thirds say they believe in heaven and just over half believe in hell. What is likely to become obvious with more qualitative research is that heaven and hell are concepts of an 'afterlife', which may be widely shared while not being religious. Conventional religious words like heaven hell are generally inadequate to reflect what seems to be the common theme: more than heaven, hell or ghosts – most people believe in the continuity of the human soul. Words or phrases that may be more adequate could be: continuing bonds, extraordinary relationality or, as discussed below, the social, sensuous secular supernatural.

A comparatively young religion, founded in the 1800s, spiritualism has apparently seen growth recently in the numbers of young people joining. The way such beliefs are practised may not be the same as, say, the popular practice of seances in the late 19th and early 20th centuries. While some may attend spiritualist churches, others will simply keep their extraordinary experiences to themselves or share them with close friends and families. In spiritualism, people believe that contact with the dead is possible, and they actively encourage such experiences. Census evidence in the UK, for example, shows that the number of people who define themselves as 'spiritualist' (the belief that it is possible to communicate with the dead) grew 22 per cent between 2001 and 2011. While some may attend spiritualist churches, others will share their extraordinary experiences with close friends and families.

In my (Day 2011) research on what people in Britain 'believe in' there were atheists who believe in ghosts, humanists who believe in life after death and Christians who prefer praying to their dead relatives than to God or Jesus. One-third of my research participants reported feeling the presence of their deceased relatives, even though I did not ask people directly about uncanny or supernatural experiences. Reports varied from feeling the presence of God or deceased relatives and most did not describe such experiences as either spiritual or religious.

Definitions of a ghost, a spirit or a strong sense of an immaterial, immortal 'other' are difficult to agree upon because they are culturally located and may reflect religious contexts and other social constructs (as discussed in Chapter 2) contributing to social learning, memory, cultural artefacts and shared discourse. It is not just the report of such events that is interesting, but the way it is culturally produced. As David Oswell (2006, 3) noted, 'Culture in all its flexibility allows us to think not just of the stuff that is carried, but also all that goes on in the carrying.'

That many non-religious people experience what may be described as supernatural, paranormal or extraordinary events may present as a mystery, but not if we try to understand these experiences in social rather than religious terms. Most religions base their philosophies on a distinct binary between 'this world' of the material and present, and an 'other world' of the immaterial and eternal. Christian Protestants are taught that people will go to heaven or hell after they die, while Catholics insert a staging zone, a liminal state of 'purgatory'. Jews and Muslims also generally hold views that deceased people are either dead and gone forever or live in another heavenly realm. Believers of monotheistic religions are discouraged from trying to continue relationships with their deceased relatives. Adherents to Buddhism, Taoism, Hinduism and Sikhism, may not accept such clear-cut distinctions and often believe in 'hungry ghosts', being the former humans still trapped in a karmic cycle by their unresolved, unsatisfied earthly cravings and desires.

The living may also feel trapped in something unresolved and require explanation or understanding from their deceased loved ones. A dissertation by Yuan Zhu (2017) examines a documentary film focused on the 'Phone of the Wind' a telephone box which functions as a ritual for people who lost their family members during the 2011 Japanese tsunami. It is situated on a hill overlooking Otsuchi, a region devastated by the earthquake and tsunami, and was originally placed by someone who wanted to remember his cousin who died in the disaster: 'In the builder's own words, "Telephone line won't carry my voice. So I let wind do it instead. That's why I call it the Phone of the Wind"' (Zhu 2017, 4). Once people heard about it, they came to use the phone as a means of connecting to their dead relatives. They would speak into it, as if making a real phone call, and express their emotions, both sorrow and anger.

A sensed (and, less commonly, seen) ghost or spirit may be human, other-than-human, divine or demotic, benign, harmful or neutral. There were several sensory experiences at work involving deceased loved ones in my (Day 2011) study in the UK: sight (dreamlike qualities of grandparents; candles mysteriously relit), smells (a favourite flower; a cigarette; aftershave), hearing (footsteps) and touch (a prickly sensation as if someone was standing close behind). Significantly, for the sociologist, most such experiences involve figures already known. Indeed, the appearance of deceased friends or relatives was a phenomenon that influenced one of the most prevailing definitions of religion as a belief in spirits.

Edward Burnett Tylor (1871, 1958) developed theories of animism – the belief that everything, material and non-material, has a soul – and argued that the origins of religion lay in the experience people had of what they thought were visions of their deceased ancestors. Such beliefs, he argued, would diminish as societies modernized. He may have been surprised to know that, a century later, people in modern, urban societies still believe in spirits and witchcraft (as discussed in Chapter 1), and the power of Jedi Knights (as discussed in Chapter 3).

Ancestor communication, care and veneration are widespread and appear to be growing in Euro-American countries where institutional religiosity is decreasing. In Norway, Olaf Aagedal (2013) found that the practice of lighting candles on graves increased from 40 per cent in 1991 to 59 per cent in 2008. Further, several studies of ancestor veneration belief and practices in Africa and Asia show similar structural frameworks and purposes, principally relating to a movement from death to a temporary place and then ultimately to a relocation of a post-death home. Meyer Fortes (1987, 67) argued that the effect and social purpose of ancestor worship is not simply about sacralizing an individual's memory but reinforcing social boundaries and norms. Raymond Firth (1955) described it as a restatement of symbolic structures to ensure that the social structure, not just the individual, continues.

Maurice Halbwachs (1992) developed theories of memory to explain how memory serves as an element in a framework to support wider social relations, such as a family. They are what connect the individual to the group, and the group to the individual. Other scholars, notably Tonkin 1992, have worked to fill the gaps in his ideas, particularly uncovering the important mechanisms of socialization, recognizing that memory is shared through story-telling and other group activities, such as commemorative events. There is no such thing as a stable entity called 'social memory', but rather processes that produce both continuities and discontinuities.

In her socio-philosophical exploration of 'nothing', Susie Scott explores how people try to make connections between things, and sociologists define their craft as an examination of things but neglect the study of nothing. And yet, something apparently as insubstantial as memory, and ghosts, is the glue that binds people together. It may also be an important part of grieving. As Janet Carsten (2007, 24) wrote, accepting and incorporating loss into one's biography is 'an integral part of adulthood, and of creating new kinds of relatedness in the present and the future'.

People report that their ancestor spirits exist to protect the living, and many people will recount instances of escaping from an accident or recovering from an illness that might otherwise be described as 'miraculous': the intervention by the ancestor is a more accepted cultural explanation. A story related to me by a young woman who was missing her deceased grandfather stressed that role of protector. Lin was on a bus and heavily laden with shopping when she started to climb up the interior stairs of the double-decker. Suddenly, the bus sped up and, although she was not holding the rail, she never fell. This, she explained, was due to the intervention of her grandfather spirit. On another occasion, she said, she had fallen downstairs holding a glass but was, in her view, miraculously unhurt due to the intervention of her grandfather.

There may be a need to continue to tell stories about the ancestors, particularly accounts of being visited by them. This might be one reason why participants resist being given other, perhaps science-based, explanations. Other research has emphasized the extent to which participants wanted to be treated seriously, with their stories viewed as authentic. Dennis Waskul and Michele Waskul (2016, 17) found in their American study that participants wanted to have their experiences recognized as genuine, 'not only a product and reflection of culture'.

It was apparent to me in my research that people's accounts were well-polished and, in that sense performative (Day 2011, 107):

> I suggest that my informants were creating and sustaining beliefs in their continuing relationships by performing those beliefs through the telling. Their act of describing the experience with me and others was a repetitive performance (recalling Butler 1990; 1993), enriching, renewing, and rendering more plausible their beliefs. The experiences of sensing deceased relatives were not frequently repeated; for most people those experiences happened rarely, but their smooth narrative performances had the quality of practice through repetition.

Considering this phenomenon sociologically, what becomes apparent is not just the frequency of such beliefs, but their specificity and relationship to a wider milieu. Ghosts, good luck charms, extra-sensory perceptions, experience with religious and non-religious angels (and see Terhi Utrianen (2014) for a detailed and sensitive exploration of how Finnish women relate to angels), messages from mediums and fortune tellers tend to have one thing in common: they are *relational*. Frequently, the figure being sensed or the dreams being experienced are related to loved ones, usually those who have died. The characteristics described in both qualitative and quantitative research seem to indicate that those experiences share four characteristics:

1   Social binder
2   Comforter, protector, portender
3   Embodied, sensuous
4   Exhibiting same relationship on earth as beyond

The definitional problem remains. Much of academic religion-related literature stems from theology, and therefore may categorize such events as 'religious experiences' when what is more often experienced is something qualitatively non-religious and rejected as such by those who experience it. Tom Rice (2003) notes that religious scholars generally ask questions about supernatural beliefs that are already embedded in religious language. The Alister Hardy Trust, based at the University Wales, Trinity St David, has been collecting people's accounts of sensing a presence outside of themselves since 1969. A review of the accounts people had described (Hay 1982, 152) found that, other than the named experience of God, experiences such as 'premonitions, encounters with the dead and encounters with an evil presence were often ruled out of the category religious'. Nevertheless, Hay continued to use the term 'religious'.

The conundrum this presents is one that complicates categories: should such experiences be labelled as religious, when most of the time people rule that category out? And if not religious or spiritual, what should they be called? A more recent study conducted by the Centre into Religious Experience in China (www.uwtsd.ac.uk/library/alister-hardy-religious-experience-research-centre/research/ last accessed June 2020) discovered that while only 8.7 per cent of the Chinese people surveyed described themselves as 'religious', 56.7 per cent report that they have experienced the sense of 'a kind of power that people cannot control or explain clearly'.

James Spickard (1993) reviewed literature of 'religious experiences' and found that how to label them was problematic, particularly when some would describe them as religious but many did not. In an earlier study with Mary Jo Neitz (1990) they found that a common feature of some 'religious' experiences was a 'flow'-like quality. 'All sense of individual self vanishes. The person feels in a time out of time, connected to "the way things really are"' (Neitz and Spickard 1990, 24). As Spickard notes, most accounts of research into religious experience stress the emotional or psychological aspects, not the sociological. And yet, he adds (1993, 3): 'A sociology of religious experience must be more than a sociology of ideas about religious experience – at least if it is to be worth furthering.'

His analytical framework can be applied both to those experiences named as religious by the participant and those that are not. Spickard suggests that such experiences are learned, or at least presupposed.[2] These are then, in his words (Spickard, 1993, 6), 'social products'. The social nature of extraordinary, supernatural or paranormal experience was described, for example, in Chapter 11 through research on faith healing, and also in the case example above on the secular sacred.

In another example I found, a young woman called Becca related her experiences of sensing her deceased grandmother, who promised her that she would send a sign after her death (through the smell of violets). This promise presumed her family already to some extent believed in that possibility. Becca and her mother thought that thunderstorms often carried messages related to their deceased relatives (Day 2011) and when discussing this with the researcher, Becca often used the plural pronoun 'we'. In his research, Piers Vitebsky (2006) found that indigenous people of northern Siberia talked about sharing experiences of deceased relatives. One woman reported 'This man had been appearing in the dreams of all our relatives', she said, 'they were all having the same dream.'

Spiritual but not religious?

Case example: a spiritual revolution?

Some claim that religion is being replaced by spirituality. A research team at Lancaster University in the UK led by Paul Heelas and Linda Woodhead (2005) set out to investigate that, and the theories they developed were arresting. A strong methodological implication also arose, reinforcing the validity of using a single case site, in this case the small, mainly white population of Kendal in northern England. It is an excellent example of the generalizability of the theories emerging from a single case study.

During two years the team conducted surveys, interviews, observations and archival research to explore what they described as the 'contemporary patterns of the sacred', searching for the less obvious, nuanced examples in people's religious and spiritual lives. They divided the population into two broad areas: the 'congregational domain', composed of churches, chapels and other Christian institutions, and the 'holistic milieu', a diverse and often hard to identify population whose activities had, in their own terms, a spiritual dimension. These included discussion groups meeting in private homes, circle dancers, yoga practitioners, Tai Chi groups and complementary therapy practitioners.

One of the differences was where people located authority. People in the congregational domain professed their beliefs in a higher, external power, such as God, while those in the holistic milieu focused internally, on their own bodies and emotions or, in the researchers' words, 'subjective lives'. They found that 7.9 per cent of the Kendal population belonged to the 'congregational domain', while 1.6 per cent were in the 'holistic milieu'. The authors did not conclude that religion would diminish entirely and be replaced by spirituality, but rather that some kinds of religion lose their appeal and credibility as some forms of spirituality increase theirs. They concluded that, if the current rates of respective decline and growth continued in Kendal, within 40 years the 'holistic milieu' would grow proportionately and the congregational domain would decline, reversing position.

Nancy Ammerman (2014) has shown that many of her research participants feel that they are both religious and spiritual. She questioned the 'spiritual but not religious' category and concluded (Ammerman 2014, 50) that: 'in the vast majority of our participants, religious participation and spiritual engagement occur alongside talk that intermingle the two' and, correspondingly, 'spiritual and religious disengagement talk is also similarly entangled'. One disciplinary issue she raised is the feasibility of studying something scholars tend to see as highly individualized, such as spirituality. She suggests (Ammerman 2013, 59) that 'Accepting that individualized view has often meant that sociologists have ignored spirituality entirely, sticking to measures of organized religiosity and relegating spirituality to the domain of psychologists and religious studies scholars'. She agrees that defining spirituality is difficult, and quotes one of her research participants, (Ammerman 2013, 265) who struggles to put it in words: 'Spirituality is certainly something that, first of all it's hard to define in a way, but, um, it's important to me and I still do believe that it's, you know, the focus of my life really. It should be the focus of everybody's life. I mean we all have spirits and our spirits are going to live forever.'

On a similar note, Lori Beaman and Peter Beyer (2013, 131) heard from those they studied who identified as 'spiritual but not religious' that religious identities 'were not central to their lives'. Lack of scholarly consensus on what spirituality might 'be' does not, for many people, detract from what it 'does'. When Lori Beaman (2017) studied people who participated in a sea-turtle conservation project she found that they expressed deep commitment to the creatures they accepted as equal to humans in their rights to live well on our planet, with the turtles 'positioned at the center and in relationship with human beings, rather than hierarchical, and as integrally tied to human well-beings' (Beaman 2017, 24). Speaking about the study of religion more generally, Beaman suggests that academics should look beyond just religion 'to the interaction between religion and non-religion and to the environment that supports us and with which we are intimately connected' (Beaman 2017, 27).

The connection between the environment and spirituality is being studied by Paul Bramadat, focusing on a region known by some as the 'Cascadia' bioregion: Washington and Oregon states in the USA and British Columbia in Canada. The region has some of the lowest rates of religious adherence and highest of those affiliated as spiritual, but not religious. Bramadat (2020,10) writes that for many 'people in Cascadia "religion" and "religious" are increasingly problematic and sometimes even inert terms that would not just fail to capture what is occurring in the region, but also fail to resonate with many residents'. He describes 'reverential naturalism' as the way Cascadians think and talk about religion, spirituality and nature. That may best be encapsulated by their attitude (Bramadat 2020, 1) 'of deference to and, for many, a veneration of nature is framed as a distinctive, even definitive, feature of what it means to live well here'.

Other movements closely connected to nature are forms of neo-paganism, Wicca or witchcraft. As discussed in Chapter 3, paganism is growing and represents more than a stereotypical description of a superstition, or people in pointy hats casting spells.[3] Modern witches (see e.g. Cush 2010, 1997; Berger and Ezzy 2007) are more likely to be involved in small, supportive groups and focus on well-being and conservation.

As this chapter has shown, the categories of none, religious, secular and spiritual are all complicated, and much depends on how such categories are understood and measured.[4] As Andrew Copson (2017, 140) concludes in his historical, sociological and at times philosophical study of secularism worldwide, the number of people claiming religious identity is increasing in some countries, including those who 'barely practise a religion and have no personal religious beliefs increasingly claim them as a cultural self-identity', as we saw in detail in earlier chapters here. There may be several, not traditionally 'religious', reasons why people would align themselves with a religious organization or identity. Nina Rageth (2018) explored the relationship between Siddha medicine and Santhigiri, a Hindu guru organization in South India. She examined how Santhigiri positions itself as a necessary agent to valorize and restore Siddha medicine. Its international network helps to distribute the medicine beyond the Tamil community, and, in return, Santhigiri's appropriation of Siddha medicine gives it positive symbolic capital.

It might be possible that religion grows because of different and new allegiances. Following Pippa Norris and Ronald Inglehart (2004) it is also possible that people may become more 'religious' as existential and material insecurity increases in a post-pandemic, economically damaged world.

Whatever the future may look like, one thing is certain: it will be more important in an increasingly interconnected and fragmented world to develop the skills to understand a variety (and not always 'western' as James Spickard 2017 urges) of religious and non-religious positions. This may require reducing preconceptions and learning better forms of research exploration, teaching and engagement with established religions, new forms of non-religion and something 'in between' (Day et al. 2013), perhaps emphasizing the connections and sense of belonging in all of them – not so much the religion but the 'we'-ligion, as Jay Demerath (2013) put it.

It will also be necessary to use analytical frameworks that direct attention to important dimensions of what we study. In earlier work (Day 2011), I developed seven: the content, the sources, the practice, the salience, the function, the place and the time. I concluded then, and will do so now, that the way of understanding people as either religious or non-religious will not give a full picture. Rather, I suggested, perhaps the real difference is a matter of orientation, of whether people derive meaning, mores and authority (and see also Mark Chaves 1994) from external divine sources – theocentric – or more from people and everyday places – anthropocentric. It may be this orientation, and the way it shifts over time and place, that best explains many of the differences, and similarities, in our increasingly complex world.

Sample questions for private study

1   Which of the above ideas to explain non-religious sacred experience do you find most convincing, and least?
2   How does the idea of social memory help revise other theories about individualism?

Sample class exercise

Bring examples of social media where themes of non-religion are discussed or illustrated.

Notes

1   For more discussion about 'belief' see e.g. Day and Lynch 2013; Day 2010, 2011; Day and Coleman, 2010; Lindquist and Coleman 2008; Robbins 2007, 2003).
2   Tanya Luhrmann (2007, 1989) applied the idea of social learning from others in the same milieu to both conventionally and non-conventional spiritual experience.
3   The first major anthropological study (Evans Pritchard [1937].1976) into witchcraft was significant for the study of religion for not dismissing the Azande witchcraft beliefs as silly

superstition. He could see how they not only made sense at that time and in that place but were vital for calibrating and maintaining a social system.

4   As Ingrid Storm (2009) points out, single-scale measurements are not useful for measuring multi-dimensional phenomena.

Indicative reading

Aagedal, Olaf. 2013. *Deconstructing Death: Changing Cultures of Death, Dying, Bereavement and Care in the Nordic Countries*. Odense: University Press of Southern Denmark.

Ammerman, Nancy T. 2013. 'Spiritual But Not Religious? Beyond Binary Choices in the Study of Religion.' *Journal for the Scientific Study of Religion* 52, no. 2: 258–78. doi.org/10.1111/jssr.12024

Ammerman, Nancy T. 2014. *Sacred Stories, Spiritual Tribes: Finding Religion in Everyday Life*. New York: Oxford University Press.

Arat, Alp. 2017. '"What it Means to be Truly Human": The Postsecular Hack of Mindfulness.' *Social Compass* 64, no. 2: 167–79. https://doi.org/10.1177/0037768617697390.

Beaman, Lori G. 2017. 'Living Well Together in a (Non)Religious Future: Contributions from the Sociology of Religion.' *Sociology of Religion: A Quarterly Review* 78, no. 1: 9–32.

Beaman, Lori G., and Peter Beyer. 2013. 'Betwixt and Between: A Canadian Perspective on the Challenges of Researching the Spiritual But Not Religious.' In *Social Identities between the Sacred and the Secular,* edited by Abby Day, Giselle Vincett and Christopher R. Cotter, 127–44. Aldershot: Ashgate.

Berger, Helen and Douglas Ezzy. 2007. *Teenage Witches*. New Brunswick, NJ: Rutgers University Press.

Bramadat, Paul. 2020. *Religion and Bioregionalism in Cascadia: The Trouble with Categories*. MMG Working Paper 20-05. Göttingen: Max Planck Institute for the Study of Religious and Ethnic Diversity.

Brown, Callum G. 2015. 'How Anglicans Lose Religion: An Oral History of Becoming Secular'. In *Contemporary Issues in the Worldwide Anglican Communion, Powers and Pieties*, edited by Abby Day, 245–66. Aldershot: Ashgate.

Bullivant, Stephen, and Lois Lee. 2016. *A Dictionary of Atheism*. Oxford: Oxford University Press.

Calhoun, Craig, Mark Juergensmeyer and Jonathan Van Antwerpen (eds). 2011. *Rethinking Secularism*. Oxford: Oxford University Press.

Campbell, Colin. 1971. *Towards a Sociology of Irreligion*. London: Macmillan.

Carroll, Tony, and Richard Norman (eds). 2016. *Beyond the Divide: Religion and Atheism in Dialogue*. London: Routledge.

Carsten, Janet (ed.). 2007. *Ghosts of Memory: Essays on Remembrance and Relatedness*. Oxford: Blackwell.

Catto, Rebecca, and Janet Eccles. 2013. 'Dis)Believing and Belonging: Investigating the Narratives of Young British Atheists.' *Temenos – Nordic Journal of Comparative Religion* 49, no. 1. https://doi.org/10.33356/temenos.8616.

Chaves, Mark. 1994. 'Secularization as Declining Religious Authority.' *Social Forces* 72, no. 3: 749–74.

Contractor, Sariya, Tristram Hooley, Nicki Moore, Kingsley Purdam and Paul Weller. 2013. 'Researching the Non-Religious: Methods and Methodological Issues, Challenges and Controversies.' In *Social Identities between the Sacred and the Secular,* edited by Abby Day, Giselle Vincett and Christopher R. Cotter, 173–90. Aldershot: Ashgate.

Copson, Andrew. 2017. *Secularism: Politics, Religion, and Freedom*. Oxford, New York: Oxford University Press.

Cush, Denise. 1997. 'Paganism in the Classroom,' *British Journal of Religious Education*, 19, no. 2: 83–94. DOI: 10.1080/0141620970190205.

Cush, Denise. 2010. 'Teenage Witchcraft in Britain.' In *Religion and Youth,* edited by Sylvia Collins-Mayo and Pink Dandelion, 74–81. Abingdon, Oxon: Routledge.

De Graaf, Nan Dirk, and Manfred Te Grotenhuis. 2008. 'Traditional Christian Belief and Belief in the Supernatural: Diverging Trends in the Netherlands between 1979 and 2005?' *Journal for the Scientific Study of Religion* 47: 585–98.

Davie, Grace. 1994. *Religion in Britain since 1945: Believing without Belonging.* Oxford: Blackwell.

Day, Abby. 2009. 'Researching Belief without Asking Religious Questions.' *Fieldwork in Religion* 4, no. 1: 89–106. doi: 10.1558/fiel.v4i1.86.

Day, Abby. 2010 'Propositions and Performativity: Relocating Belief to the Social.' *Culture and Religion* 11, no. 1: 9–30.

Day, Abby. 2011. *Believing in Belonging: Belief and Social Identity in the Modern World.* Oxford: Oxford University Press.

Day, Abby. 2012. 'Sensing the "Social Sacred"'. Conference Paper, Society for the Scientific Study of Religion, 9 November, Phoenix, AZ.

Day, Abby. 2013. 'Euro-American Ethnic and Natal Christians: Believing in Belonging.' In *Social Identities between the Sacred and the Secular*, edited by Abby Day, Giselle Vincett and Christopher R. Cotter, 83–104. Aldershot: Ashgate.

Day, Abby, and Simon Coleman (eds). 2010. 'Broadening the Boundaries of Belief.' Special issue of *Culture and Religion* 11, no. 1.

Day, Abby, and Gordon Lynch, guest editors. 2013 'Belief as Cultural Performance'. Special issue of the *Journal of Contemporary Religion* 28, no.2.

Day, Abby, Giselle Vincett and Christopher R. Cotter. 2013. 'Introduction: What Lies between: Exploring the Depths of Social Identities between the Sacred and the Secular.' In *Social Identities between the Sacred and the Secular,* edited by Abby Day, Giselle Vincett and Christopher R. Cotter, 1–6. Aldershot: Ashgate.

Day, Abby, Giselle Vincett and Christopher R. Cotter. 2013. *Social Identities between the Sacred and the Secular.* Abingdon: Routledge.

Demerath, N. Jay III. 2000. 'The Varieties of Sacred Experience: Finding the Sacred in a Secular Grove.' *Journal for the Scientific Study of Religion* 39, no. 1: 1–11.

Demerath, N. Jay III. 2001. *Crossing the Gods: World Religions and Worldly Politics.* New Brunswick, NJ: Rutgers University Press.

Demerath, N. Jay III. 2013. 'Afterword.' In *Social Identities between the Sacred and the Secular,* edited by Abby Day, Giselle Vincett and Christopher R. Cotter, 191–201. Aldershot: Ashgate.

Douglas, Mary. 1966. *Purity and Danger: An Analysis of Pollution and Taboo.* London: Routledge.

Drescher, Elizabeth. 2016. *'Choosing our Religion: The Spiritual Lives of America's Nones'.* New York, London: Oxford University Press.

Durkheim, Émile. 1915. *The Elementary Forms of the Religious Life: A Study in Religious Sociology.* London: G. Allen & Unwin; Macmillan

Evans-Pritchard, E. E. 1937 (1976). *Witchcraft, Oracles, and Magic among the Azande.* Oxford: Clarendon.

Firth, Raymond. 1955. *The Fate of the Soul.* Cambridge: Cambridge University Press.

Fortes, Meyer. 1987. 'Ancestor Worship in Africa.' In *Religion, Morality and the Person: Essays on Tallensi religion*, edited by Jack Goody, 65–6. Cambridge: University of Cambridge Press.

Goffman, Erving. 1959. *The Presentation of Self in Everyday Life.* New York: Doubleday.

Halbtranslated and edited by L. A. Coser. Chicago, IL: Chicago University Press.

Haraldsson, Erlender. 2006. 'Popular Psychology, Belief in Life After Death and Reincarnation in the Nordic Countries, Western and Eastern Europe.' *Nordic Psychology* 58, no. 2: 171–80. https://doi.org/10.1027/1901-2276.58.2.171.

Hay, David. 1982. *Exploring Inner Space: Scientists and Experience.* Harmondsworth: Penguin.

Heelas, Paul, Linda Woodhead, Benjamin Seel, Bronislaw Szerszynski and Karin Tusting. 2005. *The Spiritual Revolution: Why Religion is Giving Way to Spirituality.* Oxford: Blackwell.

Hutchings, Tim. 2016. 'Angels and the Digital Afterlife: Studying Nonreligion Online'. https://nsrn.net/2016/05/18/blog-seriesangels-and-the-digital-afterlife-studying-nonreligion-online/.

Kettell, Steven. 2014. 'Divided we Stand: The Politics of the Atheist Movement in the United States.' *Journal of Contemporary Religion*, 29, no. 3: 377–91, DOI: 10.1080/13537903.2014.945722.

Kleeb, Sarah Lynn. 2013. 'Anonymous Believers in Bron Taylor's Dark Green Religion.' *Studies in Religion* 42, no. 3: 309–14

Knott, Kim. 2013. 'The Secular Sacred: In between or both/and?' In *Social Identities Between the Sacred and the Secular,* edited by Abby Day, Giselle Vincett and Christopher R. Cotter, 145–60. Aldershot: Ashgate.

Kosmin, Barry A., and Ariela Keysar. 2009. *American Religious Identification Survey 2008.* Hartford, CT: Institute for the Study of Secularism in Society and Culture.

Lee, Lois. 2015. *Recognizing the Non-Religious: Reimagining the Secular.* Oxford: Oxford University Press.

Lindquist, Galina, and Simon Coleman 2008. 'Introduction: Against Belief?' *Social Analysis* 52, no. 1: 1–18. www.jstor.org/stable/i23182441.

Luhrmann, Tanya. 1989. *Persuasions of the Witch's Craft: Ritual Magic in Contemporary England.* Cambridge, MA: Harvard University Press.

Luhrmann, Tanya. 2007. 'How do you Learn to Know that it is God Who Speaks?' In *Learning Religion, Anthropological Approaches,* edited by David Berliner and Ramon Sarró, 83–102. New York, Oxford: Berghahn Books.

Mitchell, Jon P. 1997. 'A Moment with Christ: The Importance of Feelings in the Analysis of Belief.' *Journal of the Royal Anthropological Institute* 3: 79–94. 10.2307/3034366.

Needham, Rodney. 1972. *Belief, Language and Experience.* Chicago, IL: Chicago University Press.

Neitz, Mary Jo, and James V. Spickard. 1990. 'Steps toward a Sociology of Religious Experience: The Theories of Mihaly Csikszentmihalyi and Alfred Schutz.' *Sociological Analysis* 51, no. 1: 5–33.

Norris, Pippa, and Ronald Inglehart. 2004. *Sacred and Secular: Religion and Politics Worldwide.* Cambridge: Cambridge University Press.

Oswell, David. 2006. *Culture and Society: An Introduction to Cultural Studies.* London: SAGE.

Rageth, Nina. 2018. 'A Reciprocal Relationship: Siddha Medicine in the Context of a Hindu Guru Organization.' *Asian Medicine* 13: 222–46. doi:10.1163/15734218-12341414.

Rice, Tom W. 2003. 'Believe it or Not: Religious and Other Paranormal Beliefs in the United States.' *Journal for the Scientific Study of Religion* 42: 95–106. https://doi.org/10.1111/1468–5906.00163.

Ruel, Malcolm. 1982. 'Christians as Believers.' In *Religious Organization and Religious Experience,* edited by John Davis, 9–32. Asa Monograph 21. London: New York.

Robbins, Joel. 2003. 'What is a Christian? Notes Toward an Anthropology of Christianity.' *Religion* 33, no. 3: 191–9.

Robbins, Joel. 2007. 'Continuity Thinking and the Problem of Christian Culture.' *Current Anthropology* 48, no. 1: 5–17.

Scott, Susie. 2019. *The Social Life of Nothing: Silence, Invisibility and Emptiness in Tales of Lost Experience.* Abingdon, Oxon, New York: Routledge.

Sjöborg, Anders. 2013. 'Mapping "Religion" – or "Something, I don't Know What"? Methodological Challenges Exploring Young Peoples' Relations with "Religion".' In *Social Identities between the Sacred and the Secular,* edited by Abby Day, Giselle Vincett and Christopher R. Cotter, 191–200, Aldershot: Ashgate.

Spickard, James V. 1993. 'For a Sociology of Religious Experience.' *Our House Book Chapters and Sections* 37. https://inspire.redlands.edu/oh_chapters/37.

Spickard, James V. 2017. *Alternative Sociologies of Religion – Through Non-Western Eyes.* New York: New York University Press.

Storm, Ingrid. 2009. 'Halfway to Heaven: Four Types of Fuzzy Fidelity in Europe.' *Journal for the Scientific Study of Religion* 48: 702–18. doi:10.1111/j.1468-5906.2009.01474.x.

Tonkin, Elizabeth. 1992. *Narrating our Pasts: The Social Construction of Oral History*. Cambridge: Cambridge University Press.

Tylor, Edward Burnett. 1871 (1958). *Primitive Culture*. New York: Harper.

Utrianen, Terhi. 2014. 'Angels, Agency and Emotions: Global Religion for Women in Finland?' In *Finnish Women Making Religion: Between Ancestors and Angels* edited by Terhi Utrianen and Pävi Salmesvuori, 237–54. New York: Palgrave Macmillan.

van der Veer, Peter. 2017. 'Urban Planning and Secular Atheism in Shanghai, Beijing, and Singapore'. In *Religion and the Global City*, edited by David Garbin and Anna Strhan, 47–61. London: Bloomsbury.

Vitebsky, Piers. 2006. *The Reindeer People: Living with Animals and Spirits in Siberia.* New York: Houghton Mifflin Harcourt.

Waskul, Dennis D., and Michele Waskul. 2016. *Ghostly Encounters: The Hauntings of Everyday Life.* Philadelphia, PA: Temple University Press.

Woodhead, Linda. 2016. 'The Rise of "No Religion" in Britain: The Emergence of a New Cultural Majority.' *Journal of the British Academy* 4: 245–61. DOI 10.5871/jba/004.245.

Zhu, Yuan. 2017. 'Traumatic Men and Dramatic Women: How the Relationship with Deceased Relatives is Mediated by Social Construction of Gender.' Unpublished master's dissertation, Goldsmiths, University of London.

Zuckerman, Phil. 2011. *Faith No More: Why People Reject Religion*. New York: Oxford University Press.

Index

Made in the USA
Las Vegas, NV
09 July 2024

92089486R00129